COLUMBUS METROPOLITAN LIBRARY

150
1873
2023

CELEBRATING 150 YEARS

COLUMBUS METROPOLITAN LIBRARY

1873 2023

CELEBRATING 150 YEARS

Orange *frazer* Press

Wilmington, Ohio

ISBN 978-1949248-692
Copyright ©2023 Columbus Metropolitan Library
All Rights Reserved

Published for the copyright holder by:
Orange Frazer Press
37½ West Main St.
P.O. Box 214
Wilmington, OH 45177
937.382.3196
www.orangefrazer.com

For more information, call: 614.645.2275
Or visit: columbuslibrary.org

Book and cover design:
Orange Frazer Press with Catie South

Library of Congress Control Number: 2023902448

First Printing

We want to thank our customers, Franklin County Commissioners, Judges of the Court of Common Pleas, state legislators and elected leaders, our Board of Trustees, donors and community leaders.

Your support has made it possible for Columbus Metropolitan Library to continue its work to achieve a *thriving community where wisdom prevails*.

TABLE OF CONTENTS

FOREWORD

Honoring our past and looking forward to the future.

One hundred fifty years ago, shortly after the cruel crucible of the Civil War, a group of dedicated citizens formed the first library in our capital city. The Public Library and Reading Room opened on March 4, 1873, as a single room inside the original Columbus City Hall. Those modest origins were born out of a simple idea – to provide all people access to the resources they need to enrich their minds and transform their lives, their communities and our greater society.

From our humble beginnings in one room to the profound gift from Andrew Carnegie to build Main Library, from civic support that formed our first branches to community support that builds 21st century libraries, we owe much of our present to the work of so many in our past.

Today, we stand on the shoulders of dedicated staff and community members who have come before us – trailblazers who have forged pathways for us to become the library we are today, and the library we aspire to be in the future.

Our sesquicentennial celebration in 2023 marks 15 decades of commitment to inspire reading, share resources and connect people. We have served our customers through two pandemics and two world wars. Card catalogs held the key to our treasures within for many years, replaced by computers as the internet age took hold and we rode the wave of digital change, innovating and evolving to meet our customers' needs. Through it all, Columbus Metropolitan Library, now 23 locations strong, remains a constant presence, providing access for all.

I am truly grateful to the residents of Franklin County, our elected leaders, donors and community leaders who have contributed to the vitality of our library system. To mark our sesquicentennial, Columbus Metropolitan Library is proud to produce *Celebrating 150 Years* to capture the spirit and history of the library.

Columbus Metropolitan Library was founded on the tenets of opportunity, accessibility and community. It was shaped by the millions of customers, community supporters and staff who believed in the power of access and information for all. Just imagine what we can achieve together in our next 150 years.

Sincerely,

Patrick Losinski

Patrick Losinski
Chief Executive Officer
Columbus Metropolitan Library

COLUMBUS METROPOLITAN LIBRARY

CELEBRATING 150 YEARS

1873
2023

OPEN TO ALL
SINCE 1873

The new library opened with 1,500 books and 54 magazine and newspaper subscriptions.

Rules for the Library and Reading Room

1.

Every person desiring to take books from the library shall first register his or her name and residence with a promise to obey the rules, and if personally unknown to the Librarian, shall name one or more persons, who shall give to the Librarian satisfactory assurances as to the good faith of the applicant, and whose names shall be recorded by him; or, if preferred, the applicant may deposit, as security while using the Library, the sum of Five Dollars with the Librarian.

2.

The reading room and library shall be free to every resident of the city of Columbus over fifteen years of age, and, by permission of the Librarian, to persons under such age, provided however, that books shall be given out to minors, to be taken away from the library room, only on the written request of their parents or guardians and on their making themselves responsible for the books so taken, and also to strangers visiting the city, who shall be introduced to the Librarian by persons known to him to be reliable, and whose names shall be by him recorded, subject however to such rules and regulations for maintaining order and for the safety of the books and other property, as the Trustees shall prescribe. The Librarian may, in his discretion, require of strangers taking books from the Library as security a deposit of five dollars.

EARLY LIBRARIES IN COLUMBUS

Columbus has a storied history of supporting libraries. Calls for a public library in Columbus grew with the population of the city. As early as 1821 the *Columbus Gazette* newspaper reported that "the apprentices of Columbus" came together to form a library. Other early libraries were subscription-based or supported with proceeds from lecture series. Library advocates met in the old City Hall in 1871 to plan an appeal to the City Council for funds for a public library that would be free and open to everyone. The ordinance for the establishment of a library space in City Hall passed and the library opened on March 4, 1873. John W. Andrews, the first president of the library Board of Trustees, emphasized that the library would be "open to all" at the dedication ceremony. He said, "I congratulate you…our City Council, backed by the unanimous vote of the citizens, has established and liberally endowed a free library and reading room, free to the whole population of the city."

Left: Excerpt from the Board of Trustees meeting minutes that declared, "the public library and reading room will be free to every resident."

Right: The first Columbus library was one room in the old City Hall, located at the current site of the Ohio Theatre.

Above: Rev. James Grover served as chief librarian from 1873 to 1896.

THE CITY HALL LIBRARY

Rev. James Grover, pastor of St. Paul's Episcopal Church, was named the first librarian and given a salary of $800 per year. He was the library's only staff member until 1879.

Until 1891, the original City Hall library included the Columbus City Schools' library. Even after the school library moved in 1891, the original library room on the first floor of City Hall was overcrowded with books and customers. In 1896, the city appropriated funds to expand the space using vacant land to the east of the building. Visits continued to grow to nearly 100,000 with 13,000 cardholders. By 1900, the library was running out of space again.

Below: John J. Pugh *(center)* was hired in 1881 and became chief librarian when Grover retired. Blanche Roberts *(second from left, front row)* became the first woman employee in 1893 and the first female chief librarian/director in 1946.

Newspapers were a major draw. The expanded space was used as a newspaper and magazine reading room.

Andrew Carnegie funded 103 public libraries and eight academic libraries in Ohio. He once said, "A library outranks any other one thing a community can do to benefit its people. It is a never-failing spring in the desert."

GOV. FORAKER'S RESIDENCE.

Above: Although the original plan for the library included a brick façade, the Board asked Carnegie to fund another $50,000 for marble to make the building "an ornament to the city."

Left: The T. Ewing Miller property at State Street and Grant Avenue was purchased for the site of the new Carnegie library. The site was also known as Swayne Mansion and the first Governor's Mansion. The home was built circa 1847 for attorney Noah H. Swayne. He would go on to be appointed a Supreme Court Justice by Abraham Lincoln.

ANDREW CARNEGIE

As library use continued to grow, it was clear that Columbus needed a new library building. The Board tapped chief librarian John Pugh to meet with industrialist Andrew Carnegie to ask for funds to build a standalone library. Carnegie typically funded rural or branch libraries. It was not clear if he would consider funding an urban library. However, when Pugh met with Carnegie in New York, they bonded over their shared experiences as sons of immigrants. Although the meeting went well, several months passed with no word from Carnegie.

On December 31, 1901, Carnegie wrote to offer $150,000 for building a new library, with the condition that the library Board find a suitable site and the city appropriate at least $20,000 per year for maintenance. City Council quickly passed a resolution for the maintenance fee and the Board set out to find a location. The initial suggestion was to build the library at the corner of State and Third streets, across from the Statehouse, but ultimately land for the library was purchased at State Street and Grant Avenue.

GROUNDBREAKING FOR A NEW LIBRARY

Librarian John Pugh *(left)* and Wilbur T. Mills, supervising architect for the new library.

Left: Groundbreaking for the new library was held on October 12, 1903. It took nearly four years to build.

Above: An exhibit of American birds was built on the second floor to appeal to children. In 1938, the birds were donated to the Ohio State Museum.

Upper right: A 200-seat auditorium in the basement offered a gathering space.

Right: Books were positioned behind a reference desk on five floors of stacks.

A NEW LIBRARY

The Columbus Public Library building was dedicated on April 4, 1907, and regular library service began on April 8. The new library included an auditorium and space for exhibits and cultural displays. The building was considered fireproof, since the only wood used was on railings leading up to the second floor and down to the basement.

The new library included a children's space.

THE 1910s–1920s

The new library quickly became a community gathering place. During the 1913 flood that devastated the city, the library registered family members who were separated from loved ones and worked to reunite them. When City Hall burned in 1921, the mayor, City Council and other government offices moved to the library's basement until the new City Hall building opened in 1928. During World War II, the library served as Columbus' official civilian information center. It was also home to the Franklin County Historical Society (now doing business as COSI) from 1948 to 1956.

After the catastrophic 1913 flood, the library helped to reunite families. The Ohio Flood Relief Committee was appointed by Governor James Cox *(second from right)* and was comprised of Ohio businessmen. James Kilbourne *(second from left)* served as President of the Board of Trustees of the Columbus Public Library for four terms.

Above: Visitors to the gallery in February of 1910. Photo courtesy of the *Columbus Dispatch*.

Right: An exhibit organized by artist George Wesley Bellows in 1911, included nudes which were placed in a separate room deemed the "chamber of immorality" by some.

ART GALLERIES

Until 1931, the library was home to the Columbus Gallery of Fine Arts, the predecessor of the Columbus Museum of Art. The gallery hosted exhibits of artists such as Alice Schille and Emerson Burkhart. The Carnegie Gallery continues to be used for art exhibits today.

An East High School student standing next to her artwork on display in 1970.

SUMMER READING: 1930s–1940s

One of the most gratifying accomplishments for John Pugh was the creation of the Children's department. With a dedicated space in the Carnegie building, the Children's department created displays and programs for children of all ages to enjoy, like "Story Hour," which was first held in 1909. In 1937 children's librarians Blanche C. Roberts and Lillian Skeele developed a reading contest to keep children engaged during the summer months when they were not attending school. The first "summer reading contest" took place at Columbus Public Library's Main Library, May 15–July 15, 1937. The 165 participants ranged from third grade to eighth grade. The program had a baseball theme, with participants' names entered on a large scoreboard so they could see where they stood on the leaderboard. Prizes for the top readers were books donated by library staff.

After a successful first year, the library decided to make Summer Reading Club (also known as Vacation Reading Club) an annual event. The second contest was extended to children from third grade to twelfth grade and was open to kids at Main Library, Hilltop and Linden branches. In 1942, the number of books to "graduate" was reduced from 15 books to 12 and the library extended the program to all branches and county station libraries.

Right: Fifty-seven children received diplomas for completing the 1939 Summer Reading Club by reading and reporting on 15 books. Carolyn High, age 7, is shown here getting her diploma from Lillian Skeele, the librarian in charge of the Children's department.

Above: The winners of the first Summer Reading Club in 1937. *Left to right:* Dino Pappas, age 8, read 69 books. Jeanne F. Chavous, age 10, read 101 books. Bobby Weisberg, age 11, read 80 books.

Parsons Branch Librarian Margaret Bausch with a rocket display for "Space Exploration," 1958's Summer Reading Club theme. Over 10,000 children participated that year.

SUMMER READING CLUB: 1950s–1960s

The 1950s saw a surge of participants in Summer Reading Club as themes changed and programs in locations were promoted. In 1951, it was extended to customers who accessed the library through the bookmobile, which made 29 stops around the county. In 1953, the library began to bring in guests to promote Summer Reading Club. Among them was "Aunt" Fran Norris, a children's television show host on WBNS-TV. Norris was a popular personality and precursor to *Luci's Toyshop*. In 1955, the Zoo theme attracted over 9,000 sign-ups from 10 branches and 83 bookmobile stops. The prize for reading 10 books was a free one-day pass to the Columbus Zoo.

1961's Summer Reading Club theme was the Civil War, to mark the 100th year of the beginning of the war. Pictured here are the Eastside Branch winners.

Aerial view of Main Library with the brick addition in the back.

MAIN LIBRARY BUILDING ADDITION: 1950s

Columbus experienced enormous growth after World War II ended in 1945. Enrollment at The Ohio State University tripled and the population of Franklin County grew to over 500,000. In 1951, when the library celebrated the 50th anniversary of Andrew Carnegie's gift, it was clear that more space was needed, especially for cataloging and outreach services. Council member Henry Koontz, who remembered borrowing books from Main Library soon after it opened in 1907, led the effort to raise funds for an addition. Although construction was delayed a year due to restrictions on purchasing steel as a result of the Korean War, the new library service building opened in 1953. A second addition was built between 1959 and 1961.

Construction of the 1953 addition.

Home Movies

By PAUL GAPP

Film Librarian Mary Rupe checks out reels to Police Sgt. Joe Foster, movie fan who's a regular patron.

IF you're a home-movie fan, there's really no reason you must show the same old thing over and over again. At the Columbus Public Library you can borrow any one of 244 16-mm. sound films, merely by presenting your library card. The service is open, of course, to groups and organizations, as well as individuals.

The library started its film department last May with the purchase of 146 reels. Now the collection is growing at the rate of about 10 new films a month.

Just about every type of educational movie is available. But don't let "educational" frighten you away; the films are entertaining. Indeed, your guests will probably welcome them as a relief from the home-made, painfully routine productions on Junior at the age of one, 2 and 3.

Among the topics available are history, religion, sports, travel, art, music, civil defense, community planning, democratic living and *March of Time* subjects. There are films for children ranging from stories about animals to animated cartoons.

Upon presenting your library card, you fill out a simple form and take the reels you want. One important tip: there's a 25-cents-an-hour fine for overdue films. This is pretty stiff, librarians admit, but it isn't very often that people keep the reels longer than the 24-hour lending period.

TECHNOLOGICAL ADVANCEMENTS

Long before computers, the library helped citizens gain access to new technology. The Microfilm Reading Room opened in 1948 with one reader and several cabinets of microfilm. Record and film collections began in the 1950s and the library purchased its first Xerox copier in 1966.

Records and a room with facilities for listening to them are among the many services provided patrons by the Columbus Public Library.

Newspaper files are photographed on Micro-Film for study on a viewer in full-size reproduction. Films save wear on original copies.

Healthline debuted in October 1977. Customers could call in, listen to tapes about health topics and get help from librarians.

REFERENCE SERVICES

Reference services in the 1970s and 1980s saw many advancements, from new electronic resources to innovative access tools. The library's first public computer was installed in 1977. Staff in the Business & Technology, Magazines & Newspapers and Fine Arts divisions responded to thousands of customer questions each year. The expanded Columbus and Ohio Room was dedicated in 1975 to answer local history and genealogy questions.

Judge Thomas Moyer *(left)* presents Assistant Director Charles Brown *(right)* with tapes for the Law Line service.

WLWC-TV (now WCMH-TV) donated a film collection to the library in 1970. Head Librarian Edward Daniels (left) and Martin Luther King Branch Verdi Fitz accepted the donation.

COLLECTION FACTS

Branch book circulation first topped that of Main Library in 1938.

Overall Columbus Metropolitan Library circulation passed the one million mark for the first time in November 1954.

Videos were added to the library's collection in 1978.

Compact discs were added to the library's collection in 1985.

Fax machines were installed at Main Library and five branches in 1987 and at all branches in 1990.

The library started offering eBooks in 2005.

In 2017 the library stopped charging fines for overdue items to remove barriers to access.

The author that has the most titles in our collection is James Patterson.

PROGRAMS FOR CHILDREN AND TEENS

The library's focus on youth continued in the second half of the 20th century. Storytimes, teen events and programs for preschoolers expanded. At Main Library, the Center for Discovery opened in November 1978 to "give very young children a chance at development before they start school." It featured a treehouse, story pit and puppet theater.

Teen disco party at Driving Park Branch, 1980.

Story Web, a Storytime for preschoolers, began in the late 1970s.

Treehouse in the Center for Discovery.

Bubbles activity in front
of Main Library.

Storytime in the Center for Discovery.

Making its first appearance in 1991, Metro Mouse encouraged kids to read.

AUTHORS AND SPECIAL EVENTS

The library has hosted many famous authors over the years, including Marc Brown, Jason Reynolds and Diana Gabaldon. Others include Bill Bryson, Ashley Bryan, Bob Greene and Jeff Kinney. The library has also sponsored author talks at other venues in Columbus, including events with Toni Morrison and Rick Steves.

Photo by Kojo Kamau.

Above: James Patterson Author Talk, 2022.

Author Wil Haygood at a 1993 talk at the library for the launch of his book *King of the Cats: The Life and Times of Adam Clayton Powell, Jr.*

Laura Numeroff, author of *If You Give A Mouse A Cookie*, visited Hilliard Branch in 1997.

Librarian Gail Milner and children during a Summer Reading Club activity at the Martin Luther King Branch in 1977.

Channingway Branch promoting Big Foot, 1978's Summer Reading Club theme.

Yachtman, the first mascot to promote summer reading, debuted in 1977.

SUMMER READING: 1970s

Summer Reading Club continued to grow under the leadership of Phyllis Thompson, children's head librarian, who became head of the department in 1968. Expanded programs included more Storytimes, adventure and nature movies on Saturdays at Main Library and the Bookworm Club for students who had completed fourth, fifth and sixth grades. In 1976, free coupons for fast food were given out for the first time to children who read 12 books. The library aired its first television commercial for 1979's Summer Reading Club, featuring a superheroes theme. Superheroes Word Woman and Super Reader fought villain Dr. Dolt, who was stealing books from library shelves. The library initially ordered 10,000 custom t-shirt transfers proclaiming "I'm a Super Reader" to give participants after they read 12 books. By the end of the program, the library had awarded 75,000 transfers.

SUMMER READING: 1980s–1990s

Summer Reading Club entered the 1980s with a roar with the theme "Bring a Dinosaur Up to Date." Other themes of the decade included "Join the Space Reading Crew," "Reading is Cool" and in 1988 the entire summer was dedicated to a Maurice Sendak celebration. In 1981, just over 8,000 children registered for the program and by 1989 that number had increased to almost 18,000 children.

Above: A special visitor greets participants in 1985 to celebrate the library's "Reading is Cool" theme.

Right: In 1981, Summer Reading Club participants were invited to join the "Space Reading Crew."

Far right: 1980's Summer Reading Club featured Geniusaurus, a dinosaur who was newly thawed out. Participants helped bring him up to date on all the books he missed.

JOIN THE Space Reading Crew

There is Space For You!

The 1981 Summer Reading Program of The Public Library of Columbus and Franklin County

JUNE 17—AUGUST 5

Sign up at all PLCFC branches, Main Library and the Bookmobile

It's a summer of interplanetary reading achievements ! Join the LIBRARY, COSI, ROACH, INC., and McDONALD'S for a star-studded summer featuring a galaxy of books, programs and out-of-this world prizes !

Read one book and sign up at your local library. You'll receive your SPACE READING LOG and coupon for $1 off admission to COSI or to an exciting COSI summer workshop.

Read four books and win a SPACE READING CREW T-shirt iron-on from ROACH, Inc.!

Read 10 books and receive a SPACE POSTER.

Read 16 books and you'll earn a coupon good for an astronomical meal from McDONALD'S.

SEE BACK FOR MORE DETAILS

GENIUSAURUS (jeen-yes-sawr-us) n. [learned lizard] An American dinosaur known for his keen intelligence. Lived about 120 million years ago; about 20 feet high, 65 feet long. The geniusaurus was the only dinosaur who realized that the climate he lived in was becoming too cold to survive. He built shelter and managed to survive for millions of years after all the other dinosaurs.

Scientists say the geniusaurus was caught in the Great Ice Age and a glacier probably carried him up North. One has been discovered recently in the Arctic and is being brought to Franklin County for a meltdown. The dinosaur is an avid reader, and scientists want to have a list of good books ready for him when he is completely melted. They have asked the children of Franklin County to read as many books as they can this summer so they can give a list to the geniusaurus to read — after all, he has a lot of catching up to do! It's called: Operation Meltdown.

Children who participate will be rewarded for their contributions. After one book, they will be eligible for their "Official Thawmometer" Reading Record to keep track of their books, and a dinosaur mobile. As they read more, they will receive a Roach iron-on dinosaur transfer for their T-shirts, a Dairy Queen sundae and a McDonald's meal.

Dr. Terri Dactyl, head of the dinosaur program, urges all children to join the program. "We are really depending upon you," she says. Readers can get information on the project by dialing 864-8050 and asking for Dr. Dactyl, or by visiting their local library.

EVERYBODY LOVES THE LIBRARY

another FREE program from the Public Library of Columbus and Franklin County because,

WE DELIVER

A VolunTeen helps a child sign up for Summer Reading Club in 1987.

Summer Reading Challenge Kickoff, 2018.

Summer Reading Challenge Kickoff, 2019.

SUMMER READING CHALLENGE: 2000s

In 2018, Summer Reading Club's name changed to Summer Reading Challenge, featuring the Reading League, a team of pro-literacy caped crusaders. Superheroes like Captain Read and Page Turner encourage everyone to make reading a habit.

All ages participate by reading, completing activities and attending programs. Our locations come alive with music, fill up with laughter and celebrate special guests like artists, magicians, goats, or even hedgehogs! It's the perfect blend of fun activities and reading to prevent summer learning loss.

During 2020 and 2021, Summer Reading Challenge changed to navigate the obstacles faced due to the COVID-19 pandemic. In-person activities moved online and prizes were mailed to homes. In 2022, the library resumed in-person Summer Reading Challenge and more than 40,000 kids, teens and adults registered.

WHAT'S IN A NAME?

As the library grew, its name changed to keep up with the times. The 1873 ordinance that created the library simply called it the "Public Library and Reading Room." In 1903, the standalone library was named Columbus Public Library. In 1976, the Board changed the name to Public Library of Columbus and Franklin County to reflect the inclusion of county libraries. In 1989, the Board changed the name to Columbus Metropolitan Library, as it remains today.

Left: Main Library Director Meribah Mansfield announces the new name of the library.

No. 544255 J Expires 5-57

Nancy Agnes Miller

604 Berkeley Road - Holy Rosary

Present this card each time you borrow a book.
You are responsible for books borrowed on it.
Please notify the Library at once of a change of Address.

Columbus Public Library
Columbus, Ohio   3051   30M

Expires 1-72

Gregory Allen Zachariah

4885 Northtowne Blvd. (29)

is responsible for all books borrowed on this card.
Present this card each time you borrow a book.
If card is lost there will be a charge for replacement.

Columbus Public Library
Columbus, Ohio

B   7316

COLUMBUS PUBLIC LIBRARY SYSTEM

Expires

53 179 142 5   J   10/74
KYLE L DENNISON
5496 PINE BLUFF RD
COLUMBUS   OHIO   43229

The Public Library of Columbus and Franklin County

Use this library card to check out Books, Records, Films, Toys, Large Print Books, Tapes and other materials available for loan free from your neighborhood library. We know you'll return them on time and in good library considers it the responsibility of parents or materials borrowed by youngsters.

DISCOVERY PLACE
L I B R A R I E S

This card may be utilized at any Discovery Place Library (Columbus Metropolitan Library, Franklin University, Southwest Public Libraries and Worthington Public Libraries). The Library is not responsible for lost or damaged cards, or value added to this card. The library cannot refund any unused value on the debit card.

COLUMBUS METROPOLITAN LIBRARY
COLUMBUSLIBRARY.ORG
614-645-2275

Left: Kwanzaa celebration at Driving Park Branch, 1980.

Bottom left: The Weasle Borough has been displayed at Main Library during the holidays since the early 1990s. It was created in 1990 for Children's Hospital by students at the Columbus College of Art and Design.

Bottom right: Many Columbus families have memories of visiting the library during the holidays. The Huntington Holiday Train was displayed at Huntington National Bank between 1992 and 2008. The display moved to Main Library in 2009 as part of a partnership with Huntington.

Construction of the 378-space parking garage for Main Library.

Above: The collections processing and outreach building was demolished to make room for the addition.

Children enjoying the groundbreaking celebration.

MAIN LIBRARY EXPANSION GROUNDBREAKING: 1987

Funded by the passage of a 2.2 mill levy in 1986, the expansion of Main Library began in 1987. There were two phases since buildings behind the library had to be torn down and the parking garage built. The new library expanded from 87,000 square feet to 255,400 square feet of much needed space.

MAIN LIBRARY EXPANSION OPENING: 1991

The expanded Main Library officially opened on April 13, 1991, with a "Celebration of the Family" that included a breakfast Storytime and alphabet-shaped cakes. Events continued for more than a week, including programs with artists Aminah Robinson and Todd Slaughter, local history classes and a wellness fair. The library was officially dedicated on Tuesday, April 30, 1991, in a ceremony that included First Lady Barbara Bush, Ohio Governor George Voinovich and Columbus Mayor Dana Rinehart.

Above: NBC meteorologist Willard Scott *(right)* aired segments of the *Today Show* from Main Library. Also pictured are Board President Terry Casey *(left)*, Ohio Governor George Voinovich and First Lady Janet Voinovich *(center)*.

Below: First Lady Barbara Bush read a story to children as part of the festivities.

The library hosted the first Black Caucus of the American Library Association meeting in 1992. Assistant Director Rubye Kyles, Library Services & Programming Administrator Wendy Ramsey and Director of Communications Larry Allen presented a session.

LIBRARY SERVICES: 1990s

Library services continued to expand in the 1990s. Many new services incorporated digital databases and internet connectivity. The first online library services began at Main Library, including the creation of an online catalog. The library launched its first website in March of 1998 so library customers could access services at home.

Business & Technology was the first library division to receive computerized databases. John Davidson of Society National Bank reviews financial statistics on Compact Disclosure, a CD-ROM database.

Director Larry Black with the first Discovery Place public computer terminal in 1989. The new terminals allowed library customers to search the electronic card catalog for the first time.

Library Channel, an index of websites, began on July 30, 1997 and ended in 2001.

InfoTrac debuted in 1994, giving customers the ability to search periodical indices. Shelton P. Kang, a customer at Livingston Branch, used the database.

CEO Patrick Losinski *(right)* with artist Aminah Robinson *(left)*, who created the mural on Main Library's stairway.

MAIN LIBRARY'S CENTENNIAL CELEBRATION

In April 2007, Main Library celebrated the 100th anniversary of its April 1907 grand opening. To mark the occasion, the library held two events. On April 21, the library's Foundation hosted the Party of the Century black-tie gala on the library lawn. Guests enjoyed dancing and dinner by Chef Handke. Then on April 28, the Friends of the Library held a Community Open House with cake and ice cream for everyone. Those attending enjoyed activities for all ages. The library was also recognized with a historical marker. Several thousand people visited the library during this centennial celebration.

Library leaders celebrate the centennial. *From left to right:* Steve Prater, Chris Taylor, Scott Fothergill, Patrick Losinski, Susan Studebaker, Dewitt Harrell and Kerry Bierman.

LIBRARY SERVICES: 2000s

Library services expanded in the 2000s. In 2004, the first School Help Center opened at the new Linden Branch; by 2012, all locations had Homework Help Centers. The library began offering eBooks on OverDrive in 2005; about 600 eBooks grew to a collection of 10,000 eBooks, audio and video files by 2010. In May 2013, the library joined the Central Library Consortium, giving customers access to more than a million more resources, including books, audiobooks, DVDs and CDs. In 2018, the library gained access to SearchOhio, a consortium of public libraries and OhioLINK, a consortium of Ohio's college and university libraries. Borrowing also became easier during this time. Automatic renewals began for checked out items in 2014. On January 1, 2017, the library stopped charging fines for overdue books and other materials since overdue fines often prevented people, especially kids, from using the library.

Teen Read Week, 2001.

Upper far left: In 2018, staff digitized the one-millionth item for My History, the library's digital collection.

Upper left: More than two dozen central Ohio artists exhibited as part of the Ohio Artist Registry Juried Show, which has since become an annual event.

Left: Main Library opened its Homework Help Center, the 10th in the system, in 2009.

The renovated Main Library opened on June 25, 2016.

MAIN LIBRARY RENOVATION: 2016

On February 24, 2015, Main Library's newest renovation kicked off with a wallbreaking event. The renovation connected the library to Topiary Park, reimagined the Children's area, created more meeting and study rooms and featured a new Reading Room to host author talks and events. The removal of the exterior marble from the front and back of the library revealed spectacular views of downtown and Topiary Park.

City Council members Shannon Hardin *(left)* and Jaiza Page *(center)* tour the construction site with CEO Patrick Losinski *(right)*.

Main Library under construction.

Excited customers with librarian Ann Ogg *(center)*.

MAIN LIBRARY EVENTS: 2010s–2020s

The 2016 renovation of Main Library made it a popular location for big events, such as Cartoon Crossroads Columbus and the Ohioana Book Festival. The Carnegie Author Series hosted dozens of authors and filled the Reading Room with customers who love to read.

Upper left: Guests at the opening of the Creative Women of Color exhibit in the Carnegie Gallery, July 2016.

Upper right: Storyteller Jim Gill entertained the crowd in 2017.

The Job & Resource Fair at Main Library in 2022 hosted a crowd of job seekers.

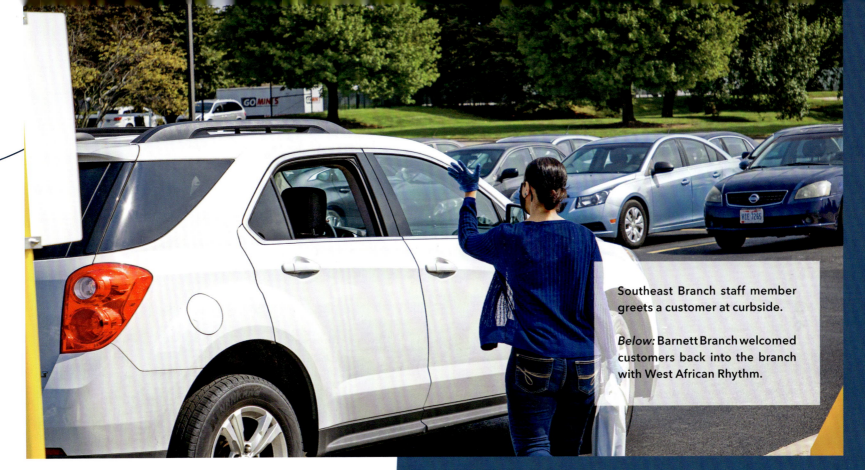

Southeast Branch staff member greets a customer at curbside.

Below: Barnett Branch welcomed customers back into the branch with West African Rhythm.

COVID-19 PANDEMIC

The COVID-19 pandemic in 2020 prompted the shutdown of the library system for nine weeks. The library reopened with limited services as soon as it responsibly could. Library staff developed innovative ways to support the community, from curbside pickup to virtual events like Storytime. As the pandemic evolved and guidelines eased, customers were invited back into library locations with an Open House celebration in August 2021.

BUILDING COMMUNITY

IN NEIGHBORHOODS

The second Clintonville Branch at 14 W. Lakeview Ave.

Soon after Main Library opened in 1907, it became clear that there was a need for branch libraries in Columbus neighborhoods. Horse-and-buggy traffic along Grant Ave. led to congestion and hitching posts near Main Library were often at capacity. Also, Columbus residents wanted library locations closer to home. However, Andrew Carnegie was no longer funding libraries and City Council did not have funds for branch libraries. The Board of Trustees decided to create library "deposit" locations in fire stations, settlement houses and schools. Deposit locations had about 100-500 books for visitors to read. The Godman Guild was the first deposit location in 1910. Others included Bellows Avenue Recreation Center, the Crittenden Home, the B'nai B'rith Social Center, the Hague Avenue School, the Juvenile Detention Home and the South Side Settlement House.

After World War I, there were repeated calls for branch libraries. Fred J. Heer, president of the library Board, appealed to the Federation of Women's Clubs

Left: The Milo Branch at 768 Leona Ave. was dedicated on January 18, 1930, as the system's fifth branch. In 1950, the Milo Branch was replaced by a bookmobile stop. Most of the book collection was donated to the Franklin County Children's Home.

Below: Margaret Bausch, Parsons Ave. Branch librarian and Marie Zapp, assistant.

for help. On January 17, 1928, the women marched to City Hall to demand funds for branches. Two weeks later, City Council appropriated $40,000 to build four: Clintonville, Linden, Parsons and Hilltop branches.

There was an enormous public response to the new branches. Within 10 years, the combined branches exceeded the annual circulation numbers of Main Library. Rose G. Beresford was tapped to lead the Department of Extension Services in 1928, where she served until 1942. Under her leadership, the Milo Branch opened in 1930. The Great Depression took a toll on libraries, however. Staff took a 50% pay cut and purchases of new books and materials virtually ceased between 1930 and 1939. As a result, State Senator Robert A. Taft drafted a bill that allowed library boards to request funds from the County Commissioners if they offered services county-wide. The law passed in 1933 and in July 1934, Columbus Public Library became a county-wide library.

To support library services around the county, new facilities called "county stations" were established. They were typically a room in a school and were often staffed by teachers. Canal Winchester was the first county library station in 1937 and was followed by Briggsdale, Dublin, Fornof, Gahanna, Galloway, Harrisburg, Hilliard, Lockbourne, New Albany and Reynoldsburg.

Right: Children at Godman Guild. Photo courtesy of Ohio History Connection.

Left: Canal Winchester's county station was in the old school.

By 1960, five bookmobiles like this one checked out over half a million books in one year. By 1969, bookmobiles served 118 locations around the county.

The Metro Mouse Mobile with driver David Scott and librarian Ruth Pettibone.

A home delivery customer in 1981. The service continues today but residents receive items by mail.

OUTREACH SERVICES

Bookmobile service began in November 1950 to reach parts of the county that were not served by a library branch or county station library. In its first year, over 75,000 books were borrowed from the bookmobile. By 1958, there were four bookmobiles that together made up one-quarter of all library circulation that year.

In 1995, two bookmobiles were redesigned to become "Metro Mouse Mobiles" and visited area preschools to promote early literacy skills. The last two large bookmobiles were retired in 2014. One small bookmobile is still in use for library sponsored and community events.

Home delivery service began in 1972 and continues as a mail service for customers who are unable to visit in person. Lobby Stop service to senior residential sites began in 1995. Many of the original sites are still on the roster.

Delivery of classroom collections of books to 23 area schools began in 2014 and became part of Outreach Services in 2016.

First location in the Berwick Manor Shopping Center.

BARNETT BRANCH

- Opened in November 1963 at 3669 E. Livingston Ave. as the Livingston Branch.
- Moved in 1978 to 3655 E. Livingston Ave., a former A&P Super Market.
- New building opened in 1992 at 3434 E. Livingston Ave.
- Renovated and renamed the Barnett Branch in 2019.

Did You Know? The Livingston Heights Place neighborhood to the west of the library was the first suburban land in Columbus to be purchased and developed by African Americans. The neighborhood was founded in 1945 by Charles E. Jones and Dr. Harley S. Manuel.

The second branch included a "Magic Mountain" children's area with raised levels for seating.

Local WBNS-TV anchor Angela Pace spoke at the 1991 groundbreaking.

Upper left: For several years the branch held a popular dreidel spinning competition.

Bottom left: Barnett Branch opening, 2019.

Current location at 3434 E. Livingston Ave. designed by Moody Nolan, Ltd.

Canal Winchester was served by a bookmobile for many years after the county station closed. The bookmobile came to Canal Winchester twice a week.

CANAL WINCHESTER BRANCH

- Opened in 1937 as the first county station library in the old Canal Winchester school.
- Closed in 1963 and later served by bookmobile.
- Reopened in 2016 as express branch at 115 Franklin St.
- Became a full service branch in 2021.

Did You Know? By 1953, Canal Winchester was one of the most active station libraries in the system. It closed in 1963 to make room for additional classrooms at the school.

Below: Children at the 2016 ribbon-cutting of the Canal Winchester Branch.

The location that opened in 2016 is next to the same building that housed the county station library in 1937.

DRIVING PARK BRANCH

- Opened in 1972 at 1566 E. Livingston Ave.
- New building opened in 2014 at 1422 E. Livingston Ave.

Did You Know? Driving Park Branch was the first new building in the library's ambitious 2020 Vision Plan building program.

Left: Pop-up book author Robert Crowther visited Driving Park Branch in 1989.

Below: Customer Geneva Jackson checked out the branch's 100,000th item in 1995.

The first branch on Livingston Ave. in 1972.

The new building designed by NBBJ opened on July 12, 2014.

Above: The portable branch on its way from Gahanna to Dublin along Route 161 in 1971.

Right: Librarian Jean Walker *(middle)* and staff at the Dublin Branch in 1976.

DUBLIN BRANCH

- Opened on St. Patrick's Day in 1971 at 75 N. High St. as a portable branch.
- New building opened in 1980 at 75 N. High St.
- Renovated in 1990.
- New building opened June 6, 2019, at the same 75 N. High St. location.

Did You Know? A time capsule was sealed in the floor of a closet on September 18, 1980, and was recovered before construction began on the new branch in 2017. It was filled with history and photos of old Dublin, information on the portable branch and photos of children's programs.

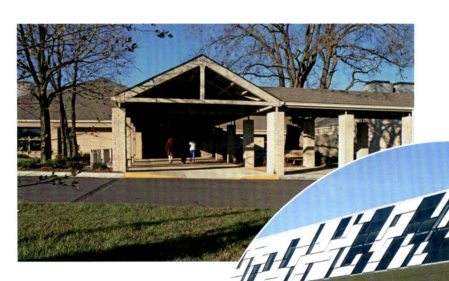

Above: Dublin Branch, 1990.

Right: Dublin Branch, designed by the NBBJ architecture firm.

Storytime at the Dublin Branch.

FRANKLINTON BRANCH

- Opened in 1943 at 840 Sullivant Ave.
- Moved in 1976 to 1061 W. Town St.
- New building opened in 1995 at 1061 W. Town St.

Did You Know? In the 1980s and 1990s, the branch had a cat named Smoke that was featured in a documentary about library cats.

Above: Franklinton Branch Story Hour, 1999.

Right: Franklinton Branch designed by the Moody Nolan architecture firm.

Far right: Librarian Jean Hessler working with children, 1950s.

Far bottom right: The original Franklinton Branch on Sullivant Ave.

GAHANNA BRANCH

- Opened on April 7, 1969 in a portable structure at 160 N. Hamilton Rd.
- New building opened in 1971 at the municipal complex at 480 Rocky Fork Blvd.
- New building opened in 1991 at 310 Granville St.
- Renovated in 1998; addition doubled the branch size to over 21,000 sq. ft.
- New building opened on March 4, 2023 at 310 Granville St.

Did You Know? In 1990, a coin-operated computer with software was offered at the branch. The software included word processing, graphics and spreadsheet capabilities. A coin-operated typewriter was also available.

Below: Staff and volunteers, 1986.

Gahanna Branch, 1991.

Baby Laptime, 2019.

PUBLIC LIBRARY OF COLUMBUS & FRANKLIN COUNTY GAHANNA BRANCH

The new Gahanna Branch
designed by NBBJ.

Hilliard Branch, 1960.

Opening day of the Homework Help Center, 2010.

Top: The newest branch was designed by the architectural firm DesignGroup at 4500 Hickory Chase Way.

Middle: Banjo performance during Summer Reading Club.

Left: Hilliard Branch customers in the 1980s.

HILLIARD BRANCH

- Opened in 1939 as a county station library in the old Hilliard High School.
- Bookmobile service started for Hilliard in 1952.
- New building opened in 1960 at 3730 Main St.
- New building opened in 1978 at 5657 Scioto Darby Rd.
- New building opened in 1996 at 4772 Cemetery Rd.
- New building opened in 2018 at 4500 Hickory Chase Way.

Did You Know? Hilliard Branch circulated over one million books a year for the first time in 1999.

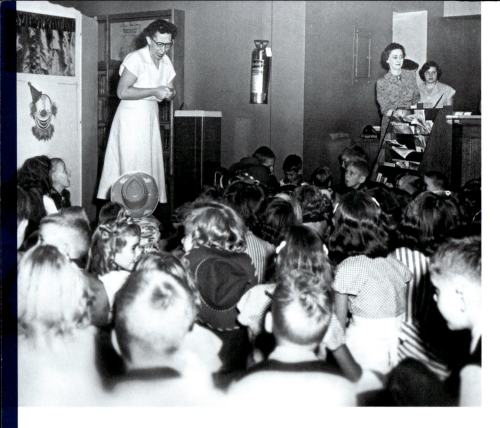

HILLTOP BRANCH

- Opened as the Hilltop Branch in 1928 at 21 N. Hague Ave.; one of the first four branches.
- New Hilltop Branch building opened in 1950 at 2955 W. Broad St.
- New Hilltop building opened in 1996 at 511 S. Hague Ave.; branch merged with the Hilltonia Branch.
- New building opened in 2021 at 511 S. Hague Ave.

Did You Know? *Outlander* author Diana Gabaldon visited the branch for a program in September 1997.

Upper left: Storytime with Patty Gibson, 1950s.

Left: Balloon launch at Hilltonia Branch in the 1970s.

Below: Hilltop Branch at 2955 W. Broad St., 1950.

The Hilltop Branch was originally designed by Schooley Caldwell Associates and renovated and expanded by Gresham Smith.

Customers enjoying the new Hilltop Branch at the grand opening in 2021.

Above: Stained glass windows from the Columbus State Hospital were hung in the 1996 Hilltop Branch and were restored for the new building in 2021.

Groundbreaking for the new Hilltop Branch, 511 South Hague Ave., took place on March 22, 1995.

Hilltop USA: History And Homes

Staff member Rosie Bayer *(right)* on Historic Preservation Day, May 26, 1987.

School bus in the children's area, 2021.

Morse Road Branch.

Information desk, 1995.

Karl Road Branch Dedication Ceremony, 1988.

KARL ROAD BRANCH

- Opened in 1968 as Morse Road Branch at 1421 Morse Rd.
- New building opened in 1988 as the Karl Road Branch when it moved to 5590 Karl Rd.
- New building opened in 2021 at 5590 Karl Rd.

Did You Know? In 1968, the branch was the first in the system to have a collection of 100 phonograph recordings of music and spoken word.

Duarte Brown from Transit Arts creates a multimedia mural with customers, 2022.

New Karl Road Branch, 2021. Designed by the Moody Nolan architectural firm.

This mural was designed by Ohio Dominican Professor of Art, Mel Rosen, in 1977. Staff and customers helped Rosen paint scenes from around the neighborhood.

LINDEN BRANCH

- Opened in 1928 at 1751 E. Aberdeen Ave.; one of the first four branches.
- New building opened in 1935 at 2416 Cleveland Ave.
- New building opened in 1952 at 2432 Cleveland Ave.
- Renovated in 1984 and opened with Alex Haley as guest speaker.
- New building opened in 2004 at 2223 Cleveland Ave. The new branch was the first to include a Homework Help Center, with $500,000 in capital donations raised for the project.

Linden Branch, 2004. Designed by the Moody Nolan architectural firm.

Did You Know? In 1984, Wally "Famous" Amos visited the branch to promote his book *The Famous Amos Story: The Face That Launched a Thousand Chips*. He spoke about the importance of literacy and dedicated the library's new adult learning center.

The adult book and coffee club started at the Linden Branch in 1970 and continued into the 2000s.

Linden Branch location at 2432 Cleveland Ave., 1952.

LINDEN BRANCH COLUMBUS PUBLIC LIBRARY

Teens checking out the new collection of LPs.

Marion-Franklin Branch.

MARION-FRANKLIN BRANCH

- Opened in 1938 as a county station library at 156 Dering Ave. in the Fornof School.
- Bookmobile provided service after closure of county station in 1957.
- Reopened in 2014 in the former Beery Middle School, 2740 Lockbourne Rd.

Did You Know? Marion-Franklin Branch was the first "express" branch in the system when it opened in 2014.

Upper right: Beery Middle School was built in 1956 and named after George C. Beery, Superintendent of Franklin County Schools from 1924–1958.

Right: Children participate in a Summer Reading Challenge program, 2019.

Grand opening of the Marion-Franklin Branch, 2014.

MARTIN LUTHER KING BRANCH

- Opened as the Eastside Branch in 1953, in an old pharmacy building at 1479 E. Long St.
- New building opened in 1969 at 1600 E. Long St. with Martin Luther King, Sr. as guest speaker; renamed the Martin Luther King Branch.
- Renovated in 1993, with a steel structure added to the outside entrance.
- New building opened in 2018 with Martin Luther King III as guest speaker.

Did You Know? The branch is the first public library building in the nation named after Dr. Martin Luther King, Jr.

Left: Summer Reading Club winners at the Eastside Branch.

Right: After the 1992-93 remodel.

"I HAVE A DREAM ..."

1600

Top: Members of the Eastside Library Council, members of the library's Board of Trustees and others at the groundbreaking for the new Martin Luther King Branch, 1968.

Bottom: The 2018 Martin Luther King Branch at Taylor and Long streets designed by Moody Nolan, where the Eastside Branch originally stood.

THE AFRICAN TREASURE CHEST

The African Treasure Chest was developed as a result of a journey to Africa in 1983 by four members of Friends of Arts for Community Enrichment (FACE) led by Dr. Jacqueline Chanda, an African Studies professor from The Ohio State University. They accompanied local artist Queen Brooks on a residency trip to Africa. The group sought to acquire authentic pieces of art from Africa and bring them back to the branch to help the residents of the Near East Side better understand their history.

U.S. Air Force Colonel and NASA astronaut Guion "Guy" S. Bluford signs an autograph during a program at the branch in 1987. He was the first African American in space.

The 2003 opening of the New Albany Branch marked the first time that the library received significant private funding, with $1.2 million raised for the branch's book collection.

New Albany opening ceremony, 1998.

NEW ALBANY BRANCH

- Opened in 1938 as a county station library in the New Albany school.
- Bookmobile served the community beginning in the 1950s.
- Moved to 7600 Fodor Rd., in New Albany High School, in 1998.
- New building opened in 2003 at 200 Market St.
- Renovated in 2021 with an updated children's area, more study rooms and a view of Rose Run Park.

Did You Know? Historian David Mc-Cullough was a guest speaker at the 2003 branch dedication.

Left: New Albany Branch designed by Acock Associates Architects.

Reading Buddies, 2019.

NORTHERN LIGHTS BRANCH

- Opened in 1956 at Northern Lights Shopping Center.
- Renovated in 1966, expanded to neighboring storefront.
- Moved in 1977 to a larger and more visible storefront in the shopping center.
- New building opened in 1993 at 4093 Cleveland Ave.
- New building opened in 2016 at 4093 Cleveland Ave.

Did You Know? In 2002, a touch screen computer kiosk was installed at the branch to assist English-as-a-second-language customers in getting a library card.

Summer Reading Club, 1996.

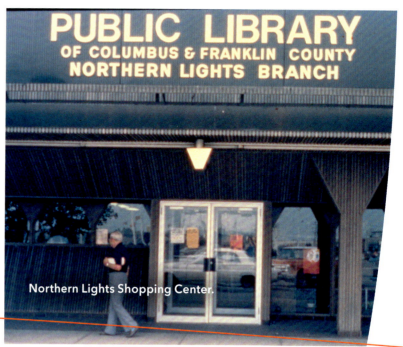

Northern Lights Shopping Center.

The 2016 Northern Lights Branch was designed by the architectural firm DesignGroup.

Northern Lights Branch, 1993.

Young customer with her new library card.

Original location of the Northside Branch at 944 N. High St.

NORTHSIDE BRANCH

- Opened in 1940 at 944 N. High St.
- Moved in 1958 to 1100 N. High St. in the old Brown Dye House dry cleaners.
- New building opened in 1975 at 1260 N. High St. shopping plaza.
- New building opened in 1990 at 1423 N. High St. with The Ohio State University President E. Gordon Gee as guest speaker.
- New building opened in 2017 at 1423 N. High St.

Did You Know? A bookmobile served as the temporary location for the branch while the new branch was being built in 2017.

Opening the new branch, 2017.

The building designed by NBBJ won awards in 2017, from the Columbus Chapter of the American Institute of Architects and in 2018, won the James B. Recchie Design Award from Columbus Landmarks.

Children's program, 1961.

The Ohio State University President E. Gordon Gee at the 1990 branch dedication. Seated behind Gee are library Assistant Director Rubye Kyles and Director Larry Black. Library Board of Trustees members Cynthia Hardy and Terry Casey are seated to the left of Gee and Board President Robert N. Wistner is standing to the right.

Right: The fourth location of the Northside Branch at 1423 N. High St.

NORTHWEST LIBRARY

- Opened in 1996 at 2280 Hard Rd.

Did You Know? The Northwest Library was the first library in Ohio – and only the second in the entire nation – to be built and operated by two library systems.

Worthington Libraries Director Meribah Mansfield *(fourth from left)*, cuts the ribbon with Columbus Metropolitan Library Director Larry Black *(fifth from left)*. Mansfield was a Main Library director for Columbus Metropolitan Library before joining Worthington Libraries.

The Northwest Library, designed by DesignGroup, is a cooperative project of Worthington Libraries and Columbus Metropolitan Library, staffed and managed by Worthington Libraries.

OPERATIONS CENTER

- Opened 2002 at 101 S. Stygler Rd.

Did You Know? The building, now owned by Mifflin Township, is home to the library's Collection Services team who orders and processes all new material and the Transportation team who delivers books, movies, music and more to all library locations.

The Operations Center was designed by DesignGroup with the purpose of housing the Information Services, Technical Services and Transportation departments to expand library services.

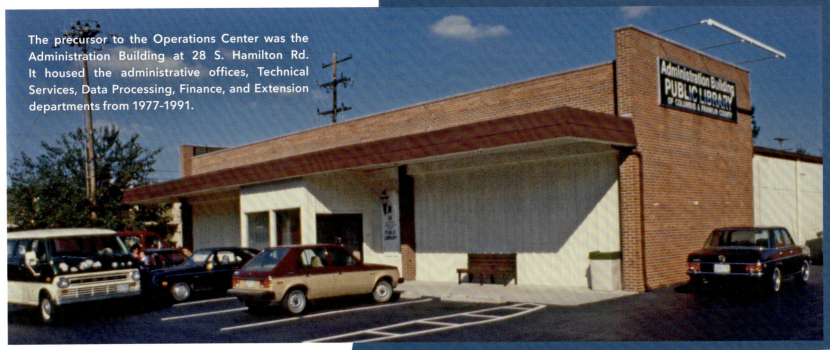

The precursor to the Operations Center was the Administration Building at 28 S. Hamilton Rd. It housed the administrative offices, Technical Services, Data Processing, Finance, and Extension departments from 1977-1991.

PARSONS BRANCH

- Opened in 1928 at 1124 Parsons Ave.; one of the first four branches.
- New building opened in 1956 at 845 Parsons Ave.
- Renovation in 1991 included expansion.
- New building opened in 2016 at 1113 Parsons Ave.

Did You Know? Margaret Bausch was chosen to be the first chief librarian at Parsons because she could speak German, which was a commonly used language in the area at that time.

Parsons Branch Pet Show participants show off their pets and ribbons.

The 1991 renovated and expanded Parsons Branch.

The Parsons Branch designed by Moody Nolan opened June 4, 2016.

The first branch at 1124 Parsons Ave., 1928.

Mayor Jack Sensenbrenner *(center)* at the opening in 1956. Librarian Margaret Bausch *(left)* points out an illustration to three-year-old Barbara Blankmann.

New Reynoldsburg Branch, designed by the Gund Partnership and Jonathan Barnes Architecture and Design.

REYNOLDSBURG BRANCH

- Opened in 1938 as a county station library in Reynoldsburg Elementary School.
- New building opened in 1964 at 7094 E. Main St. in the Reynoldsburg Shopping Center.
- New building opened in 1980 at 1402 Brice Rd.; branch merged with the Channingway Branch.
- Renovation in 1990 included expansion.
- New Reynoldsburg Branch is scheduled to open at 1402 Brice Rd. in 2024.

Did You Know? In the 1970s, the Channingway Branch had two parakeets in the children's area named Cakes and Ice Cream.

Below: Paying tribute to Reynoldsburg's history and the annual Tomato Festival, the 1990 building opened with a tomato soup can play structure.

Top: The expanded and renovated branch opened in 1990.

Middle: In 1980, the new Reynoldsburg Branch at 1402 Brice Rd. combined Channingway and Reynoldsburg branches into a single branch.

Bottom: Reynoldsburg Branch at 7094 E. Main St., 1964–1980.

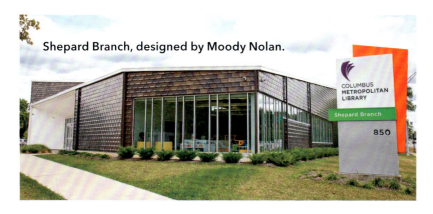
Shepard Branch, designed by Moody Nolan.

1985 branch.

The first Shepard Branch, 1939.

SHEPARD BRANCH

- Opened in 1939 at 2185 E. Fifth Ave.
- Moved to 2424 E. Fifth Ave. in 1978.
- New building opened in 1985 on the site of the historic William Shepard's water cure sanitarium.
- Renovated in 1997.
- New building opened in 2016 at 850 N. Nelson Rd.

Did You Know? During World War II, Shepard Branch was a collection site for the USO's "Victory Book Campaign."

State Representative Ray Miller speaking at the 1985 branch dedication.

The South High Branch was designed by DesignGroup.

South High Branch, 1970s.

South High Branch dedication, 1992.

Holidays, 1970s.

Story Hour, 1981.

SOUTH HIGH BRANCH

- Opened in 1971 at 2912 S. High St.
- New building opened in 1992 at 3540 S. High St.

Did You Know? The branch offered disco lessons in the 1970s.

SOUTHEAST BRANCH

- Opened in 1991 at 4575 Winchester Pike, the first new branch in the system since Channingway opened in 1974.
- New building opened in 2000 at 3980 S. Hamilton Rd.

Did You Know? The clock tower was built so the branch could be seen from Route 33.

Left: Summer Reading Club Open House featuring Metro Mouse, 1995.

First Southeast Branch, 1991.

The building with the clock tower was designed by Schooley Caldwell Associates.

Author visit with Denise Fleming.

Whetstone Branch circulation desk.

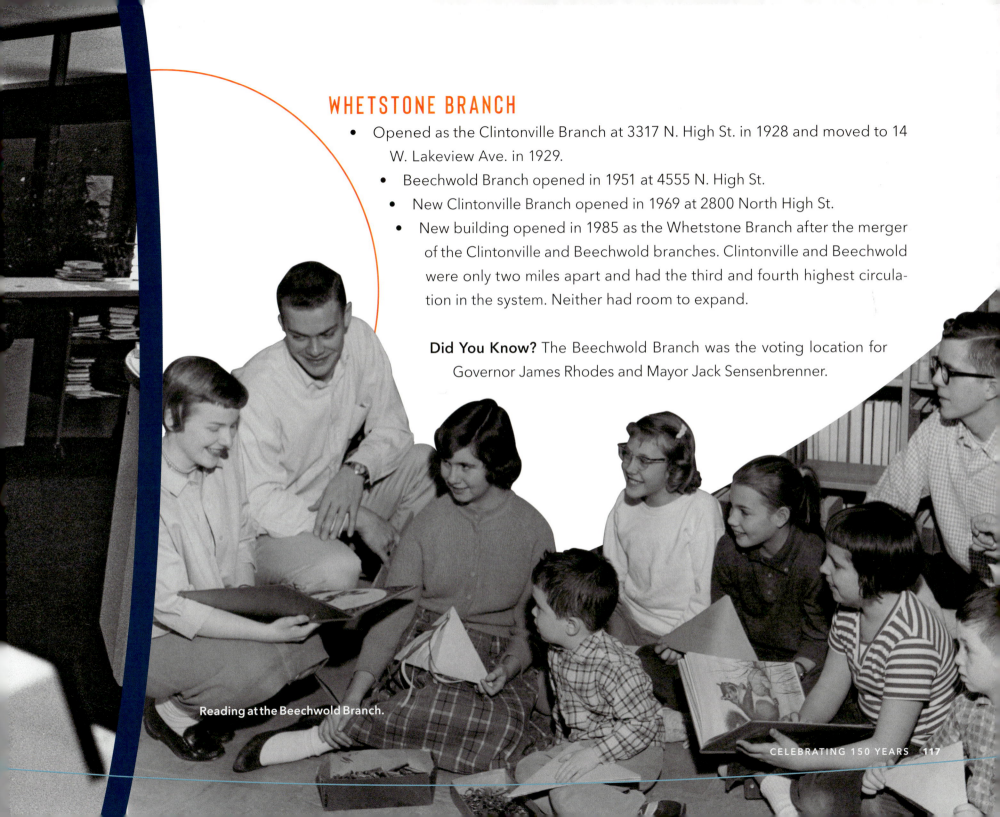

WHETSTONE BRANCH

- Opened as the Clintonville Branch at 3317 N. High St. in 1928 and moved to 14 W. Lakeview Ave. in 1929.
- Beechwold Branch opened in 1951 at 4555 N. High St.
- New Clintonville Branch opened in 1969 at 2800 North High St.
- New building opened in 1985 as the Whetstone Branch after the merger of the Clintonville and Beechwold branches. Clintonville and Beechwold were only two miles apart and had the third and fourth highest circulation in the system. Neither had room to expand.

Did You Know? The Beechwold Branch was the voting location for Governor James Rhodes and Mayor Jack Sensenbrenner.

Reading at the Beechwold Branch.

The first annual Duckling Day event was held on April 18, 1987, and it remains one of Whetstone Branch's most popular events.

Beechwold Branch, 1954.

DesignGroup was the architect for the Whetstone Branch.

The third Clintonville Branch at 2800 N. High St.

WHITEHALL BRANCH

- Opened as the Town & Country Branch in 1950 in the Town & Country Shopping Center.
- Whitehall Branch opened in 1959 at the corner of Yearling Rd. and E. Broad St.
- Renovated in 1982 to increase book space and create a lounge area.
- Renovated in 1993 with a 2,400 sq. ft. addition.
- New building opened in 2015 at the site of the historic Norton Field.

Did You Know? Whitehall Branch was one of three libraries in the nation to test the new Regiscope "Rapidex" photo charging machine in 1963. The machine took a photo of the customer's library card placed on the book pocket. The roll of exposed film was then sent to the local office that used a microfilm reader to perform customer overdue notices once a week.

Below: Homework Help Center, 2016.

YouMedia Center, 2019.

Upper left: Town & Country location.

Bottom left: The new Whitehall Branch designed by Jonathan Barnes Architecture and Design opened in 2015 and won an award from the American Institute of Architects for its design.

Whitehall Branch at 4371
E. Broad St.

COMMUNITY SUPPORT
FOR THE LIBRARY

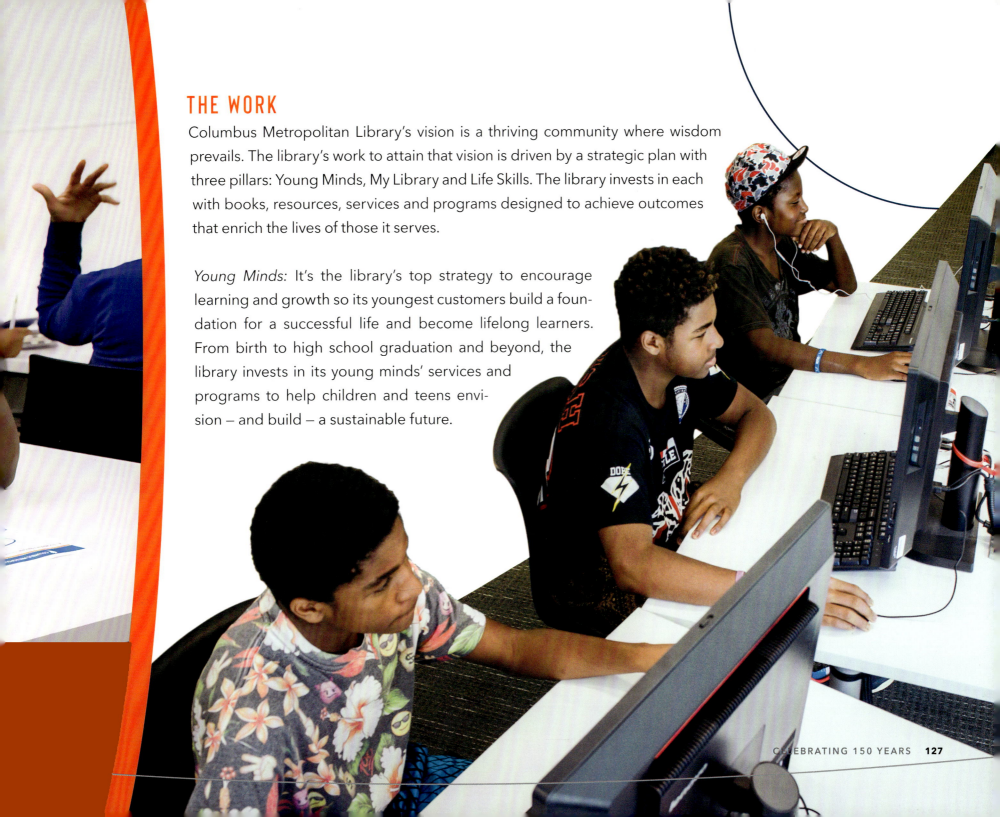

THE WORK

Columbus Metropolitan Library's vision is a thriving community where wisdom prevails. The library's work to attain that vision is driven by a strategic plan with three pillars: Young Minds, My Library and Life Skills. The library invests in each with books, resources, services and programs designed to achieve outcomes that enrich the lives of those it serves.

Young Minds: It's the library's top strategy to encourage learning and growth so its youngest customers build a foundation for a successful life and become lifelong learners. From birth to high school graduation and beyond, the library invests in its young minds' services and programs to help children and teens envision – and build – a sustainable future.

My Library: Libraries evolve to meet customer needs in a rapidly changing world. By creating innovative physical and digital spaces, the library aspires to anticipate those changing needs and provide access to all. The library's continued investment in new libraries is a testament to its commitment to building spaces where all feel welcome.

Life Skills: The library is committed to digital equity, workforce development, adult education and providing access to social services resources. This work is accomplished through strong community partnerships. By identifying challenges and providing opportunities to help, the library supports the community in reaching its full potential.

Above: Annie Norton Battelle was a suffragette who became the first woman to serve on the library's board in 1920. *Image courtesy of Battelle.*

BOARD OF TRUSTEES

The library's seven-member Board of Trustees is responsible for setting the strategic direction for the library and making financial decisions. This includes everything from capital projects like building new libraries to supporting vital services like School Help and Ready for Kindergarten. The Board is instrumental in guiding library leadership as it looks to the future for viability and sustainability.

The ordinance establishing the library and its board, including selection of trustee members, passed on Jan. 15, 1872. Four members were selected by City Council, and there were three ex-officio members, including the mayor, the President of the Council, and the President of the Board of Education. The first board included Otto Dresel,

Below: Left to right are board members Dr. Evelyn Luckey, A. Leonard Nusbaum, Robert Carlile, and A.C. Strip, 1975.

Board members on the Finance Committee complete their purchase of the land for the Hilltop Branch on March 4, 1946, from Harry and Alberta Markins. Here they exchanged a check for $7,000 for the abstract of title and warranty deed. From left to right are Alberta and Harry Markins, board members Rose Briggs Ferguson and Jacob A. Meckstroth, and head librarian John Pugh.

From left to right are 1957 board members Walter H. Kropp, Harold F. Adams, R. Carlisle Moffitt, Jacob A. Meckstroth, Margaret E. Carroll (the Head Librarian), Marion E. Smith and Rose B. Ferguson. Meckstroth is the longest-serving board member, having served from 1929 to 1970. Rose Briggs Ferguson was one of three trustees, along with Frank Warner and Emilius O. Randall, to serve for more than 30 years.

Alfred S. Glenn, William B. Hayden and John W. Andrews, as well as the ex-officio trustees Mayor James G. Bull, Board of Education President Fred Fieser and President of the City Council Luthor Donaldson. In 1890, the state legislature passed the "Heffner Ripper Law" that disbanded some city-appointed offices, including the library board. The board was re-established in 1891, although the Board of Education no longer appointed an ex-officio trustee since they had formed a new school library.

In 1902, the State of Ohio passed a law on municipal codes that changed how all city library boards in Ohio were established. The mayor would select six trustees, and there was a bipartisan requirement that no more than three trustees were from the same party. Board members had to live in the city of Columbus.

As the library expanded county-wide, the board organization changed. In 1976, Columbus City Council voted to create the County Library District. The Ohio Revised Code's library board requirements for county library districts went into effect, providing the structure that exists today: the Franklin County Board of Commissioners selecting four trustees and the Franklin County Court of Common Pleas selecting three. Trustees have a term of seven years.

Left: Dr. Evelyn Luckey was elected the first Black president of the library's board in 1985 and served on the board from 1973-1988. Dr. Luckey was an educator and started teaching first grade at Beatty Park School in 1957. After several promotions she became an assistant superintendent for the Columbus City Schools.

Right: The Reverend Ward S. Parham was the first Black member of the library's board. In addition to his work with the library, he was the president of the Columbus NAACP, and a pastor at Bethany Presbyterian Church. He was appointed in 1970 and served until 1973, when he resigned to go to the Woodland Avenue church in Camden, New Jersey.

Annie Norton Battelle, the first woman trustee, joined the board on February 1, 1920, and there has been at least one woman on the board ever since. In 1934, three women were trustees together for the first time: Elizabeth Norman, Cora Brickell and Lora Kirk. The first time the board included four women trustees was 2022, with Katie Chatas, Sandy Doyle-Ahern, Catherine Strauss and Carla Williams-Scott.

EARLY DONORS & ALCOVES

Contributions from citizens were part of the library's history from its founding. Soon after City Council passed the ordinance to fund the library, a "victory party" was held and raised $49 for books and supplies. At the dedication of the first library in City Hall in 1873, Board President John W. Andrews encouraged fellow citizens to give to the library and your gift "will bless successive generations of citizens and will have an influence on children and children's children."

The Deshler family was the first to make a large contribution to the library. In memory of their father, John and William Deshler donated $1,200 to support the purchase

Above: The E.S. Mattoon is the only surviving alcove. It was donated in honor of Edmund S. Mattoon, "one of the city's most distinguished musicians" by P.J. Huntington in 1909.

of books, with the stipulation that the library "shall remain public and free to every resident of Columbus, without distinction of race, sex, color or religion."

Early gifts came in the form of "alcoves" where donors would sponsor the purchase of a collection of books. Eighteen alcoves were created: Deshler, Noble, Hubbard, Andrews, Brickell, Kilbourne, Women's Music Club, Medical, Dental, Mattoon, Lyman, Sessions, Battelle, Mooney, Moore, Braun, Stevenson, and Soldiers & Sailors.

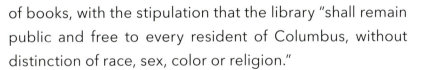

Retired school teacher Carroll S. Kennedy donated funds to start a library in Dublin in 1967. He is shown here on the far right at the dedication ceremony for the temporary building.

Above: Sheila A. Castellarin is thanked by Director Larry Black at a retirement reception in her honor. Castellarin served on the Board of Trustees for six years (1991-1997). Her time on the board was devoted to establishing the library's development program.

Left: Former Library Board of Trustees President Dr. Cynthia Hardy helped create the Carnegie Society and was instrumental in developing the library's art acquisition process. During her tenure the library hosted the first Black Caucus of the American Library Association.

Charlotte Kessler, former Library Board of Trustees President, speaking at the opening of the Hilltop Branch in 1996.

COLUMBUS METROPOLITAN LIBRARY FOUNDATION

The Columbus Metropolitan Library Foundation began as the Carnegie Society in 1990 by Ellen Bachmann, Ann Hoaglin, Charlotte Kessler, Cordelia Robinson and Andrew Sonderman. The name was officially changed to the Foundation in 2005. The Foundation is a 501(c)(3) charitable organization whose mission is building resources for the sole purpose of advancing the library for generations to come.

CAROL SNOWDEN
CHILDREN'S ROOM

toddobo - siete - seven 7
two - dos - labo 2
lix - seis - six 6
shan - cinco - five 5
afam - cuatro - four 4
one - uno 1
three 3

FAMILY
PRIVACY
ROOM

Carol Snowden, a librarian at the Whitehall Branch for 30 years, donated $600,000 for the children's room at the new branch. Her generosity has inspired several other staff members to become legacy donors. Shown here is Youth Services Manager Christy Meister presenting Storytime in the space.

RECENT CAMPAIGNS

Since its founding in 1990, Columbus Metropolitan Library Foundation has successfully completed several campaigns, secured funding for many of the library's signature programs and received generous donations from community members. The people in the community love their library and show it through continued commitment with increasing donations each year.

THE SPIRIT OF GENEROSITY

In 1994, there were 35 gifts to the library. In 2021, 7,017 gifts were received.

Upper left: The Martin Luther King Branch Campaign had a goal to raise $50,000 but concluded with raising over $90,000. Most gifts came from the local community and averaged $50. The names of every donor are on a mural displayed in the branch.

Left: At-risk families, and particularly children, have benefited from Barbara and Al Siemer's vision and extraordinary generosity. They care deeply for the community and want to create opportunities for families to thrive and for students to achieve academic success. From Barbara serving more than two decades on the Foundation board to their family investing through philanthropic gifts to the library, they have made a lasting impact.

Above: The Great Libraries Create campaign launched in 2013 with the goal of renovating or rebuilding 10 libraries in Phase I of the library's building program: Main Library, Driving Park, Dublin, Hilliard, Martin Luther King, Northern Lights, Northside, Parsons, Shepard and Whitehall branches.

Below: Phase II of the library's building program began in 2019 and includes Gahanna, Hilltop, Karl Road and Reynoldsburg branches. Lisal and Don Gorman established a significant estate gift to support the new Gahanna Branch building, set to open in 2023. The building will be the second to bear a donor's name.

Kiwanis Club of Columbus has proudly contributed a portion of the proceeds from their annual Regatta, held at Main Library, for more than 20 years in support of Summer Reading Challenge.

A VERY SPECIAL DONATION

The library received this note from a donor in 2021 in honor of her 80th year as a library cardholder.

"I just made a donation of $80 in honor of my 80th year as a library card holder. I am eighty-five years old, and this was a momentous occasion in my life. In 1941 when I got my card it was required that I sign my name in cursive. I learned to do this as a five-year-old child to receive a passport to the world. The head librarian at that time was Ms. Zapf, and she was a powerful and wise person who was both stern and compassionate. I wish I knew more about her as she was the embodiment of the ideal librarian. I am sure she had a first name, but at the time I would never have dared to ask! This card and the library system has been the most valuable thing in my possession.

I wish I could give much much more, but just know how this changed my young life and be proud of this amazing gift to the community."

Wil Haygood donated a collage of his works to Columbus Metropolitan Library during the 2013 Celebration of Learning, when Haygood was the featured author.

GIVING SOCIETIES

Carnegie: Named in honor of Andrew Carnegie whose $200,000 gift built Main Library.

Pugh: Named in honor of John Pugh, city librarian who convinced Carnegie to build a library in Columbus, Ohio.

Noble: Named in honor of Henry C. Noble who established the second trust fund in memory of his father, John Noble, in 1876.

Deshler: Named in honor of John G. Deshler and William G. Deshler who established the first trust fund in honor of their father, David W. Deshler, in 1869.

Roberts: Named in honor of Blanche C. Roberts, the first woman library director in 1946.

Janney: Named in honor of John Jay Janney who introduced into Columbus City Council an ordinance for establishing our public library on January 15, 1872.

CELEBRATION OF LEARNING

The Foundation held the first Celebration of Learning — the Foundation's signature fundraising event — in 1993 to raise funds for the library's greatest needs and highest priorities. Typically held on the first Friday of November, the event features remarks from a well-known author and dinner from one of the area's finest restaurants. It culminates in the presentation of the Julian Sinclair Smith Award given to a central Ohio resident who demonstrates a dedication to education and a passion for lifelong learning. Occasionally, the Foundation Award is also presented to a dedicated volunteer who has made a significant impact on the legacy of the library.

Below: From left to right, Julian Sinclair Smith award winners Tad and Nancy Jeffrey pose with author Isabel Wilkerson and CEO Patrick Losinski, 2011.

Guests at the 2016 Celebration of Learning admire the gallery of previous authors who have spoken at the event.

JULIAN SINCLAIR SMITH (JSS) AWARD WINNERS & CELEBRATION OF LEARNING SPEAKERS

YEAR	JSS AWARD WINNERS	SPEAKER
1993	Clifford Tyree	Ray Bradbury
1994	William T. Gillie	Ellen Goodman
1995	Donn Vickers	Calvin Trillin
1996	Judy R. Garel	Doris Kearns Goodwin
1997	Rose-Marie Dilenschneider	Shelby Foote
1998	Josiah H. Blackmore III and Yvonne A. Bell	Frank McCourt
1999	Rowland C.W. Brown	Margaret Atwood
2000	Catherine T. Willis	Arthur Golden
2001	Phyllis Greene	Joyce Carol Oates
2002	Donald and Thekla Shackelford	Michael Cunningham
2003	Wayne P. Lawson	David McCullough
2004	Robert and Shirley Duncan	David Halberstam
2005	Annie Glenn	Richard Russo
2006	Loann Crane	Scott Turow
2007	Carl Kohrt	Walter Isaacson
2008	Linda Stern Kass	Roy Blount Jr.
2009	Stefanie and Chris Spielman	Azar Nafisi
2010	Marci and Bill Ingram	Colum McCann
2011	Nancy and Tad Jeffrey	Isabel Wilkerson
2012	Jay Jordan	Michael Chabon
2013	Tanny Crane	Wil Haygood
2014	Ann and Tom Hoaglin	Wes Moore
2015	DeeDee and Herb Glimcher	Carl Hiaasen
2016	Barbara and Al Siemer	Jeffrey Toobin
2017	Robert J. Weiler	Suzan-Lori Parks
2018	Donna and Larry James	Bill Bryson
2019	Jack and Suzi Hanna	Candice Millard
2020	Mary Lazarus	Abraham Verghese
2021	Algenon L. Marbley	Jacqueline Woodson
2022	Ann and Ron Pizzuti	Jon Meacham

1999's Celebration of Learning drew a large audience to hear featured author Margaret Atwood.

FRIENDS OF THE COLUMBUS METROPOLITAN LIBRARY

Friends of the Library is a nonprofit 501(c)(4) organization made up of everyday customers and advocates passionate about Columbus Metropolitan Library. Its purpose is to build awareness and resources to champion the vision of the library. The Friends began in 1975, with James R. Hull as the first president. By January 1976, it had 120 members before quickly growing to over 2,500 by 1981. The first Friends' book sale was held March 22-27, 1976, at Main Library in the Bookmobile garage. In its early years, some Friends activities included selling salt, baked goods, plants and handmade bookmarks.

The Friends opened a bookstore at Main Library called "Secondhand Prose" in 1977. It was renamed the Library Store in 1992. At the 1997 American Library Association's conference, the organization was awarded a Friends of the Library USA award for its outstanding membership drive, newsletter and coffee kiosk. Today, Friends of the Library manages revenue-generating library amenities that enhance the library experience and maintains a membership program of library lovers who champion grassroots advocacy in support of Columbus Metropolitan Library.

Right: Friends of the Library Book Sale at Main Library, 1987.

Upper Left: Friends of the Library holds multiple book sales each year. It's their longest running revenue generator.

Left: Friends of the Library won the Ohio Friends of the Library Recognition Award in 2011.

Friends of the Library hosted a reception for the opening of the Touched...Recognizing Artist Queen Brooks exhibit in 2022.

A volunteer puts out a yard sign in support of the library's levy in 1981.

LEVY CAMPAIGNS

Taxpayer support has been a crucial part of the library's funding from the beginning in 1873. The first levy to go on the ballot, however, was not until 1976. Voters approved a 0.6 mill, 5-year levy by a margin of 63% to 36%. The levy was renewed in 1981 with approval of nearly three-quarters of voters. At the time, it was the largest margin of victory for any county-wide library levy issue in Ohio's history.

By 1986, it was clear that a new levy was needed. The Board of Trustees asked voters to approve a 2.2 mill, 15-year levy to allow for long-term planning. It would allow the library to increase staff by 44%, add evening and Sunday hours at certain locations, increase the book budget, renovate Main Library, expand and create new buildings for other branches, and, most importantly, improve service to all our customers. It passed by a margin of 53% to 47% and was renewed in 2000 with 67% approval.

The 2000 levy was a 10-year renewal of the 1986 appropriation, which meant that a new ballot initiative was necessary in 2010. Recent cuts in the state budget meant that salaries had been cut by 5%, staff hours were reduced by 10%, hours of operation

Dear Neighbors,

Our top-rated Columbus Metropolitan Library does great work every day. It means so much to children and youth, seniors and families, small businesses and working people.

So we support Issue 4 because it keeps library branches open, provides books, funds reading and homework help programs and helps adults without computers look for jobs.

Issue 4 is the library's only local support – half its budget. It's a necessity after millions in cuts by the state, staff reductions and pay freezes at the library.

Without Issue 4, up to half the branches could close, we would have many less books at the library, and much-needed programs and services would be greatly reduced.

After 24 years with no new local levy funds, and huge state cuts, please vote for Issue 4. Keep our library strong. It's the only local support.

Thank you,
Friends of the Library

A Community Letter
FOR ISSUE 4
Columbus Metropolitan Library

VOTE FOR **4**

were cut by 18%, and the acquisition budget was cut by 40%. The proposed 2.8 mill permanent levy would restore all services. It passed overwhelmingly with 66% of the vote.

The passage of the levy was a testament to the value the library brings to the community, and to the dedicated staff who work every day to enrich the lives of the customers they serve.

Above: A bumper sticker showing support of the library's levy in 1986.

Upper left: A letter to the community to support the library's levy in 2010, when the library was trying to restore services after state budget cuts.

Left: Four board of trustees members look at a sign in support of the library's first levy in 1976.

ESTABLISHED THE CHILDREN'S HOUR WHICH HAS BEEN A GREAT SUCCESS.

ONE OF THE TREASURES THAT IS WITHIN.

HE IS AN AUTHORITY ON THE CULTURE AND TREATMENT OF BOOK WORMS

JOHN KNOWS RIGHT WHERE TO PUT HIS FINGER ON 'EM!

THE ARTS

THE LOVERS

WIFE

OLD AGE

CHRIS

FARMER

YOUTH

SCIENTIST

CLERICAL

STUDENT

EVERYONE WHO HAS TAKEN BOOKS FROM THE CARNEGIE LIBRARY HAS NOTED THE GREAT SYSTEM WHICH IS USED THERE.

THE NEEDS OF ALL QUICKLY SUPPLIED.

JOHN J. PUGH
Secretary and Librarian Columbus Public Library

LIBRARY LEADERS

Columbus Metropolitan Library is fortunate to have had several long-serving directors. In the early days of the library, the title "chief librarian" was used. As the number of staff increased, it was changed to director and finally Chief Executive Officer. The first three directors were with the library from the time period when it was at City Hall. Rev. James Grover (namesake of author James Thurber) became the first director in 1872, and was succeeded by John Pugh, who served until his death in 1946. Blanche Roberts, the first woman hired at the library and the assistant director for 40 years, became the library's first woman director in 1946.

CHIEF LIBRARIANS, LIBRARY DIRECTORS AND CHIEF EXECUTIVE OFFICERS

James Grover, 1872–1896
John Pugh, 1896–1946
Blanche Roberts, 1946–1947
Will Collins, 1947–1956
Margaret E. Carroll, 1956–1962
Edward B. Daniels, 1962–1974
James E. Ahlstrom, 1974–1975
Donald J. Sager, 1975–1978
Hoyt Rees Galvin, 1978–1979
Richard Sweeney, 1979–1984
Larry Black, 1984–2002
Patrick Losinski, 2002–present

Far left: Caricature of librarian John James Pugh from the book *Club Men of Columbus*, 1911. Pugh began at the library in 1881 and became director in 1896. In total, he served for 65 years until his death in 1946.

Far bottom left: Richard T. Sweeney *(right),* shown here with assistant director Charles Brown, conducted the first experiment in checking out materials by a television-computer network. The library increased its circulation 20% during his five years as director.

1: The first woman hired by the library, Blanche Roberts also founded the first children's Story Hour prior to World War I. She served for 53 years as a librarian, assistant director and director.

2: Margaret E. Carroll, alumna of North High School and The Ohio State University, previously ran the Memorial Library in West Palm Beach, Florida. At Columbus Metropolitan Library, she was head of Circulation before becoming Director. She was Director during the library's fastest growing decade, the 1950s, which included the expansion of Main Library and several new community branches, as well as new bookmobiles.

3: Donald Sager was instrumental in passing the 1976 Levy and saved four branches from closing due to funding during his tenure.

4: Larry D. Black served Columbus Metropolitan Library for 24 years, 18 as library director. He guided the library through decades of technological advancements and established the library as an industry leader in customer-focused service. The auditorium at Main Library was named in his honor when he retired in 2002. The Larry D. Black Fund through the library's foundation was also established to recognize his commitment to the library.

5: Patrick Losinski was named Columbus Metropolitan Library's chief executive officer in 2002. Among his breadth of work is leadership of the library's $250 million investment in 16 new or renovated buildings as part of the library's ambitious building program launched in 2013.

Staff picnic at Olentangy Park, 1948. Director Will Collins is on the far left. Image courtesy of Helen Allison.

DEDICATED STAFF THROUGHOUT THE YEARS

From its humble beginning with one staff member in 1873, to nearly 900 employees in 2023, Columbus Metropolitan Library has invested heavily in its people. John Pugh, the second chief librarian, was the longest-serving staff member at 65 years. Carrie Ingle, technical services assistant, was a close second at 60 years.

Finance team works on the library's budget.

Above: Magazines and Newspapers Division staff, 1990.

Far left: Security Operations Center is the hub of safety and security services, monitoring buildings across the system.

Left: Drivers and sorters keep materials moving across central Ohio.

Many Columbus Metropolitan Library staff members have been recognized as leaders in their fields. They have gone on to become library directors across the country as well as hold nonprofit, government and for-profit leadership positions. In addition to their dedicated work for the library, many employees are also musicians, poets, artists and community leaders, giving even more back to their communities.

Property Management team members work across the system to maintain high standards in library buildings.

Staff and their families at the opening of the renovated Main Library, 2016.

> Library staff care deeply about serving our customers and community. That dedication extends to all: the student who makes the honor roll because of our school help efforts, the customers who come to us for help finding their place in the workforce, and the child getting their first library card to start their journey to becoming a lifelong learner. We are the sum of our community.

—Patrick Losinski
CEO, Columbus Metropolitan Library

Bertha Campbell (*right*) and Phyllis J. Buckner (*left*) at the Eastside Branch. Buckner was one of the first African American librarians hired at the library in 1953. In 1954, she was promoted to head librarian at the Franklinton Branch. Campbell became head librarian at the Eastside Branch in 1964.

APLE held a Staff Appreciation Party for library staff and families in 2013, at Wolfe Park.

2019 APLE picnic.

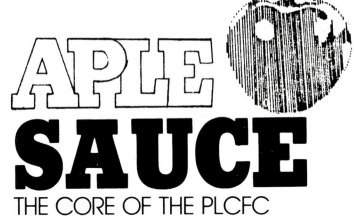

Above: Logo for the "APLE Sauce" column from *Contents*, the staff newsletter in 1978.

ASSOCIATION OF PUBLIC LIBRARY EMPLOYEES

The Association of Public Library Employees (APLE) chapter at Columbus Metropolitan Library began in 1965. Its purpose stated, "to promote the welfare and mutual understanding of the staff of the Columbus Public Library and to further the progress of library service in the Columbus area." APLE's first fundraising project in

Left: Driving Park Branch manager Gloria Campbell receives a commendation from Board President Robert Ramage for her work as President of APLE.

1966 involved selling canisters of Easter candy. The project raised $50. The organization sponsored social events such as picnics and holiday parties and at one time even organized a softball team.

APLE facilitates the Staff Relations Committee, which began with a suggestion box placed in the staff room in the fall of 1969. APLE also supports staff through financial assistance for education. In 2013, the Ohio Secretary of State certified APLE as a nonprofit, domestic corporation and in 2018, the IRS granted APLE status as a tax-exempt charity under IRC 501(c)(3). During the COVID-19 pandemic, APLE committed to providing staff with tools and connections to local businesses as ways to help staff cope.

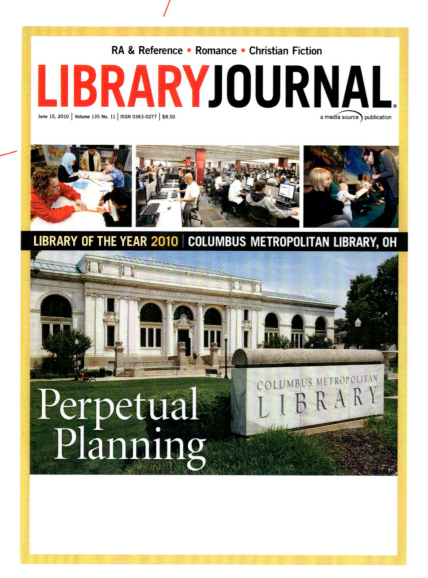

Right: The Whitehall Branch was recognized by the American Institute of Architects/American Library Association (AIA/ALA) with a Library Building Award in 2017.

AWARD-WINNING LIBRARY

Columbus Metropolitan Library has long been recognized as a leader in library services. The Institute of Museum and Library Services awarded the library its highest honor, the National Medal for Museum and Library Service, in 2011. A year earlier, *Library Journal* named Columbus Metropolitan Library "Library of the Year" at a reception at the American Library Association Conference in Washington, D.C. The library first won the John Cotton Dana Library Public Relations Award in 1978, then again in 1979, 1992, 1993 and in 2017 for the Great Libraries Create campaign that raised $21.5 million.

Columbus Metropolitan Library is also recognized for its stewardship of public funds. It routinely receives the Auditor of State Award with Distinction, and has been

awarded the Government Finance Officers Association of the United States and Canada Certificate of Achievement for Excellence in Financial Reporting for over 35 years.

The library's commitment to inspirational architecture for its new libraries has resulted in numerous awards. The Driving Park (2015) and Northside (2018) branches won

the Columbus Landmarks Foundation's James B. Recchie Design Award in 2018.

Johnathan Barnes Architecture and Design (Whitehall Branch, 2017) and Moody Nolan Inc. (Martin Luther King Branch, 2015) won American Institute of Architects (AIA) Merit Awards for their designs.

Patrick Losinski announces Columbus Metropolitan Library as the recipient of the National Medal for Museum and Library Services, 2011.

WHAT DOES THE FUTURE HOLD?

As Ohio's capital city, Columbus continues to experience incredible growth. Planning studies estimate that the Columbus region will gain 1 million new residents by the year 2050. The current U.S. Census Bureau results report that Columbus' population grew 15.08% from 2010 to 2020, which makes Columbus one of the fastest growing cities in the Midwest, and one of only 14 cities nationwide to gain at least 100,000 residents over the past 10 years. Intel's investment in U.S. chip manufacturing, with a "mega-site" on 1,000 acres in Licking County, also heralds a new age of growth for central Ohio and its workforce.

What does this mean for Columbus Metropolitan Library's vision of a thriving community where wisdom prevails? It means the library keeps growing and keeps innovating. It has an enduring history of evolving to meet customer needs as the world around it changes, and the world is changing more rapidly than ever before.

Community activism resulted in the library's expansion from a single reading room to a library with 23 locations. Community support continues to help the library provide access to books, resources, technology — and knowledge — so the library can be the space that meets the promise of the words etched above Main Library's front doors: Open to All.

Library work is steeped in the tradition of helping others. Its legacy is service; the future of that service is shaped by the wants and needs of the people who walk through the doors of every library, every day.

WHAT DOES THE FUTURE HOLD FOR COLUMBUS METROPOLITAN LIBRARY?

Ohio is fortunate to have many talented authors who were either born here or found their passion for writing here. A few have shared their thoughts about the library's future.

" When I was a kid growing up in Columbus in the 1960s, one of the popular cartoons was *The Jetsons*. They were a family who lived in outer space, traveling around a moonlit galaxy on individualized spaceships. The spaceships looked mighty hip. My everyday reality, of course, was more down to earth. There was not a car in our family and I walked everywhere. Or caught the city bus on special occasions. On Saturdays my grandmother would give me money to catch the bus downtown to go to the Main Library on Grant Avenue. There were always school projects that took me to the big library to do research! I'd dive into the history and art sections, scouring for books. History fascinated me. So did maps. Wouldn't it be amazing if there were a train system to pick people up – especially students who hailed from families without cars – and deliver them to the downtown library? The only stop it would make would be to the front door of the library. And it would deliver them back home. Like the experiences of outer space Jetsons family. I want there to be a future where young students can get to the Main Library with as little effort as possible."

—Wil Haygood
Journalist and award-winning author

" The library of the future looks much like a gathering place for the community to come together, no matter your walk of life, and safely have discussions about politics, religion, race, art, education, and personal growth just to name a few. We have lost the tolerance for healthy debate in this country and I truly believe that there's more that connects us than that divides us. The library of the future has the opportunity to be the catalyst of that change in the narrative."

—Achea Redd
Author, public speaker and mental health advocate

" I was raised on books. My mother Betty knew the importance of reading. But growing up, we didn't have a lot of money. My father Glen was a mechanic and welder, while my mother had manual labor jobs like tending an orchard and cleaning houses. Libraries gave me the opportunity to discover books without limitation. Though some things in my childhood have faded, I still remember the layout of the library. The grand entry with the Dewey Decimal cabinet, its brass pulls tarnished by the years. The large oak desk of the librarian just to the left, leading to the room full of dusty reference books. To the right, the children's room where I could spend hours. Oftentimes I would sneak into the adult section that existed in the back. I still remember the metal shelves painted blue, peach, and cream. The line of windows opened to the outside. And there in the corner, a spot where the sun shined and where I could take a thick book off the shelf to be lost with the cool air and the sunshine. That's what the future of the Columbus Metropolitan Library looks like to me. It looks like a girl reading a book like a secret in the crisp air and sunshine. It looks like those memories already made, and new ones yet to be. Because in a library, the story is never finished. Here's to the next 150 years of falling in love with books and celebrating the libraries we call home."

—Tiffany McDaniel
Award-winning novelist and artist

"I'm certainly not a great prognosticator. After all, I'm the one who famously said, "No one is going to pay good money for water in plastic bottles." However, I believe the challenges that libraries will face will be competently met by the people who have dedicated their working lives to library science – the people who create the pro-

grams, purchase materials, research the archives, and keep our libraries open. We must rely on them to see the future and meet the needs of our public in general and our children in particular. Thirty years ago, few could have foreseen the digital revolution, but our libraries did and adjusted accordingly. I don't know what the next revolution will be, but I have every confidence that our libraries and the individuals who run them will be ready for that challenge."

—Robin Yocum
Journalist and best-selling novelist

"These days predicting the future can be frightening, but I am not at all scared to imagine the future of Columbus Metropolitan Library. In an ever-changing world, the library will continue to be what it is now: a place where learning, community, and democracy thrive. During my years in Columbus, the city has undergone rapid growth and change, but the libraries have been a constant, whether I am visiting online for research or in-person for a community event with my daughter. I am sure the library will continue to evolve to meet the needs of the future, just as libraries have incorporated computers, eBooks, and most recently, COVID tests, in the years since my childhood, when my local library offered little more than words on paper. Still, I have great nostalgia, not just for that modest space, but for all the imagined places I visited in the pages of its books. Those places, even if they aren't real, can exist forever, and I have faith that they will live on in Columbus Metropolitan Library."

—Janet Beard
Award-winning novelist

"The Library of the Future is here today. Thanks to the digital media revolution, libraries have transformed into architecturally interesting and inviting spaces. Peaceful. Calm gathering places for the curious who seek out knowledge, while providing access to all the information that now resides in the clouds. Naturally, the library of the future still has books and most importantly, Librarians. The future is good."

—Jeff Smith
Cartoonist and award-winning author

"In Ray Bradbury's 1950 short story "The Long Rain," human colonists on Venus seek shelter in Sun Domes, strategically based reprieves from the planet's constant rain and dangerous inhabitants. I imagine Columbus library branches of the future as similar respites from an increasingly chaotic world. Libraries today are some of the country's last remaining public spaces where people can gather free of corporate rules and political interference. I imagine this role expanding years from now as branches serve as welcoming public chambers of information, imagination, and physical and intellectual safety."

—Andrew Welsh-Huggins
Journalist and novelist

"The Columbus Metropolitan Library of the future will be a place for information, education, collaboration, community, and compassion."

—Terry Eisele
Educator and graphic novelist

Time It!

Marg Melanson
Teaching Master
Business and Commerce Department
Seneca College of Applied Arts and Technology
Willowdale, Ontario

Copp Clark Pitman Ltd.
Toronto

© Copp Clark Pitman Ltd. 1983

ISBN 0-7730-4319-5

Editing/Carol Ring
Design/Linda Hosso and Patti Brown
Typesetting/Trigraph

Canadian Cataloguing in Publication Data
Melanson, Margaret C.
Time it!

ISBN 0-7730-4319-5

Copp Clark Pitman Ltd.

Printed and bound in Canada

Table of Contents

Acknowledgements

The following authors and publishers have given permission for the adaptation of their material in the pieces listed below. Thanks is extended to all, with special appreciation to those individuals who wrote pieces especially for this publication. In particular, I would like to thank Ann Thornton for contributions above and beyond the call of sisterly duty.

Baker, Sandy
PARACHUTING THE FIRST TIME Adapted from "I can not think ...." by Sandy Baker; Toronto, Canada.

Banks, Joan Brix
VINE GIANT Adapted from "The Mile-a-Minute Vine" by Joan Brix Banks from *Ranger Rick's Nature Magazine*, July 1980, Washington, U.S.A.

Berton, Pierre
BILLY BISHOP Adapted from "Billy Bishop: The Lone Hawk" by Pierre Berton, *My Country*, used by permission of The Canadian Publishers, McClelland and Stewart Limited, Toronto, Canada.

Canadian Government
HOME INSULATION Adapted from "Highlights from the History of Canadian Insulation" leaflet distributed by Energy, Mines and Resources Canada. Reproduced by permission of the Minister of Supply and Services Canada.

Churchill, Sir Winston
IN THE WORDS OF SIR WINSTON Adapted from *A History of the English Speaking Peoples* by Sir Winston Churchill, used by permission of The Canadian Publishers, McClelland and Stewart Limited, Toronto, Canada.

Cunnington, Joan
MARTHA SEEKS EMPLOYMENT and MARTHA'S JOB INTERVIEW Adapted from "You're Not Going to Believe This, But ..." by Joan Cunnington; Toronto, Canada.

Elliott, Marion
OFFICE OF THE FUTURE Adapted from a report by Marion Elliott; Toronto, Canada.

Holliday, Jon
OPERA Adapted from "A Too Comic Opera" by Jon Holliday, *WineMine, A First Anthology*, edited by Anthony Hogg, published by Souvenir Press. By permission of Peter Dominic Publications; Harlow, England.

Kemp, Murdina
CHILDHOOD Adapted from "My childhood days ...." by Murdina Kemp; London, Canada.

Kipness, Jean
ON TIME Adapted and reprinted from "Just In Time" by Jean Kipness, published in *World of Work*, with permission of Webster/McGraw-Hill, New York, U.S.A.

Kucharski, Joyce
NEW WORLD Adapted from "It Happened One Day" by Joyce Kucharski; Toronto, Canada.

Leacock, Stephen
HUMOUR Adapted from "Humour As I See It" by Stephen Leacock, *Leacock Roundabout*, used by permission of The Canadian Publishers, McClelland and Stewart Limited, Toronto, Canada.
MOTHER'S DAY Adapted from "How We Kept Mother's Day" by Stephen Leacock, *Leacock Roundabout*, used by permission of The Canadian Publishers, McClelland and Stewart Limited, Toronto, Canada.
SMITH'S HOTEL Adapted from "The Hostelry of Mr. Smith" by Stephen Leacock, *Sunshine Sketches of a Little Town*, used by permission of The Canadian Publishers, McClelland and Stewart Limited, Toronto, Canada.

SPRING Adapted from "First Call for Spring" by Stephen Leacock, *Leacock Roundabout*, used by permission of The Canadian Publishers, McClelland and Stewart Limited, Toronto, Canada.

Macdonald, John
NULLARBOR PLAIN Adapted from "I often thought ...." by John Macdonald; Melbourne, Australia.

McNulty, Velma
WHY ME? Adapted from "Why Me" by Velma McNulty; Toronto, Canada.

Money, Dr. Herbert
DISASTER Adapted from "The Ranrajirca Disaster" by Dr. Herbert Money and Mrs. Netta Money; Christchurch, New Zealand.
REVOLUTION Adapted from "My First Revolution" by Dr. Herbert Money; Christchurch, New Zealand.

Ontario Science Centre
ROBOTS Adapted from "Men of Steel?" from *Newscience*, October 1982, published by the Ontario Science Centre, Toronto, Canada.

Petersen, Susan
HOMEMAKER Adapted from a letter by Susan Petersen published in *Homemakers Magazine*, October 1980, Toronto, Canada.

Ring, Dr. W. A.
ESKIMO ART Adapted from "Eskimo Art ...." by Dr. W. A. Ring; St. John's, Canada.
QUILTING Adapted from "Quilting ...." by Dr. W. A. Ring; St. John's, Canada.

Soriano, Zilla
SKIING Adapted from "To Ski or Not to Ski" by Zilla Soriano; Toronto, Canada.

Thompson, Tommy
OTHER SIDE OF THE WINDOW Adapted from "Message to Members" by Tommy Thompson, *Trellis*, January 1983, published by the Civic Garden Centre, Toronto, Canada.

Thornton, Ann
COUNTRY MOUSE Adapted from "The little country mouse ...." by Ann Thornton; London, Canada.
HOGS Adapted from "The hog ...." by Ann Thornton; London, Canada.
HOUSEHOLD SCIENCE Adapted from "The Family Studies classroom ...." by Ann Thornton; London, Canada.
LIGHTNING AND THUNDER Adapted from "Lightning is ...." by Ann Thornton; London, Canada.
MUSICAL TRAINING Adapted from "All Children ...." by Ann Thornton; London, Canada.
SALT Adapted from "The chemical compound ...." by Ann Thornton; London, Canada.
VIOLIN - FIRST STRING and VIOLIN - HISTORY AND CARE Adapted from "The Violin - Queen of Instruments" by Ann Thornton; London, Canada.

Vanstone, Kay
EXERCISE NEEDED and LETTER WRITING Adapted from *Develop Your English Skills* by Kay Vanstone, published by Copp Clark Pitman, Toronto, Canada.

Preface

Ever since the first typewriter invaded the office, employers have used keyboarding speed as the major indicator of typing abilities. Many people have argued that this practice is unfair to those who have a relatively low input speed but who are highly accurate and, therefore, highly productive. As a result, some employers have implemented production tests, but the speed test remains as the standard form of measuring keyboarding skills.

Because employers do seek adequate keyboarding speeds from word processor and typewriter operators and also from many other personnel - even at the executive level - timed testing of speed/accuracy achievements is of prime and increasing concern to educational institutions. It has been shown that students perform best when using an abundance of varied and interesting materials and *Time It!* provides this. In addition, many of the timed writings are speed scored and paced so that they may also be used for speed/accuracy building.

Part 1 ▪ Warm-up Drills

Part 1 is comprised of 75 warm-up drills. Each drill contains three lines: an easy line for speed, a variable line for building proficiency on a specific element, and a line of challenging difficulty for reinforcing accuracy.

The syllabic intensity (SI) of easy lines progresses in difficulty from 1.00 SI to 1.30 SI. The challenging lines progress from 1.50 SI to 1.72 SI.

All lines are 70 characters long.

Part 2 ▪ Timed Writings

Part 2 is comprised of 115 timed writings. The content of these writings covers a broad range of topics and stories that students will find interesting. Students are not expected to type the titles of the writings as they have not been included in the word counts. The format used for typing such elements as dashes and ellipses is that which is most compatible with the word wraparound feature found on most word processors and other computer stations. Accents have been omitted from words of foreign derivation to avoid confusing students as to how to handle them.

Three difficulty levels are provided for as follows:

Easy Copy

There are 15 easy (1.20 SI - 1.30 SI) timed writings for use as timed tests. Because these writings are speed scored and paced for each minute, they may also be used for building speed/accuracy. Speeds start at 28 gross words per minute (gwpm) and increase four words with each timing up to 100 gwpm.

Average Copy

There are 85 average (1.35 SI - 1.45 SI) timed writings for use as timed tests. The first fifteen average writings, which are speed scored and paced for each minute, may also be used for building speed/accuracy. Speeds start at 28 gwpm and increase four words with each timing up to 100 gwpm.

Challenging Copy

There are 15 challenging (1.50 SI - 1.65 SI) timed writings for use as timed tests. Because these writings are speed scored and paced for each minute, they may also be used for building speed/accuracy. Speeds start at 28 gwpm and increase four words with each timing up to 100 gwpm.

Diamonds

100
GWPM

Diamonds have long been hailed as a girl's best friend. Chemi- — 13
cally speaking, however, a diamond is the same as a hunk of coal. — 26
Diamonds are pieces of crystallized carbon that were formed in the — 39
depths of the earth eons ago and brought up to the surface by volcanic — 53
pressures. When cut into facets, the diamond is the most brilliant of — 67
all gems. It is also the hardest – so hard, in fact, that it is used — 81
in drills and other tools for cutting hard materials. — 92

The second hardest stone, the cubic zirconium, has created some — 106
problems for diamond merchants. Fabricated from the metallic element, — 120
zirconium, and cut into facets, it, too, is very brilliant and, to the — 134
naked eye, cannot be distinguished from a diamond. Even using a — 147
strong magnifying glass, some experts cannot tell the difference. — 160

Diamonds are priced in accordance with their carat, cut, colour, — 174
and clarity – the four Cs. Most diamonds appear to be clear and — 187
white, but if held up to the light and looked at through their sides — 201
against a white background, a touch of colour can usually be seen. A — 215
few diamonds are completely coloured. The Hope diamond is blue, and — 229
the Tiffany diamond is canary yellow. Diamonds contain natural flaws, — 243
such as spots, fractures, etc. In the gem trade, these are called — 256
inclusions. The fewer inclusions a diamond contains, the more valu- — 270
able the gem. Like snowflakes and fingerprints, there are no two — 283
diamonds exactly the same. This fact has made it possible for a form — 297
of fingerprinting to be used to positively identify diamonds in case — 311
of loss or theft. Diamonds are available in a number of different — 324
cuts. The round cut is the most common because it is the easiest to — 338
cut and is, therefore, the least expensive. Other popular cuts — 351
include the oval cut, the pear-shaped cut, the emerald cut, the — 364
marquise cut, and the heart-shaped cut. The size of a diamond is — 378
expressed in points or carats. There are 100 points to a carat. A — 392
diamond ring set with one or several diamonds is the most common sym- — 406
bol of betrothal in the western world. — 414

Diamonds are often set along with other gems, each enhancing the — 428
other's beauty. One of the best known combination settings is the — 441
engagement ring of the Princess of Wales, in which a blue sapphire is — 455
surrounded by diamonds. Dealers say that from an investment point of — 469
view, it is advisable to purchase a solitaire in a simple setting. — 482
This way, a buyer can expect to obtain a larger and better quality — 495
stone for his or her money. — 500

| 1 | 2 | 3 | 4 | 5 | 6 | 7 | 8 | 9 | 10 | 11 | 12 | 13 | 14 |

Part 1 ▪ Warm-up Drills

Purpose The first line in each drill is an easy one to limber up the fingers and promote speed. The second line provides drill on a specific aspect of keyboarding. The third line is of challenging difficulty to reinforce accuracy.

Procedure 1 Type each line three times in succession as follows:
- at a slow, accurate rate;
- at a moderate, accurate rate;
- at a rapid, but accurate rate.

Single space same lines. Double space before beginning a new line.

2 When you have finished the whole drill, proofread and circle errors.

3 If you had **up to five errors, move on** to the next drill next time.

4 If you had **more than five errors, repeat** the same drill next time.

Drill 1 ☐☐☐

Easy | Most nights, he can park the car down the street in front of the shop.
Alphabetic | I just asked him to quote a very low price for a dozen boxes of rings.
Challenging | Enclose a cheque or money order, along with your full mailing address.

Drill 2 ☐☐☐

Easy | Peas can be sown in the garden just as soon as the soil can be worked.
Home Row | He asked Dad to adjust the shelf so his glass won't skid off and fall.
Challenging | We have no service charges for travellers cheques or cash withdrawals.

Drill 3 ☐☐☐

Easy | As soon as Fran gets home, she will sew that button on your blue coat.
Third Row | It is true they wrote that the portly squire is quite worthy of power.
Challenging | Slow, gentle stretching of body muscles can reduce stress and fatigue.

Drill 4 ☐☐☐

Easy | This firm adds a service charge to all bills not paid by the due date.
Bottom Row | Can Vic and Bob give me the exact city, cove or zone which was bombed?
Challenging | For early colour indoors, he brings in cuttings from flowering shrubs.

Drill 5 ☐☐☐

Easy | You will need a list of the accounts which are two or more months old.
Adjacent Keys | A pious porter has options to buy cashews and remnants above our cave.
Challenging | Poor flying conditions have brought about a delay in flight schedules.

Drill 6 ☐☐☐

Easy | If we were all heroes, then who would clap and cheer as we marched by?
First Fingers | I gave a jaunty young man the rights to buy the timber from the grove.
Challenging | Don't forget to include your full name, address, and telephone number.

Drill 7 ☐☐☐

Easy | Your cottage is close to a clear lake in which they can swim and fish.
Second Fingers | His sidekick, who seeks to accent diet, cried at my dock like a child.
Challenging | This patient has missed several weeks of school because of infections.

| 1 | 2 | 3 | 4 | 5 | 6 | 7 | 8 | 9 | 10 | 11 | 12 | 13 | 14 |

96

GWPM

How often have we complained that there is not enough time to accomplish everything we want to do? We each have twenty-four hours available to us each day – no more, no less. Why is it, then, that some people accomplish more than others? The answer is effective time management.

Since all of our time is spent engaged in one activity or another, we are dealing with two factors: time and activities. Because we cannot increase or decrease our allotment of twenty-four hours[1] per day, time is the constant factor. Activities, however, are a variable factor; activities are something we can change. Effective time management means replacing the less important activities with more important ones. This means deciding which activities are important. Before we can do this, it is necessary to decide what our goals are.

Goals must be specific; for example, to write a children's storybook. Goals should not conflict with one another. For example[2], it would be nigh impossible to excel at a full-time job, study computer programming, train for championship tennis, and write a book all at the same time. Chances are that all of the goals would suffer and little would be achieved. Instead, we must prioritize our goals according to their importance, their ease of accomplishment, their logical sequence, or whatever criteria is suitable for us. We must also assign a completion date for each goal and draw up a plan of action which[3] includes a list of the activities required to accomplish our objectives. These are the important activities to which we should devote the bulk of our time.

Ah, but how do we go about displacing the low priority activities? First, we must get organized. This is crucial to success. It is the key to time management. Whether it takes several hours or several days, it has to be done. We can begin by making a list of the activities we currently engage in. Are there[4] any that are really not necessary? Eliminate them. Are there any that someone else could do? Delegate them. Could any be done more quickly and efficiently? Establish new systems and procedures. When all this is done, we must design a daily schedule of activities for ourselves according to our own particular situations. By following it and refusing to be detoured, we will discover that we can utilize our time so that we are more productive and accomplishing our goals.[5]

| 1 | 2 | 3 | 4 | 5 | 6 | 7 | 8 | 9 | 10 | 11 | 12 | 13 | 14 |

12
26
40
54
56
70
84
97
111
124
137
151
165
179
193
207
220
233
246
259
273
286
300
314
320
334
348
361
375
389
403
416
430
444
457
471
480

Drill 8 ☐☐☐

Easy

Third Fingers

Challenging

I plan to build a high fence around the whole yard and paint it brown.

We shall soon show those exiles who stole lassos from our saloon wall.

They are hoping for successful drilling results from the oil prospect.

Drill 9 ☐☐☐

Easy

Fourth Fingers

Challenging

I found a deep sense of pride welling up in me as I read your account.

Papa packed the prizes: a cape, a blazer, a parka, and aqua bandanas.

It appears neither of us had understood the scope of this undertaking.

Drill 10 ☐☐☐

Easy

Vertical Keys

Challenging

It is my job to open the store in the morning and lock it up at night.

Dick saw and gave Jim squeezed juice for my broiled pike and cold hen.

A shareholder may appoint someone to attend and act on his/her behalf.

Drill 11 ☐☐☐

Easy

Left Hand

Challenging

We prefer the picture of the boat scene done in tones of blue and red.

The haze made it hard to get a view of the steep descent to the river.

The fine old houses help to preserve the atmosphere of this community.

Drill 12 ☐☐☐

Easy

Right Hand

Challenging

It seems the file has been misplaced but a search for it is under way.

Young Joanie may munch on my dill pickle and dunk it in jam and honey.

The attitude of tenants has much improved over the last several years.

Drill 13 ☐☐☐

Easy

Opposite Hand Keys

Challenging

The very same day the old brick house came on the market, it was sold.

Wow! How did Jeff move, load, and tuck eighty hefty bombs below deck?

Notice the product's top quality and the attention paid to its detail.

Drill 14 ☐☐☐

Easy

Short Words

Challenging

The snow has settled in the trees and bushes and it is a lovely sight.

We know it is a long way to go to get to bask and play in sun and sea.

In a business, a good, efficient support staff makes a big difference.

Drill 15 ☐☐☐

Easy

Long Words

Challenging

The children liked the tale about a day in the life of a young prince.

General knowledge of the specialized materials available is essential.

Trade your time for equal time in another season, resort, or location.

Drill 16 ☐☐☐

Easy

One-Hand Words

Challenging

Come into our store, see what we have to offer, and let's make a deal.

Jim can pull a million crates of poppy extract up my hill in a decade.

Up until now, the education market has always been your prime concern.

Drill 17 ☐☐☐

Easy

Double Letters

Challenging

As the key witness in the case, the girl must appear in court at noon.

Appeal to Ann to keep mall dressing rooms free of attire and commerce.

It's difficult, but he tackles everything he does like a true fighter.

| 1 | 2 | 3 | 4 | 5 | 6 | 7 | 8 | 9 | 10 | 11 | 12 | 13 | 14 |

Word Processing History

92
GWPM

Word processing shares with data processing the same basic cycle 13
of input, process, and output. In word processing, input is words in 27
the form of spoken or written thoughts or ideas. Process is the 40
transformation of these words into final printed output. 51

In the first business offices, the processing was done by stenog- 65
raphers who took the words dictated by their employers and transcribed 79
them into final handwritten documents. Pens were the tools by which 93
the documents were prepared. In the late 1800s, a machine was intro- 107
duced into the processing system and revolutionized the word process- 121
ing industry. That machine, the typewriter, replaced the pen as the 135
primary tool by which final output was prepared. Over the next sever- 149
al decades, the typewriter was improved and became smaller, more 162
compact, faster, and more efficient. The next major development was 176
the electric typewriter. Although its main contribution at the time 190
was to further increase the speed at which words could be processed 203
into final copy, the electric typewriter was significant in that it 216
linked word processing with electronics, thus laying the groundwork 229
for all future developments. 235

In the 1960s, two new machines, the Magnetic Tape and the 248
Magnetic Card Selectric Typewriters, were put on the market. By in- 262
troducing the concept of stored documents, these machines represented 276
a giant step in the development of word processing. The ability to 290
store documents meant that the operator could edit and re-use material 304
that had previously been keyboarded and stored on tapes or cards, thus 318
saving valuable retyping time. These and the other machines which 331
were developed over the next few years were blind word processors. In 345
other words, the operator could not see the changes that were made 358
until the document was printed. 364

The next important advancement took place in the mid 1970s when 378
word processors with screens came onto the market. These display sys- 392
tems were a big improvement over the blind systems. The operator 405
could now see and check the work being input and the editing changes 419
that were made – before it was printed on paper. Word processing has 433
come a long way in the past hundred years, but one thing a word pro- 447
cessor has not been taught to do: it can't make coffee – yet. 460

| 1 | 2 | 3 | 4 | 5 | 6 | 7 | 8 | 9 | 10 | 11 | 12 | 13 | 14 |

Drill 18 ☐☐☐

Easy   The buzz of bees and flies is produced by the movement of their wings.

Numbers   In 1983 my restaurant had 46 beer mugs, 72 wine glasses and 50 plates.

Challenging   The company is planning a work incentive program to reverse the trend.

Drill 19 ☐☐☐

Easy   Our meetings are held at three on the first working day of each month.

Numbers/Symbols   Dunn & Park's rate for a 2-year, $4750 loan is 18% with $236 payments.

Challenging   At present, we have six operators handling the needs of twenty people.

Drill 20 ☐☐☐

Easy   The best buys at that market this week are bacon and prime rib roasts.

Alphabetic   When the viper quit the stage, Jack made his exit in a blaze of glory.

Challenging   I believe this information will assist in the research he is planning.

Drill 21 ☐☐☐

Easy   This free booklet tells what you need to know to make a wise purchase.

Home Row   The lad sulked and fidgeted till she passed along a full jar of dills.

Challenging   Newport owns and operates an emerald mine which is in full production.

Drill 22 ☐☐☐

Easy   When the soft snow clings to its branches, the tree is a pretty sight.

Third Row   Try to equip the prow with square tips; then pursue that witty porter.

Challenging   Detailed figures on the extent of the problem are still not available.

Drill 23 ☐☐☐

Easy   He has written eight books, five of which are sold in three countries.

Bottom Row   Must the canny band combine a mix of nibs, combs, and bones in a maze?

Challenging   The accused was arrested in a factory where police seized his handgun.

Drill 24 ☐☐☐

Easy   One child was laughing so hard the tears were streaming down his face.

Adjacent Keys   Many say it is obvious the pretty buyer has a passion for sporty fads.

Challenging   The proposed system would result in a significant drop in basic costs.

Drill 25 ☐☐☐

Easy   The person was caught by police and charged with nine counts of theft.

First Fingers   Junior thought he may have fumbled the trigger of the gun from fright.

Challenging   Does their program stress that sound management practices be followed?

Drill 26 ☐☐☐

Easy   The children can have fun, learn outdoor skills, and make new friends.

Second Fingers   I did accord rides to kind but derelict kids who decried the incident.

Challenging   Three agents offer discounts for homes with smoke detectors installed.

Drill 27 ☐☐☐

Easy   At the end of the day, we just sit and relax and listen to soft music.

Third Fingers   We stood still. We saw loose owls swoosh down on a slow, swollen fox.

Challenging   Take a few minutes to examine this offer; you are under no obligation.

| 1 | 2 | 3 | 4 | 5 | 6 | 7 | 8 | 9 | 10 | 11 | 12 | 13 | 14 |

88 GWPM

One of the most important requisites of a well written report is good organization. Good organization often begins with an outline which lists the topics to be covered in the report. The major topics should be prominently displayed, while less important points should be listed below the major topics to which they relate. An outline serves to put the writer's thoughts in order. It will form the basic framework on which the report will[1] be built. It is like drawing up the table of contents and then writing the report around it.

Good organization also requires that the outline and all material in the report be arranged in some kind of logical order that will render the report clear and easy for a reader to follow. There are several arrangements that may be used. One of the most common is the order in which events occur(red). A program, a resume, an agenda, and minutes[2] of a meeting would be set out in this way. Another arrangement is in order of importance. Topics or points may be arranged in ascending or descending order of importance. For example, the officers of a company would likely be listed in descending order, from the most to the least important. The reasons supporting a desired course of action might be set out in order of ascending importance, building towards a strong climax[3].

Order of space is another arrangement. It is one in which information may be arranged in the order of north to south, east to west, top to bottom, inside to outside, or in any other spatial progression that is suitable for the purpose. For example, a guide book may describe the Canadian provinces from west to east.

Order of familiarity is often used to present new ideas to readers. The writer starts off with ideas that[4] are familiar to the reader or at least are easy to understand, and works into things that may be unfamiliar or a little harder to grasp. It is an arrangement that is common in textbooks and in advertising copy. Yet another arrangement is the order of support. This order follows one of two paths. Either it begins with a concluding statement and then provides the supporting information, or it presents the data and then draws the conclusion[5].

| 1 | 2 | 3 | 4 | 5 | 6 | 7 | 8 | 9 | 10 | 11 | 12 | 13 | 14 |

WORDS: 13 26 40 54 68 82 95 106 120 133 147 161 175 189 203 217 231 245 259 264 278 292 306 319 329 343 357 371 385 399 413 427 440

Drill 28 □□□

Easy	Thank you for the offer, but I am sorry I must refuse it at this time.
Fourth Fingers	The ape has quite a craze for papaya and apples; it also eats bananas.
Challenging	To a great number of people, the telephone has now become a necessity.

Drill 29 □□□

Easy	Before I go to the store, give me a list of all the items you require.
Vertical Keys	Fran could swim, jump and kick, frolic, and dance to jazz in the loft.
Challenging	They were also strong believers in the value of our excellent library.

Drill 30 □□□

Easy	A new light bulb is needed in the laundry room and in the dining room.
Left Hand	Ask a driver the real extent of the damage caused by the diesel crash.
Challenging	All events listed are to be open to the public unless otherwise noted.

Drill 31 □□□

Easy	This may allow you the freedom to do the things you really want to do.
Right Hand	Many youths in the mob are myopic; they spoil to kick, maul and punch.
Challenging	His workload is kept at a level he can handle mentally and physically.

Drill 32 □□□

Easy	As soon as I receive the list of contacts, I can get the work started.
Opposite Hand Keys	The kiddies worked to sell the vine, lest it lose its opaque blossoms.
Challenging	The company has likely the largest reserves of gas of any gas company.

Drill 33 □□□

Easy	In fall, the bear curls up in his cozy den and sleeps the winter away.
Short Words	Put a new hat in a big box, tie it up and ship it by rail to the firm.
Challenging	Only a limited number of seats are available; so get your tickets now.

Drill 34 □□□

Easy	We are closing up our shop and every piece in the store is half price.
Long Words	Contractors did tuckpointing immediately, especially around a chimney.
Challenging	Many apartment blocks and motels could be exempt from the requirement.

Drill 35 □□□

Easy	As it happened, I returned home just in time to help with the harvest.
One-Hand Words	Fred agreed plump Barbara has oomph; you got wax or ink on my sweater.
Challenging	Our easy maintenance programs are designed to fit your personal needs.

Drill 36 □□□

Easy	He earns his living on a farm growing crops and raising pigs and cows.
Double Letters	The poor press will oppose the bill but cannot scoff at the committee.
Challenging	They pay cash dollars for estate and antique jewellery, diamonds, etc.

Drill 37 □□□

Easy	This project may be the challenge I have been seeking for a long time.
Numbers	I had 497 orders, 285 bills, 103 enquiries, and 6 pieces of junk mail.
Challenging	Those exploring for or mining these metals dominate their market news.

| 1 | 2 | 3 | 4 | 5 | 6 | 7 | 8 | 9 | 10 | 11 | 12 | 13 | 14 |

Business English Course

84

GWPM

The aim of the Business English course is to equip students to meet the English requirements of today's business office and to lay the groundwork for future language development. The course outline has been prepared on the premise that any study of English should involve the four media of communication: listening, speaking, reading, and writing. Because of the nature of the course, the application of these in business[1] should be stressed whenever possible. No attempt has been made to set out distinct teaching packages, nor to dictate time allotments, order of teaching, or depth of study. These factors may vary widely from class to class due to the needs and interests of students, the style and methodology of the instructor, and the fact that all aspects of English are continuously and concurrently being stressed throughout the[2] course. The course has four major areas of study: spelling and vocabulary, oral communication, reading, and writing.

The object of building spelling and vocabulary skills is twofold. The first is to enable the typist to recognize and spell words which are likely to be encountered in writing and in tape transcription. The second is to encourage the expansion of the student's own active vocabulary. Use of the dictionary[3], study techniques, and proofreading would, of course, be included.

The purpose of attending to oral communication is to develop the student's ability to listen and understand, to express herself or himself using correct speech and pronunciation, and, through these, to build self-confidence. Reading is a means to the end of all the other subjects outlined in this course. Too, reading can provide the student[4] with valuable knowledge.

The writing program is meant to correct weaknesses in punctuation and grammar, to develop writing skills, and to teach students how to write the most common types of business letters. As well, all students would be required to prepare a letter of application for employment and a personal data sheet. If time permits, we may be able to add the writing of reports and minutes of meetings.[5]

I have attached a list of the books currently in use. A list of sources of teaching materials is also attached. Most of these are available in the resource centre.

13	13
26	26
39	39
52	52
66	66
80	80
93	93
107	107
121	121
134	134
147	147
161	161
174	174
187	187
191	191
205	205
219	219
232	232
246	246
260	260
266	266
280	280
294	294
307	307
321	321
335	335
341	341
355	355
369	369
383	383
397	397
410	410
420	420
	434
	447
	454

| 1 | 2 | 3 | 4 | 5 | 6 | 7 | 8 | 9 | 10 | 11 | 12 | 13 | 14 |

Drill 38 ☐☐☐

Easy
Numbers/Symbols
Challenging

In the last hockey game, the star player got two goals and one assist.
He did sell 736 copies of Paul's "fun" article (4 pages) @ $2.89 each!
Brace yourself for this outstanding offer you cannot afford to resist.

Drill 39 ☐☐☐

Easy
Alphabetic
Challenging

If they wish to prevent a further loss, they must call him right away.
Judy explained my next great sequence of bleak events in the war zone.
Now really immerse yourself in the culture and traditions of Scotland.

Drill 40 ☐☐☐

Easy
Home Row
Challenging

More than one car insured with the same firm often means a lower rate.
She shuddered and hardly talked as she soaked the girl's jagged flesh.
These include a private residence, an office building and vacant land.

Drill 41 ☐☐☐

Easy
Third Row
Challenging

That club sends out a news bulletin each month to each of its members.
We wrote to enquire about the route, territory, and pay for that trip.
This public knows that huge government deficits make the dollar shaky.

Drill 42 ☐☐☐

Easy
Bottom Row
Challenging

A simple phone call could have saved a lot of time, effort, and money.
Can some men, a bobby, and a convict examine nozzles in the mauve box?
Each day, his courage and cheerful determination are called into play.

Drill 43 ☐☐☐

Easy
Adjacent Keys
Challenging

The book will be one you will cherish and consult time and time again.
Appointment of mining lads to power threw a curve at the dubious talk.
We permit no assignments of our contracts without our written consent.

Drill 44 ☐☐☐

Easy
First Fingers
Challenging

We will give them the best service they have ever had for their money.
The fifty frogs may have fun jumping for bugs on your avenue at night.
At their next meeting, nominations for the committee will be received.

Drill 45 ☐☐☐

Easy
Second Fingers
Challenging

He must change the ribbon on the printer before he can print the text.
Derek, a medic at the accident, decided to keep the sick child hidden.
You recommend that all new drivers complete a driver education course.

Drill 46 ☐☐☐

Easy
Third Fingers
Challenging

With blue skies and a very light breeze, the weather was just perfect.
All of those silly lasses still swoon as soon as Wilcox does his solo.
Try to save money through better management of your insurance dollars.

Drill 47 ☐☐☐

Easy
Fourth Fingers
Challenging

Please arrange for the carpets to be cleaned within the next few days.
Paul zipped up his parka; a palace scamp was piqued at Paul's apparel.
Your involvement was vital to bringing this to the public's attention.

| 1 | 2 | 3 | 4 | 5 | 6 | 7 | 8 | 9 | 10 | 11 | 12 | 13 | 14 |

Office of the Future

80	This report attempts to present the future shape of the business	13	13
GWPM	office. It is the result of personal interviews and research. The	26	26

This report attempts to present the future shape of the business 13 13
office. It is the result of personal interviews and research. The 26 26
study revealed that there will be two major goals in the move toward 40 40
the office of the future: integrated communication and speed. It was 54 54
the general concensus that if these goals are to be met, people needs 68 68
must be considered in the building, the organizing, and the[1] introduc- 82 82
tion of the technology required. The use of word processors, elec- 95 95
tronic typewriters, and computers will increase in small, medium, and 109 109
large firms. The use of electric typewriters will decline. There is 123 123
a definite swing away from large centralized word processing centres. 137 137
These will not be used because they tend to foster impersonal atti- 150 150
tudes, are unable to meet the needs of all people,[2] and make it diffi- 164 164
cult to achieve understanding between the principals and operators 177 177
when so many people are involved. Instead, there will be an increase 191 191
in small satellite centres of three to six operators. 202 202

There will be a tremendous growth in technology connected with 216 216
the telephone. Eventually, voice recognition will make much of the 230 230
present technology obsolete. Electronic mail will[3] reduce the need for 244 244
mail and courier services. Magnetic and microform storage systems 257 257
will replace paper ones. Micro computers are starting to appear in 270 270
both large and small offices. It is predicted that their numbers will 284 284
increase greatly as they form an integral part of the office system. 298 298

Office technology was begun at the lower end of the office cost 311 311
scale with the introduction of word processors[4] to save secretarial 324 324
time. In the future, technology will be aimed at the upper end of the 338 338
cost scale to save managerial time. As a result, we will see a grow- 352 352
ing number of terminals on managers' desks. These will be used to 365 365
analyze data, to set up financial models, to send and receive messages 379 379
and documents, to manage appointments, to write and edit reports, and 393 393
perhaps to compose correspondence.[5] 400 400

The office of the future will be in need of people who have good 414
keyboard and English skills, plus dicta and word processing. It will 428
seek people who understand the concepts of high technology and who 441
exhibit professional work habits and attitudes. Flexibility will be 455
another key requirement. 460

| 1 | 2 | 3 | 4 | 5 | 6 | 7 | 8 | 9 | 10 | 11 | 12 | 13 | 14 |

Drill 48 ☐☐☐

Easy   She will assign a date by which you should have finished this section.

Vertical Keys   I like Janice to dole out hefty sums like five or six hundred dollars.

Challenging   We have birding tours, wilderness canoeing and many high arctic tours.

Drill 49 ☐☐☐

Easy   The young hunter was trapped with no shelter or food, and little hope.

Left Hand   Several smart rovers reached over, grasped a square box, and squeezed.

Challenging   This committee asks that you support these candidates in the election.

Drill 50 ☐☐☐

Easy   We should serve praise as we do champagne - while it's still bubbling.

Right Hand   Appoint your pilot to the jury; smile at John's jokes; play his hunch.

Challenging   We have herbal teas such as peppermint, rosehip, jasmine and camomile.

Drill 51 ☐☐☐

Easy   In most cases, we would be able to save you a very large sum of money.

Opposite Hand Keys   In my movie, a lassie on a dock sells a bin of ebony wools in a jiffy.

Challenging   Donations have been made on your behalf to seven well-known charities.

Drill 52 ☐☐☐

Easy   We will need support crews that are well trained, fast, and efficient.

Short Words   He has hit the top of the list of sales each day for a year or so now.

Challenging   He reformatted the left margins to allow room for three-hole punching.

Drill 53 ☐☐☐

Easy   Could I call upon you for advice when I am ready to set up our centre?

Long Words   Explanations of the specific strategy initiated contagious excitement.

Challenging   The local chapter will get strong support from the federal government.

Drill 54 ☐☐☐

Easy   A love of nature can be seen in the beauty and spirit of her subjects.

One-Hand Words   A million jolly beavers jump in the water to scare a puppy I gave you.

Challenging   The changes are the result of a document submitted by this commission.

Drill 55 ☐☐☐

Easy   Please notify me of any change in address so that I can keep in touch.

Double Letters   Commission Scott to carry coffee and wrapped cheese food to my office.

Challenging   My report has a table of contents, some footnotes, and a bibliography.

Drill 56 ☐☐☐

Easy   He will edit the report and then give it to you to revise and reprint.

Numbers   The years 1057, 1462, and 1938 were the important ones in our history.

Challenging   This evening will begin with a reception in the true island tradition.

Drill 57 ☐☐☐

Easy   As you know, the opposite sides of a dice cube always add up to seven.

Numbers/Symbols   Pat's latest "steal" is a Soo & Lee's coat (style #30-754) for $62.98.

Challenging   I will enclose an order form and return envelope for your convenience.

| 1 | 2 | 3 | 4 | 5 | 6 | 7 | 8 | 9 | 10 | 11 | 12 | 13 | 14 |

Newspaper Survey

76

GWPM

We recently carried out a cross-country survey, via a written questionnaire, in which we asked people to tell us what daily newspapers mean to them. We wanted to know what they look for in a newspaper, how often they read and where they buy newspapers. We asked them to indicate and comment on the importance to them of the various newspaper features. We also requested that[1] they inform us of what things, if any, they didn't like in newspapers.

After tallying up the results, we found that the percentage of homes that purchase a newspaper every day has dropped in the last ten years, but that those buying just once or twice a week are on the increase. Reasons given included the observation that newspapers have become too large and take too much time[2] to read. It is faster and easier, they say, to obtain current news from radio or from television. Home delivery continues to account for the majority of newspaper sales, but many copies are sold through stores, newsstands, and newspaper boxes.

A high percentage of those surveyed said they seek a newspaper that contains comprehensive coverage of local news. They also[3] insist on being kept informed of important national and international affairs. Accompanying pictures were frequently mentioned as important news appendages. Fewer than half of those who replied read the business section regularly. Most of those who do, however, consult the stock market quotations as well. A large number of respondents, including a surprising number of men[4], enjoy reading articles about food. They like to be given recipes, especially for foods and festivals that are in season. They also appreciate cents-off food coupons and would like to see more of these. Many people regularly check the listings on the entertainment pages to find out what is going on in and around town – at the movies, theatres, galleries, auctions, etc.[5]

Articles on sports and sporting events both at home and abroad are thought to be an important part of a newspaper. A sizeable number of people find the travel section of interest. Most people consider the classified advertisements to be vital to a newspaper. It was found that a surprising number of people check the classified ads every day. Quite a few respondents said they would like to see more features about homes and gardens. A few people complained about worthwhile articles sometimes being lost in a maze of advertisements.

12	12
25	25
39	39
53	53
67	67
80	80
89	89
103	103
117	117
130	130
144	144
157	157
170	170
184	184
198	198
201	201
215	215
229	229
242	242
256	256
270	270
284	284
297	297
310	310
324	324
338	338
352	352
366	366
380	380
393	
407	
421	
434	
447	
461	
474	
488	

| 1 | 2 | 3 | 4 | 5 | 6 | 7 | 8 | 9 | 10 | 11 | 12 | 13 | 14 |

Drill 58 ☐☐☐

Easy   Barrels of water were hauled on a sled pulled by a horse or a tractor.

Alphabetic   The big wet swamp froze quickly and proved just excellent for skating.

Challenging   We can offer several good reasons for having an early inspection made.

Drill 59 ☐☐☐

Easy   I am sure there is not another actor who would be better for the part.

Home Row   Jeff and a saleslady haggled over the deal for the sake of half a fig.

Challenging   Get tickets now for this gigantic celebration and avoid the onslaught.

Drill 60 ☐☐☐

Easy   Please sign the attached form and return it to me as soon as possible.

Third Row   Quit worrying about the pretty person who hurt her wrist at the party.

Challenging   Read our collection of amazing events and be prepared to be astounded.

Drill 61 ☐☐☐

Easy   The town is booming with new life but retains a reverence for the old.

Bottom Row   Can many of the brave men memorize such a complex accent for the exam?

Challenging   Call this office today and arrange an interview for a convenient time.

Drill 62 ☐☐☐

Easy   We still live up to the standards set by our founder thirty years ago.

Adjacent Keys   Jokers were poised above a cave to address you at an opportune moment.

Challenging   A magazine issue coming up will spotlight a number of success stories.

Drill 63 ☐☐☐

Easy   We look to the past for patterns which we can project into the future.

First Fingers   Marvin bought them butter, many round buns, and a big jug of vermouth.

Challenging   Develop a professional image right from the beginning of your new job.

Drill 64 ☐☐☐

Easy   That park is open to campers from early spring until late in the fall.

Second Fingers   I deceived an addict who likes dice, drinks cider, and dances on deck.

Challenging   Something must be done to reduce or eliminate the number of accidents.

Drill 65 ☐☐☐

Easy   Until the trout season opens, I will have to settle for bass or perch.

Third Fingers   Leslie will swallow our story about losing his axle in a shallow pool.

Challenging   We are confident that your company has emerged in a stronger position.

Drill 66 ☐☐☐

Easy   They suspect the links in the chain will become weaker as we go along.

Fourth Fingers   A lazy captain napped. Has Pat placed equal parts of pizza on plates?

Challenging   We had several personnel changes over the year which may interest you.

Drill 67 ☐☐☐

Easy   She saw the evil around her and grew to become the tale's moral force.

Vertical Keys   A judge decided my hubby licked Judd, wins the quiz and gets a collie.

Challenging   Even a busy work schedule doesn't deter her from an effective workout.

| 1 | 2 | 3 | 4 | 5 | 6 | 7 | 8 | 9 | 10 | 11 | 12 | 13 | 14 |

		WORDS

72
GWPM

When the will of Charles Vance Millar, a Toronto lawyer, was read | 13 | 13

in 1926, people thought he was either crazy or the biggest joker on | 26 | 26

record, for Millar left shares in a race track to well-known opponents | 40 | 40

of gambling, brewery stock to teetotallers, and money to a Roman | 53 | 53

Catholic church to say masses for the soul of a Protestant who had | 66 | 66

outsmarted him in a business [1] transaction. Even more astonishing, he | 80 | 80

left the residue of his estate to the mother in Toronto who had the | 93 | 93

greatest number of children in the ten-year period following his | 106 | 106

death. | 107 | 107

Although the last bequest was to have been confidential until the | 121 | 121

decade expired, the news escaped and the marathon was on. The news- | 135 | 135

papers kept readers posted on the latest mothers [2] who appeared to be in | 149 | 149

the running. Mothers were interviewed, pictures were taken, jokes | 162 | 162

were made, and baby births hit the headlines. When the finish line | 175 | 175

was reached, the tally showed two mothers who had delivered nine | 188 | 188

babies, three mothers who had delivered ten, and one mother who | 200 | 200

claimed eleven babies. | 204 | 204

Other questions now arose. Could illegitimate, still, [3] or unreg- | 218 | 218

istered births be counted? The courts took almost two years to | 231 | 231

decide. They ruled that neither stillborn, illegitimate, nor unregis- | 245 | 245

tered children could be included. This disqualified two mothers, | 258 | 258

including the mother who had declared eleven children. Both mothers | 272 | 272

promptly threatened to appeal to a higher court. To avoid further | 285 | 285

delay and the [4] high cost to the estate that an appeal would entail, a | 299 | 299

settlement of $12 500 was offered and each of the women accepted. The | 313 | 313

court ruled that the rest of the estate was to be divided equally | 326 | 326

among the other four mothers, each of whom had produced nine eligible | 340 | 340

babies during the baby derby decade. These mothers received the sub- | 354 | 354

stantial sum of $250 000 each. [5] | 360 | 360

The baby derby was acted out against the backdrop of the great | 374

Depression. It is likely that it was the cause of more laughter, was | 388

the subject of more discussion, aroused more indignation, kept more | 401

lawyers busy, and provided more newspaper copy than any other event of | 415

those lean years. For the winning mothers, it meant the end of pover- | 429

ty and the beginning of a financial security that they had never had | 443

before. | 445

| 1 | 2 | 3 | 4 | 5 | 6 | 7 | 8 | 9 | 10 | 11 | 12 | 13 | 14 |

Drill 68 ☐☐☐

Easy — One after another, the birds swooped down on the cat to scare it away.

Left Hand — The clever squire wants the darker flowers delivered a great distance.

Challenging — We highly recommend a purchase at the current price of eleven dollars.

Drill 69 ☐☐☐

Easy — Do not take these shopping carts beyond the limits of our parking lot.

Right Hand — Though not one ominous cloud in this glorious sky, your ship may sink.

Challenging — He owns his vacation home as a co-owner along with fellow timesharers.

Drill 70 ☐☐☐

Easy — I can convince you that our products are, in fact, better and cheaper.

Opposite Hand Keys — He lies or kidded that slow drinks ruin those trying to woo and marry.

Challenging — Symbol of human courage and endurance, it tested both body and spirit.

Drill 71 ☐☐☐

Easy — They compete for the glory of sport and the honour of their homelands.

Short Words — I will pay the bill for the two pots he sent me just as soon as I can.

Challenging — We give you thoughtful service, friendly attention, and happy results.

Drill 72 ☐☐☐

Easy — We are both pleased and honoured that our new hotel has been selected.

Long Words — Intelligent individuals reacted spontaneously to a proposed adventure.

Challenging — I have included numerous pictures, graphs, maps, charts, and diagrams.

Drill 73 ☐☐☐

Easy — The four leaders will decide what action should be taken in this case.

One-Hand Words — Look at my best pony, Pinky, in the fastest races in its great career.

Challenging — Most classmates entered a profession, like medicine, law, or teaching.

Drill 74 ☐☐☐

Easy — Of course everyone knows that a door cannot be a door when it is ajar.

Double Letters — Snooze or sleep better on a queen, rubber-filled mattress and bedding.

Challenging — Give the document a more professional look; justify all right margins.

Drill 75 ☐☐☐

Easy — The product has sold well in this region and right across the country.

Numbers — Of 1286 who ran, 739 dropped out and only 547 crossed the finish line.

Challenging — Readers relive the drama and excitement of bygone peoples and empires.

| 1 | 2 | 3 | 4 | 5 | 6 | 7 | 8 | 9 | 10 | 11 | 12 | 13 | 14 |

Part 2 ▪ Timed Writings

Test Speed/Accuracy

1 Take 3-minute, 5-minute or 10-minute timing(s).
2 Calculate net words per minute:
   NWPM = (total words ÷ number of minutes) − 2 for each error.

Build or Stabilize Speed

1 Select the **paced** easy, average or challenging timed writing that is closest to the speed you wish to achieve.
2 Take 3-minute or 5-minute timing(s) during which a tape or someone signals each minute. If, when the signal is given, you are typing more than three characters behind or ahead of the interval marker, adjust your speed (faster or slower) so as to be as close as possible to the next marker when the next signal is given.

Conversation

68
GWPM

Regardless of our age or vocation, we all engage in the game of conversation. The game is played wherever there is social contact of two or more persons. The game may be played for pleasure or for profit. As with other games, successful players require certain basic equipment. They require a good command of words, clear diction, a[1] pleasing voice, an interest in other people and the world around them, and some interesting ideas to exchange. The ability to set other people at ease and to draw them into conversation is also an asset, and an essential one for people who are required to conduct interviews.

Skillful players in the game of conversation develop a sensitivity[2] to the needs and aspirations of others. Recognizing and responding to the rationale of others is essential if one is to acquire a most important tool of conversation – tact. Tact is the knack of knowing when to speak, what to say, and how to say it. A player who is proficient in the use of tact has elevated his/her game[3] to the level of an art.

When we stop to consider what profound effect our skill at conversation can have on our lives – personal, social, and business – it becomes apparent that conversation is a most worthy art to develop. Just as some people have a natural aptitude for music or drawing, some have a natural flair for conversation.[4] Many others are not so gifted. Where do the ungifted go for instruction and guidance in developing conversation skills? There are schools that train in music and drawing; there are schools that instruct in the art of public speaking; but there are few schools that train in the art of private speaking – the art of conversation.[5]

Developing conversation skills requires much practice; but the opportunities for practice are becoming more and more difficult to come by. Modern society and lifestyles tend to discourage conversation. Television has probably been the biggest single culprit in stifling conversation. If the art of conversation is going to survive, courses will have to be developed in the schools, and we will each have to make a conscientious effort to talk, to listen, and to share ideas and opinions – in other words, to converse.

13	13
27	27
41	41
55	55
68	68
82	82
95	95
109	109
122	122
123	123
137	137
151	151
165	165
178	178
192	192
206	206
209	209
223	223
237	237
251	251
265	265
279	279
293	293
307	307
321	321
335	335
340	340
	354
	368
	382
	395
	409
	423
	437
	448

| 1 | 2 | 3 | 4 | 5 | 6 | 7 | 8 | 9 | 10 | 11 | 12 | 13 | 14 |

28
GWPM

This timed writing is a collection of brain games designed to test not only your typing speed, but your mental agility too. When you are finished, check your answers with the timed writing on the next page.

In this first group, explain why the odd fact in each story is true. My friend held an egg over a concrete floor, then dropped it one metre without breaking it. Two mothers and two daughters were out shopping and each of them bought a new coat. However, only three coats were purchased. A thief and a doctor sat talking in a room. The thief was the doctor's son, but the doctor was not the thief's father. Two girls played three games of tennis one morning and they each won three games.

	12	12
	26	26
	39	39
	41	41
	55	55
	69	69
	83	83
	96	96
	109	109
	122	122
	136	136
	140	140

32
GWPM

Next, try your skill at these riddles. A man has a fox, a goose, and a bag of grain. He has to cross the river, but his boat is small and he can take only one thing with him at a time. Figure out how he can transport all three safely. On a high shelf are three boxes which you can reach but cannot see into. The boxes are labelled red balls, blue balls, and red and blue balls. Somehow the labels were mixed up and each box has the wrong label on it. By reaching up and removing just one ball, how can you determine which box contains what? In a drawer are thirty socks, fifteen blue and fifteen brown. If the light is burned out and you must find a pair of socks in the dark, what would be the minimum number of socks you must remove from the drawer to be sure that you have a matched pair?

13	153
27	167
41	181
55	195
69	209
83	223
97	237
111	251
125	265
138	278
152	292
160	300

36
GWPM

A boy scout is lost in a forest in which two brothers live, one of whom always tells the truth and the other always tells a lie. The scout finds a path but doesn't know which way to go. Along comes one of the brothers but the scout can't tell whether he is the truthful one or the liar. What one question can he ask to learn the direction out of the woods?

Now see how well you can respond to this quiz. Some months of the year have thirty days and some have thirty-one. How many months have twenty-eight days? Two days ago, my son was two years old. Next year he will be five years old. Can you explain that one? If your friend has just one match and he enters a cabin that has a wood stove, a candle, and an oil lamp, tell me which he should light first. If you take three grapes from ten grapes, how many grapes do you have? Could a woman living in Quebec be buried in Alberta?

13	313
27	327
41	341
55	355
69	369
73	373
87	387
101	401
115	415
129	429
143	443
156	456
170	470
180	480

| 1 | 2 | 3 | 4 | 5 | 6 | 7 | 8 | 9 | 10 | 11 | 12 | 13 | 14 |

Computers

64 GWPM

In the late 1930s, a math professor found all the calculations required of him just too much, and he decided to do something about it. What he did was to design the first electronic digital computer. — 13 / 26 / 40

During the Second World War, there was an urgent need for a machine that would calculate ballistic tables much more[1] quickly than the current methods were capable of. This need provided the opportunity for the development of the first large-scale digital computer, the ENIAC. The machine could multiply two numbers in about three milliseconds. It weighed thirty tonnes and took up the space of a large room. It contained thousands of wires[2] and switches, as well as 18 000 vacuum tubes for the storage of data. One of the problems was that when a new program was required, all of the switches and wires on the machine had to be changed. To alleviate this, the concept of a stored program was developed. — 53 / 67 / 80 / 94 / 107 / 120 / 134 / 148 / 162 / 175 / 181

In the early 1950s, the computer entered the business[3] arena. New programming languages were introduced that were faster and easier to write, and were, therefore, less prone to errors. However, the vacuum tubes were a problem. Not only did they take up a lot of space, heat up, use a lot of electricity, and were expensive, but they were not all that reliable and were no[4] longer fast enough. Soon, the vacuum tube was replaced by the transistor, thus ushering in the second generation of computers. Transistors were smaller, cooler, faster, more reliable – and cheaper. This meant that more firms could now afford to buy computers. The computer market expanded by leaps and bounds.[5] — 195 / 209 / 223 / 237 / 250 / 264 / 278 / 292 / 306 / 320

The third generation of computers began in 1964 when a solid logic computer was produced in which the electronic components which made up the controlling circuitry were stored on small silicon chips, rather than on transistors. Chips were small, fast, and reliable. Because they could be mass produced, they were cheap. The chip made an astounding impact on the computer industry. In fact, the industry has grown into one of the four largest in the world. As new methods and machines for building circuits on these small chips have been devised, the capacity of the chips has increased many times over. This development continues to take place, and it is estimated that soon over one million circuit elements will be stored on a tiny chip that is less than one centimetre square. — 334 / 348 / 362 / 375 / 389 / 403 / 417 / 430 / 443 / 456 / 470 / 478

| 1 | 2 | 3 | 4 | 5 | 6 | 7 | 8 | 9 | 10 | 11 | 12 | 13 | 14 |

Timed Writings – Challenging

114

40 GWPM   This timed writing gives you the answers to the brain games. Are 13 13
you ready? Here we go. Because my friend dropped the egg from a 26 26
height of two metres, the egg fell one metre without breaking; of 39 39
course it broke when it finally hit the concrete floor. The two moth- 53 53
ers and two daughters who went shopping were a daughter, a mother, and 67 67
a grandmother. The doctor was not the thief's father because she was 81 81
his mother. The two girls who played tennis didn't play together. 94 94

The man who had to cross the river faced a serious dilemma. He 108 108
could not leave the fox and goose alone together lest the fox eat the 122 122
goose. Neither could he leave the goose and the grain alone, for the 136 136
goose would eat the grain. To solve his problem, he took the goose 150 150
across and left it on the other side. He came back and took the grain 164 164
across, left it there, and brought the goose back. Leaving the goose 178 178
on the first side, he took the fox over. Then he left the fox with 191 191
the grain while he came back for the goose. 200 200

44 GWPM   The only box of balls that will solve your problem is the one 12 212
marked red and blue balls. Remembering that all the boxes are wrongly 26 226
labelled, the ball you pick from this box has to be the colour of all 40 240
the balls in the box. From this information, you can figure out the 54 254
contents of the other two boxes. In order to be sure of getting a 67 267
matched pair of socks, you need pick just three socks from the drawer. 81 281
Should the first two be one of each colour, the third sock has to 94 294
match one of them. 98 298

To discover the direction out of the woods, the scout's question 112 312
should run something like this: If I were to ask your brother if this 126 326
is the way out of the woods, what would he say? No matter which 139 339
brother it is, if he answers no, the direction indicated is the way 152 352
out. If he answers yes, the scout must go in the other direction. 165 365

All twelve months of the year have twenty-eight days. My son's 179 379
birthday is on the thirty-first day of December. Your friend should 193 393
light the match first. You should have three grapes. The last answer 207 407
is that it is highly unlikely one would bury a person who is living. 220 420

| 1 | 2 | 3 | 4 | 5 | 6 | 7 | 8 | 9 | 10 | 11 | 12 | 13 | 14 |

Home Insulation

60
GWPM

Home insulation has been around Canada for ages. Sod structures 13   13
which have been excavated in Newfoundland date from early times. As a 27   27
matter of fact, sod houses were built right into the early twentieth 41   41
century by settlers on the Prairies where wood was scarce. Properly 55   55
cut, five centimetres of sod¹ block are the equivalent of more than two 69   69
centimetres of fibreglass. 74   74

Another type of insulated dwelling was the stovewood house which 88   88
was built by early colonists. It was basically little more than a 101   101
woodpile with four sides – hence its name. Infilling provided insula- 115   115
tion as well as a base for holding² plaster. In early Quebec, stone 128   128
houses were built with walls that were a massive 75 cm or thirty 141   141
inches thick. These were constructed in three layers with the exteri- 155   155
or and interior stone surfaces insulated from each other by a middle 169   169
section of very small stones mortared together. This created³ a crude 183   183
air chamber which kept the frost from being conducted to the interior. 197   197

Only in recent years have brick houses become common in the 210   210
Atlantic Provinces. With wood in abundant supply for both building 223   223
and heating, unpainted wooden houses sheltered rural families for 236   236
almost two centuries⁴, while a sturdy, cast-iron stove provided endless 250   250
heat. Also, each winter, planks were laid on their longitudinal edges 264   264
across upright stakes so that they formed troughs along the sides of 278   278
the house. The troughs were filled with sawdust which helped insulate 292   292
the floor level from wind and draughts⁵. 300   300

Sawdust was also the insulation used in another type of farm 313
house. This house was built with a space between the studs and the 327
inner wall. The space was filled with sawdust. This led to better 341
and more even distribution of the heat generated from the large, wood- 355
burning kitchen stove. Brick and stone houses appeared in many vari- 369
ations in most larger Canadian cities, but their hollow walls provided 383
poor insulation. However, natural gas for space heaters was cheap, 396
and so was coal to feed central heating systems. Eventually, it 409
became so costly to use energy in lieu of insulation that by the early 423
1970s, most houses had added insulation between the studs and in the 437
roof. Caulking improved, and double glazing began to replace the old 451
leaky storm window. The energy saving was significant. 462

| 1 | 2 | 3 | 4 | 5 | 6 | 7 | 8 | 9 | 10 | 11 | 12 | 13 | 14 |

48

GWPM

We tried again and again to prevent this war, but now we are at war. One bond unites us all: to wage war until victory is won and never to surrender ourselves to servitude and shame, whatever the cost and the agony may be. The long night of barbarism will descend unless we conquer – as conquer we must; as conquer we shall.

Come then. Let us to the task, to the battle and the toil – each to our part, each to our station. Fill the armies, rule the air, pour out the munitions, strangle the U-boats, sweep the mines, plough the land, build the ships, guard the streets, succour the wounded, uplift the downcast, and honour the brave. Let us go forward together. There is not a week, nor a day, nor an hour to lose. We shall defend our island home – if necessary, for years; if necessary alone. We shall not flag or fail. We shall go on to the end. We shall fight in France; we shall fight on the seas and oceans; we shall fight in the air. We shall defend our island whatever the cost may be. We shall fight on the beaches; we shall fight on the landing grounds; we shall fight in the fields and in the streets; we shall fight in the hills. We shall never surrender.

52

GWPM

Now, the old lion with her cubs at her side stands alone against hunters who are armed with deadly weapons. It has come to us to stand alone in the breach and face the worst that the tyrant may do. Should the invader come, there will be no placid lying down of the people in submission before him as we have seen in other countries. We shall defend every village, every town, and every city. If the villains drop down upon us from the skies, we will make it clear to them that they have not alighted in the poultry run, or in the rabbit farm, or in the sheepfold; but that they have come down into the lion's den. Let us therefore brace ourselves to our duties, and so bear ourselves that, if the British Empire and its Commonwealth last for a thousand years, men will still say that this was their finest hour.

Put your confidence in us. Give us your faith and your blessing; and under providence, all will be well. We shall not fail or falter; we shall not weaken or tire. Neither a sudden shock of battle nor the long-drawn trials of vigilance and exertion shall wear us down. Give us the tools and we will finish the job.

We have not flinched or wavered; we have not failed. Alone, but upborne by every generous heartbeat of mankind, we have defied the tyrant in the height of his power.

| 1 | 2 | 3 | 4 | 5 | 6 | 7 | 8 | 9 | 10 | 11 | 12 | 13 | 14 |

14	14
28	28
42	42
56	56
67	67
81	81
96	96
110	110
124	124
137	137
151	151
165	165
179	179
193	193
207	207
221	221
235	235
240	240
13	253
27	267
41	281
55	295
69	309
82	322
96	336
110	350
123	363
137	377
151	391
163	403
177	417
191	431
205	445
219	459
227	467
240	480
253	493
260	500

Knitting

56
GWPM

Needlework is an art that dates back to ancient times. It was 13 13
developed by early peoples as a means of making garments with which to 27 27
protect themselves from the weather. As time went on, new methods, 40 40
designs, colours, and materials were introduced, and a wide range of 54 54
articles¹ were made that were not only serviceable, but attractive to 68 68
look upon as well. Eventually, items that were solely for decorative 82 82
purposes became common too. Some beautiful old pieces of needlework, 96 96
such as tapestries made in the middle ages, can still be seen in muse- 110 110
ums around² the world. Needlework was considered to be mainly women's 124 124
work. In Elizabethan and Victorian days, girls were trained in the 137 137
art from a very young age. When they became ladies, they spent a con- 151 151
siderable amount of their time at their needles. They did weaving, 164 164
sewing, tatting, mending,³ embroidery, crochet, and knitting. 176 176

Knitting is one of the earliest kinds of needlework. In knit- 189 189
ting, needles made of bone, wood, steel, or plastic are used to con- 203 203
tinuously loop or knot a long string of yarn to form a very elastic 216 216
fabric that is excellent for making warm⁴ and close-fitting wearing 229 229
apparel. Early knitting was mostly confined to the making of hose or 243 243
stockings, but now countless numbers of other useful articles are 256 256
fashioned: sweaters, socks, gloves, shawls, baby clothes, cushion 270 270
covers, etc. Even fancy lace work can be knitted.⁵ 280 280

At one time, pure wool was the primary yarn used for knitting; 294
however, with the advent of easy-care fabrics like nylon, rayon, and 308
polyester, pure wool has lost ground. Knitting is most often done on 322
two needles, but for certain types of work (for example, when round 336
knitting for socks or gloves), three, four, or even five needles may 350
be required. There are two basic stitches in knitting: purl and 363
plain. By using various combinations of these two stitches, by pass- 377
ing or slipping one or more stitches over another, and/or by using 391
different colours of thread, many variations in the design can be 404
effected. Besides creating useful articles, knitting is a pleasant 418
pastime, one that may be carried on while talking or watching tele- 432
vision. It is also an easy craft for people who are invalid. For 445
this reason, it is used in many hospitals as a convalescent activity 459
for men and women alike. As with other types of needlework, popular 473
interest peaks, wanes, and revives again in a fairly regular cycle. 487
One thing seems certain, however; knitting is here to stay. 499

| 1 | 2 | 3 | 4 | 5 | 6 | 7 | 8 | 9 | 10 | 11 | 12 | 13 | 14 |

56
GWPM

From this fantastic world we live in, we now bring you a collec- 13 13
tion of facts, plus a few figures, to amaze and amuse you. 25 25

To start with, although the kiwi bird is about the size of a 38 38
domestic hen, it lays an egg that is eight times larger than a hen's. 52 52
A swift homing pigeon saved a group of soldiers. The soldiers had 65 65
ordered ahead for air assistance, but before it arrived they won a 78 78
surprise victory. They now had to deliver a fast cancellation to the 92 92
air base or be bombed by their own planes. Their only hope lay with 106 106
the speed and safety of a pigeon. The bird got the message through 119 119
just in time. 122 122

Some American Indians made their tomahawks so that they served a 136 136
dual purpose. With a hollow handle and a pipe bowl as well as a 149 149
blade, the tomahawk was a weapon in times of war and a pipe in times 163 163
of peace. One Chinese ruler was prepared to do battle even in death. 177 177
When he died, he was buried with an army of six thousand clay soldiers 191 191
and horses, all built to life size. 198 198

Crocodiles may not have tooth brushes, but some do have tooth- 211 211
picks – not our common wooden kind, but real live ones. A bird called 225 225
the plover picks out and eats the bits of food lodged between the 238 238
crocodile's teeth. Not all fish out of water are out of their ele- 251 251
ment. As well as gills, some fish, like the walking catfish, have 264 264
lungs with which they can breathe air. They are also able to walk on 278 278
their fins. 280 280

At one time, golf balls were made from pieces of leather stuffed 294
with feathers. Raincoats made out of crude rubber were worn hundreds 308
of years ago by South American natives. Long ago, the Chinese used to 322
waterproof cloth by coating it with tallow. A whip cracks in mid-air, 336
not because it has struck something, but because its tip is moving 349
faster than sound. Early clocks were built with only one hand, an 362
hour hand. 364

Some birds lay their eggs in the nests of other birds. When the 378
eggs hatch, the chicks are fed by their foster parents. Usually larg- 392
er birds, these foster chicks often knock the natural chicks right out 406
of the nest so that they can take over the roost. Vultures crack hard 420
eggs by dropping them on stones. If an egg is too large to pick up, 434
the birds drop stones on the egg. 441

| 1 | 2 | 3 | 4 | 5 | 6 | 7 | 8 | 9 | 10 | 11 | 12 | 13 | 14 |

Earthquake

48 GWPM

Of the thousands of earthquakes that occur each year, usually only about six hundred are large enough to warrant recording. Although most quakes take place under the sea or in uninhabited areas, some do occur in populated places, causing damage and sometimes loss of life. Some regions, like China, which are located in the Pacific earthquake belt, seem to be more susceptible to earthquakes than are other areas. As a result, the ancient Chinese developed a construction design that would render a building earthquake-proof. In these buildings, the roof load was balanced on an intricate arrangement of interlocking bracket sets containing thousands of mortise and tenon joints. The free movement of these joints diverted the quake's energy as it travelled up the posts. In this way, most of the energy was dissipated before it reached the roof.

It was also in China that the seismograph, an instrument that detects and records earthquakes, was invented. The seismograph was introduced there in the second century, 1 600 years before it appeared in the west. Not only did the seismograph register that an earthquake had taken place, but it also indicated from which direction the tremor had come.

52 GWPM

The seismograph looked like a large, metal urn and stood over a metre tall. Spaced equally apart on the outside were crafted eight dragons, each holding a small ball clamped in its jaws. Sitting on the ground gazing up at each dragon was a large toad with its mouth agape. Inside the urn was a heavy pendulum which hung stationary and could be triggered into motion only by a very slow vibration such as an earthquake tremor would create. When an earthquake vibrated the instrument, the pendulum swung towards the source of the tremor and lifted a lever which released the ball from the closest dragon. The mechanism then locked in position to prevent the pendulum swinging back and causing another ball to be dropped. The racket made by the bronze ball landing in the toad's mouth alerted the people in the vicinity that an earthquake had occurred. By ascertaining which ball had been released, the direction from which the tremor had originated could easily be determined.

The magnitude or destructive force of earthquakes is measured on a scale called the Richter scale. Earthquakes of magnitude 1 are hardly noticeable. Quakes of magnitude 4 or 5 could cause some damage. However, a quake that scores 7 or higher could be very destructive and would be considered a major earthquake.

| | 1 | 2 | 3 | 4 | 5 | 6 | 7 | 8 | 9 | 10 | 11 | 12 | 13 | 14 | |

There really is a vampire bat. At night, the vampire leaves its roost to seek out sleeping prey. With its sharp teeth, it bites its victim gently so as not to waken it. The bat does not suck the blood, but laps it up from the wound. The ermine and the weasel are one and the same animal. When the brown weasel dons its white fur coat for winter, it is transformed into a lovely ermine.

Before theatres were designed so that the actors and the viewers were separated, viewers sat on the stage. An actor who gave a poor performance had to be careful, for the viewers would try to bump him or her off the stage. The rarest stamp in the world has a face value of one cent but is worth many thousands of dollars. If a French horn were straightened out, it would measure seven metres.

The eyes of the squid are almost human. Its eye has an iris and pupil, and a lens that can focus for any distance. Some squids even have eyelids. The bee hummingbird, weighing in at a mere two grams and measuring just five centimetres from stem to stern, is the smallest bird in the world. One type of male moth can locate from eight kilometres away a female of its species from her scent in the air. The bat is the only mammal that can fly. The dragonfly can reach a flying speed of more than sixty kilometres per hour on wings that are thinner than paper. A flea can jump one hundred times its own height. This is like your or my jumping to the top of a building that stands sixty storeys high.

You can use a magnet to check out brass items. If it attracts, it's not brass. Before printing came into being and set up some rules, words were written all strung together with no spaces or punctuation. In the old days, tablecloths were used not so much to cover the table as to serve as a towel for wiping one's mouth and hands after a meal. The same two letters are found in many of the words that are used in connection with fowl: duck, chicken, cock, pluck, cackle, cluck, and peck. A different set of two letters occurs in many words that have to do with the nose: sneeze, snout, snort, snooty, snarl, snoop, and sniff.

| 1 | 2 | 3 | 4 | 5 | 6 | 7 | 8 | 9 | 10 | 11 | 12 | 13 | 14 |

WORDS

40 GWPM

The use of coins as a medium of exchange dates back to long · · · · · · · · 12 · · 12
before the glorious days of Greece and Rome. It is not known when · · · · 25 · · 25
numismatics, a fancy name for coin collecting, began, but it is now a · · · 39 · · 39
popular and interesting hobby which can also be financially rewarding. · · · 53 · · 53
Many collectors today began to collect coins when they were children · · · · 67 · · 67
and continued their hobby into adult life. Some numismatists collect · · · · 81 · · 81
any and all kinds of currency; others prefer to specialize in their · · · · · 94 · · 94
collections. While one collector may like commemorative coins or mint · · · 108 · 108
sets, another may zero in on gold coins, while someone else may col- · · · 122 · 122
lect only coins from a particular country. A typical collection of · · · · · 135 · 135
Canadian coins might consist of large and small pennies, nickels, · · · · · 148 · 148
dimes, quarters, half dollars, and dollars – with the coins usually · · · · 162 · 162
arranged in order of the year in which each was minted. It might also · · · 176 · 176
include old bank and provincial tokens, old paper currency like shin · · · 190 · 190
plasters, and perhaps even a few wooden nickels. · · · · · · · · · · · · · 200 · 200

44 GWPM

The popular notion has it that old is valuable. This is not · · · · · · · 13 · 213
necessarily so. Many older coins can be purchased for a few dollars, · · · 27 · 227
while some later ones may cost several hundred dollars or more. As · · · · 41 · 241
with other commodities, the value of coins is determined by supply and · · 55 · 255
demand. Usually, the scarcer the coin, the higher its value. In · · · · · 68 · 268
addition, the price of some coins, particularly gold and silver ones, · · · 82 · 282
may fluctuate according to the market value of their metal. Until a · · · · 96 · 296
couple of decades ago, it was common to find collectable coins among · · · 110 · 310
loose change; however, with the increased number of collectors, it is · · · 124 · 324
now rare to find a collectable coin in circulation. Silver coins, · · · · · 138 · 338
too, have vanished from public change purses and tills. They began to · · · 152 · 352
disappear shortly after the mints started using nickel instead of · · · · · 165 · 365
silver. A number of investors, realizing the intrinsic value of the · · · · 179 · 379
metal, were astute enough to stash silver coins away. Their foresight · · · 193 · 393
paid off, for when the price of silver rose to record highs, they were · · · 207 · 407
in a position to sell their silver coins for handsome profits. · · · · · · · 220 · 420

Most collector coins are now purchased from a dealer or, if they · · · · · · · · · 434
are new issues, directly from the mint. Mint sets and commemorative · · · · · · · 448
coins are often specially packaged to preserve their mint condition. · · · · · · · 462
Of course, an itemized record of all coins in a collection should be · · · · · · · 476
kept for insurance purposes. · 482

| 1 | 2 | 3 | 4 | 5 | 6 | 7 | 8 | 9 | 10 | 11 | 12 | 13 | 14 |

64
GWPM

The platypus has survived for thousands of years in spite of its   13 13
weird make-up. It is covered with fur; it has a tail like a beaver, a   27 27
bill like a duck, and webbed feet with cat-like claws at the ends; and   41 41
on each hind leg is a spur which carries poison. This fine swimmer   55 55
lays eggs like a reptile and nurses its young¹ like a mammal.   67 67

The Arctic is an ocean with land around it, while the Antarctic   81 81
is a land mass with ocean around it. In reading a barometer, it does   95 95
not matter what weather sign the needle is pointing at. What one must   109 109
know is in which direction the needle has moved. If the needle moved   123 123
up, the weather will improve²; if it moved down, the weather will wor-   137 137
sen. Our hair will still be around when we are long gone. Keep human   151 151
hair away from fire and it will take a long time to decay. It is not   165 165
affected by cold, heat, water, or many chemicals. That is why hair   179 179
clogs sinks and drains.   184 184

All live coral has some colour; only³ dead coral is white like   198 198
chalk. There is one type of catfish that floats upside down near the   212 212
water's surface to make it easier to feed from the surface film. When   226 226
a pride of lions has a successful hunt and feast and then lies down to   240 240
sleep, it could be as many as four days before the pride wakens. When   254 254
it starts⁴ to get cold in the late summer and early fall, some bugs   267 267
seek overnight lodgings in flowers that close their petals at night.   281 281
When the blossoms open in the morning, the bugs continue on their way.   295 295
Many folks think that cooties is just a name that children have made   309 309
up for bugs, but cooties really are a type of body lice.⁵   320 320

An odometer was in use in the horse-drawn wagons of China in the   334
early part of the first century. In the wagon were two wooden fig-   348
ures, each of which held a drum stick. Each time the cart travelled   362
half a kilometre, one of the figures struck a drum. It's much easier   376
to smile than it is to frown; in fact, it takes fewer than half as   389
many muscles to smile as it does to frown. The shortest verse in the   403
Bible has just two words, Jesus wept.   411

A snake's eggs, with their soft cover, grow up to one-third larg-   425
er after they are laid. A snake may not have a meal for over a year,   439
but when it does eat, it can swallow an animal much larger than its   453
mouth. The snake has no need to chew its meal, for its juices dis-   466
solve bone, teeth, feathers, and all. A tomato may be a vegetable in   480
your book and mine, but strictly speaking, it is a berry and therefore   494
a fruit.   496

| 1 | 2 | 3 | 4 | 5 | 6 | 7 | 8 | 9 | 10 | 11 | 12 | 13 | 14 |

28 GWPM

The first typewriter patent on record was issued in Great Britain | 14 | 14

in 1714 to one, Henry Mill. The earliest known typewriters were rath- | 28 | 28

er odd-looking machines, often incorporating features of other types | 42 | 42

of machinery. For example, at least one typewriter had a keyboard | 56 | 56

that closely resembled that of a piano. Another had a clock-like | 70 | 70

face. On yet another, the carriage was returned by use of a foot | 83 | 83

treadle, much like the treadle on an old sewing machine. Typing was | 97 | 97

done with two fingers and the typist could not see what had been typed | 111 | 111

until the paper had been removed from the machine. Most of those | 125 | 125

early typewriters were large and cumbersome and were not really | 138 | 138

practical. | 140 | 140

32 GWPM

The first practical typewriter was built in 1867 by Christopher | 13 | 153

Sholes and two associates. Sholes continued to improve on his type- | 27 | 167

writer, and seven years later it was put on the market by E. Remington | 41 | 181

and Sons, a gun manufacturing firm. The machine did not attract much | 55 | 195

interest until Mark Twain used one to prepare a manuscript for publi- | 69 | 209

cation. The resulting publicity spread the word and the typewriter | 82 | 222

era was launched. Oddly enough, although the shorthand writers at | 95 | 235

that time were men, it was mostly women who learned to operate the | 108 | 248

typewriter. The male stenographer would write the employer's letter | 122 | 262

in shorthand and then orally dictate the communication from his short- | 136 | 276

hand notes to the typist, who typed as he dictated. It was some time | 150 | 290

before the two functions were vested in one person. | 160 | 300

36 GWPM

The typewriter keyboard was designed so that the most often used | 14 | 314

keys were struck by the weaker fingers. The purpose of this was to | 27 | 327

slow down the typists who, it was found, typed faster than the ma- | 40 | 340

chines could operate, causing the machines to jam. This arrangement | 54 | 354

has become known as the "qwerty" keyboard (named after the first six | 68 | 368

keys in the second row) and is the one we still use today – not only | 82 | 382

on typewriters, but also on computers, word processors, telexes, and | 96 | 396

other communication machines. As technology developed, the speed | 109 | 409

capability of the typewriter did increase so that it reached and then | 123 | 423

surpassed the speed of the average typist. The typewriter brought | 136 | 436

about major changes in the business office. Too, it made a tremendous | 150 | 450

impact on communications and education. More than anything else, the | 164 | 464

typewriter was largely responsible for opening the doors of business | 178 | 478

to women. | 180 | 480

| 1 | 2 | 3 | 4 | 5 | 6 | 7 | 8 | 9 | 10 | 11 | 12 | 13 | 14 |

		WORDS	
68 GWPM	We are the beauty salon you have been waiting for. Our staff are	13	13
a friendly bunch and we are located right in your neighbourhood.	26	26
What's more, we offer you a new kind of styling. It's called no-risk	40	40
hairstyling. We call it no-risk styling because if you don't like it,	54	54
you don't pay for it. In other words, you risk nothing by trying us.[1]	68	68
We can make this offer because we are confident in ourselves. We are	82	82
certain that we can please you better than any other salon, and for	96	96
very good reasons.	100	100
The first reason is that we match the stylist to your needs.	113	113
When you call us for your first appointment, we will ask you some	126	126
brief questions. As a result of the information[2] you give us, we will	140	140
book you with the stylist who, we feel, would best meet your hair's	154	154
needs. Just as with all other professions, hair stylists have their	168	168
specialties and we want to make sure that you get the one who is spe-	182	182
cial for you.	185	185
The second reason for our confidence is that we listen to you.	198	198
At your first visit, you and your[3] stylist will discuss your hair. You	212	212
will talk about style preference, hair problems, the amount of time	226	226
you like to devote to your hair, etc. In other words, we study your	240	240
hair and your likes and dislikes before we undertake the work.	253	253
The third reason is that in our shop you are the judge of any	266	266
haircut or style we give you.[4] We do our utmost to combine your tastes	280	280
with our design expertise to create a look that is best suited to your	294	294
hair, your features, and your personal style. We try to come up with	308	308
a style that not only looks nice when you leave our store, but that	321	321
you can maintain until your next appointment. We even give you tips	335	335
on how to look after it.[5]	340	340
Lastly, we give you our no-risk guarantee. Our aim is to make		354
you beautiful and happy. If you decide that you are not satisfied		367
with our services, you don't pay for them. It's as simple as that –		381
no fuss, no hassle. So why not do yourself and your hair a favour?		395
Give us a call today. You just can't lose, and you have much to gain.		409
By the way, if you book your appointment for a Monday, Tuesday, or		422
Wednesday, we will give you a ten per cent discount on all of our		435
services.		437

| 1 | 2 | 3 | 4 | 5 | 6 | 7 | 8 | 9 | 10 | 11 | 12 | 13 | 14 |

Yawning

There are few of us who fail to indulge in a good old-fashioned	13
yawn now and then. In fact, many of us spend a good portion of our	27
day yawning. We yawn first thing in the morning. We yawn at various	41
times through the day. We yawn at bedtime. We started yawning quite	55
early in life. As babies, we were quite notorious yawners. Yawning	69
feels good, especially when done in private where we can put our whole	83
bodies into it. Sometimes we yawn at the wrong times in front of the	97
wrong people, and that can be embarrassing. However, yawning is con-	111
tagious and if we can get others in on the act, we can spread the	124
embarrassment around.	128

It's doubtful if yawning is often a topic of conversation in 141
scientific circles where it would likely excite only yawns. Even 154
doctors give it little thought – so little, in fact, that they haven't 168
conjured up a fancy name for it yet. It appears that yawning is one 182
of those natural phenomena, like blushing and sneezing, which has 195
drawn only passing attention. 201

Yawn is a very old word that means to be wide open or gaping, as 215
in a yawning cavern. When used in reference to people, it means that 229
involuntary action in which one takes a long, deep breath while gradu- 243
ally opening the mouth to its fullest. This causes the tongue to 256
flatten, the throat muscles to stretch, and the eyelids to droop. 269
Often at the same time, the arms and body stretch and the eyes may 282
water. 283

Pretty well all vertebrates yawn. Cats, parrots, turtles, even 297
elephants yawn. Most animals' yawning usually just means they are 310
ready to drop off to sleep. People tend to yawn when they are tired, 324
bored, or perhaps are sitting in a hot, stuffy room. Under such con- 338
ditions, our breathing becomes more shallow causing our oxygen level 352
to drop – which induces us to yawn. A nice big yawn brings added 365
oxygen into the bloodstream, which pumps it up to the brain to perk us 379
up. Yawning is the best method of clearing one's ears and relieving 393
the pain or discomfort of a change in air pressure like that experi- 407
enced on an airplane. Because so many people interpret a yawn as a 421
sign of boredom, polite folks stifle their yawns, cover them up, or 435
turn away; and almost always they apologize. 444

The subject of yawning has not been ignored by humorous writers. 458
In fact, it was defined by one wit as the act of opening one's mouth 472
in the desperate hope that other people would clamp theirs shut. 485

| 1 | 2 | 3 | 4 | 5 | 6 | 7 | 8 | 9 | 10 | 11 | 12 | 13 | 14 |

72
GWPM

My childhood days in the north of Scotland were happy times. 12 12
Life was simpler then. They were the days of candles to light one to 26 26
bed and cooking on an open grate over a wood fire. Travel was by foot 40 40
or by horse and buggy or by bicycle. In winter, there was lots of 53 53
snow. There was an old saying that a black Christmas meant a full 66 66
kirkyard. We believed it and so it was counted a bad omen if there 80 80
was no snow by the end of the year. 87 87

Most New Year's, or hogmanay as we termed it, my parents threw a 101 101
party. Father used to draw up a program and act as the master of 114 114
ceremonies. There were games like postman's knock, pass the scissors, 128 128
and yes please and thank you. The latter was a card game and, as you 142 142
may have already guessed, a very polite one. There were musical solos 156 156
and singsongs, and after it all a grand tea was laid on. 167 167

In the summer, we ran barefoot. Children played in the streets. 181 181
The boys had marbles and balls and bikes. Girls played with dolls, 195 195
knitted, and played games like catty. The catty was a thick piece of 209 209
wood that was tapered on both ends. It was laid on the ground and the 223 223
tapered end was hit with a stick which made the catty catapult up and 237 237
over. Sometimes we girls would decide to have a picnic up the hill 251 251
below which the town nestled. We would gather gooseberries from the 265 265
garden, and buy half a penny's worth of sweeties and a big bag of 278 278
broken biscuits for a penny. That, plus a few wild raspberries and 291 291
brambles that we picked on the hill, was our picnic feast. 303 303

Because so many people in the region had the same names, it was a 317 317
common custom to tack identifiers onto names. For instance, there was 331 331
Bill the wright, Dinny the grocer, and Jock the goose. My father was 345 345
renowned for his fine tenor voice, and he was widely known as Murd the 359 359
bird. 360 360

There were vagrants who wandered into town from time to time. 373
Some were tinkers, or tinks as we called them, who came to peddle 386
their wares. Some were gypsies who camped in an old quarry on the 399
outskirts of town and made a few shillings at telling fortunes. Some 413
were unusual characters like Peter the Great, a hermit who lived in a 427
small hut way up on the hill, or Eppy Cacky who would arrive round the 441
top of our street dressed in petticoats to her ankles, a wide cape, 455
and a broad-brimmed hat. She danced and sang and played the harmonica 469
and we were all enchanted. 474

| 1 | 2 | 3 | 4 | 5 | 6 | 7 | 8 | 9 | 10 | 11 | 12 | 13 | 14 |

Why Me?

At least once a day throughout my seventy-six years, I have 12
asked, "Why me?" Today, for instance, I came into the drawing room 26
with my teacup in hand. As I headed for my favourite chair, I stubbed 40
my toe on the rocking chair, spilled my tea, stumbled, and landed so 54
heavily in my chair that one of its slender legs cracked. Why me? 67

As I rested in the lopsided chair wondering whether my toe was 81
broken, I recalled the time I broke my ankle while standing on the 94
toilet. It was a sunny spring day, and while my infant son was sleep- 108
ing, I washed and ironed the bathroom curtains. When they were ready 122
for hanging, I lifted the toilet seat and stood on the rim of the bowl 136
to reach the curtain rod. As I stretched, my foot slipped and crashed 150
into the bowl with such force that it stuck and I couldn't free it. 164

Finally, I stopped struggling and, just then, I heard the screen 178
door open and the afternoon mail drop on the floor. I shouted loudly 192
for help. The door re-opened and a timid voice said, "What is it, 205
lady?" I replied that I was stuck in the toilet and needed assist- 219
ance. There was a moment's silence. Then the postman informed me 232
that he would summon my next-door neighbour. After much persuasion, I 246
coerced him into the bathroom and I was rescued. Why me? 258

A cast on my foot and a new baby were trying enough, but being 271
stuck indoors was most annoying, so one day I ventured out. Pushing 285
the baby in the pram, I was confident I could walk the short distance 299
to the store and back. I arrived with no trouble and left the baby 313
sleeping outside in the carriage while I shopped. When I came out, my 327
only thought was to reach home without dropping the milk jug. Every 341
step was an adventure, but I arrived home without mishap. I put the 355
milk in the refrigerator and sat down at the kitchen table – exhausted 369
but elated at my feat. It wasn't until I noticed the baby's dish that 383
I realized I had left my baby at the store. I was frantic. I strug- 397
gled to the telephone and called the shop. Yes, the baby was there 410
and the police had just arrived to collect the abandoned child. After 424
lengthy negotiations, tall explanations, and desperate pleading, the 438
policeman agreed to deliver the baby home. Was I embarassed as I 451
watched the officer pushing my baby pram up the street! Why me? 464

I used to think I would outgrow my calamities, but I never did. 478
The ringing of the telephone brought me back to reality, and I hobbled 492
into the kitchen, banging my head on a cupboard door that was ajar. I 506
groped for the phone and said hello. It was a wrong number. Why me? 520

| 1 | 2 | 3 | 4 | 5 | 6 | 7 | 8 | 9 | 10 | 11 | 12 | 13 | 14 |

76
GWPM

Finally, one day I decided it was time. For years, I had worked 13 13
the nine to five shift cooped up in a plush office or running from one 27 27
meeting to the next, trying to keep things running smoothly and, at 41 41
the same time, to fan the flames of new ideas. For the most part, I 55 55
enjoyed what I was doing and the nice people with whom I worked. Why 69 69
then did I suddenly up and leave it all? I left for a number of rea- 83 83
sons. Perhaps the most important was that I was drawn more and more 97 97
to the wonderful world on the other side of the window in the large 111 111
office in which I worked. 116 116

For the greater part of the threescore years and ten, I had 129 129
longed to have the freedom to watch spring emerge, not only in the 142 142
gardens, but in the meadows, along the hedgerows, in the woods and 155 155
beside the creeks and marshes. I wanted to respond to the call of the 169 169
frogs, the song of the robins, and the buzz of the bees. Every day 183 183
that passes brings me closer to that great spectrum of life repre- 196 196
sented by the flora and fauna of our native landscape. They are my 209 209
friends and I must know them better. 216 216

But the time is short, and their numbers are so great. I will 230 230
never recognize them all by name, but I will begin to know what to 243 243
expect according to their ecology. I will know that where there is 257 257
goldenrod, I am apt to find the spindle gall. I'll learn that it is 271 271
the home of a moth caterpillar, but I will likely not remember its 284 284
name, for it's so long and difficult. I will remember that wherever I 298 298
see monarch butterflies, I will expect to find milkweed; that in the 312 312
wetlands, the three-sided stems of grass-like growth are not a grass 326 326
at all but rather one of a number of sedges; and that where I hear the 340 340
frog in early spring, it will not be long before marsh marigolds will 354 354
beam from the still pond water. I simply must drink my fill of all of 368 368
these wonders and learn what I can while there is still time. 380 380

Now and then, I will take some people with me to introduce to my 394
new friends. Some of my friends can't move, but those that can will 408
wave at me in the breeze. None of my friends can talk. Nevertheless, 422
they will delight my people companions with their beauty, their 435
strange but wonderful ways, and their unique roles in this vast stage 449
called life. 452

| 1 | 2 | 3 | 4 | 5 | 6 | 7 | 8 | 9 | 10 | 11 | 12 | 13 | 14 |

The first farming settlement in the Prairies was begun by a group | 13
of Scottish families who were known as the Selkirk settlers. For some | 27
time, it seemed as though everything were pitted against these people. | 41
The fur traders saw them as a threat, and they and their Indian | 54
friends made many attempts to drive them out; but each time the set- | 68
tlers returned. As if that were not enough, the Scots were beset by | 82
drought, floods, crop disease, and even plagues of grasshoppers. | 95
Somehow, the colony survived. | 101

For those early settlers, farming was hard manual labour. They | 115
used simple tools: hoes for cutting the weeds, spades for turning the | 129
soil, sickles and scythes for harvesting, and flails for threshing. | 143
Sowing of the seeds was done by hand. With methods such as these, the | 157
homesteaders could cultivate only small parcels of land in that vast | 171
country, barely enough to give them a living. | 180

With the advent of the plow, things took a turn for the better. | 194
The settlers were able to till larger areas. Before too long, other | 208
equipment became available. Seed drills replaced hand sowing, reapers | 222
and binders made harvesting much easier, and threshing machines sepa- | 236
rated the wheat from the straw. At first, the new machines were driv- | 250
en by horses or oxen, but then the steam engine arrived to take over | 264
the job. The farmers were able to plant larger and larger crops. | 277

It was obvious to the farmers that the Prairies was a great place | 291
for growing wheat, but the varieties they were using were not really | 305
suited to short, dry summers, and they picked up diseases far too | 318
readily. What was needed was a type of wheat that would ripen quickly | 332
and be resistant to disease. | 338

Back in Scotland, a minister happened to be strolling along the | 352
dock in Glasgow when he noticed a ship unloading grain. After watch- | 366
ing for a few minutes, the minister cocked his head and his hat fell | 380
into the grain bin he was standing beside. He reached in and plucked | 394
out his hat – plus a few grains of wheat. That night, the minister | 408
wrapped up the grains and mailed them to a farming friend in Canada. | 422
From these seeds, the minister's friend, David Fife, developed a | 435
strain of wheat that was admirably suited to prairie conditions. In | 449
time, Red Fife, as the new wheat was called, became popular in the | 462
home and then the world markets; and Canada's wheat industry was | 475
launched. | 477

| 1 | 2 | 3 | 4 | 5 | 6 | 7 | 8 | 9 | 10 | 11 | 12 | 13 | 14 |

80
GWPM

Salt has some fourteen hundred known uses. Many of these can be 13 13
applied in the home where salt can be much more than just a food sea- 27 27
soner. For instance, salt is a great cleaning aid. A paste of salt 41 41
and vinegar smeared on brass, copper, or stainless steel for an hour 55 55
or more will remove tarnish. The paste should be rubbed off with a 69 69
soft cloth; and then the item can be washed and polished[1] with a clean, 83 83
dry cloth. 85 85

Wicker furniture can be cleaned with a solution of warm water and 99 99
salt. As well as cleaning, the salt solution will stiffen the wicker 113 113
and promote longer life. A deep vase may be cleaned by letting a 126 126
solution of salt and vinegar stand in it for a time. Then shake well 150 150
and rinse with clean water. A fair amount of salt[2] added to quite hot 164 164
water will set the colour in fabrics and help to prevent the colour 178 178
running. Just plunge the garment into the solution and let it stand 192 192
until the water is cold. For people who use a clothesline, a cloth 206 206
wrung out in water, to which a good portion of salt has been added, 220 220
and rubbed on the clothesline will prevent clothes sticking to the 233 233
line in cold weather. To discourage[3] snails and earthworms, sprinkle 247 247
with salt the sidewalks and damp corners where they thrive. 259 259

Some vegetables can be placed in cold, salted water for a few 272 272
minutes to allow any worms they may harbour to float to the top of the 286 286
water. Vegetables, such as sprouts and spinach, may be cleaned by 300 300
adding a handful of salt to the water in which they are to be rinsed. 314 314 306
Any sand in the greens will sink[4] to the bottom. 324 324

Salt can also be a beauty aid. A cheap, but good, facial, one 338 338
that is helpful for teenage skin problems too, can be had by mixing 352 352
two parts salt to one part olive oil and massaging the mixture into 366 366
the face and throat with gentle, upward strokes. Leave it on for five 380 380
minutes or so; then remove gently with soap and water. Follow with a 394 394
warm rinse and then a cold one.[5] 400 400

After handling onions, rubbing one's hands with salt and then 413
rinsing will remove any onion odour. Tired feet can be soothed by 426
soaking them in a foot bath to which has been added a handful of salt. 440
Salt, by itself or mixed with baking soda, is a great teeth whitener. 454
It also hardens gums, sweetens the breath, and helps to slow the 467
build-up of tartar on the teeth. In other words, it makes one a much 481
more pleasant person to be with. 487

| 1 | 2 | 3 | 4 | 5 | 6 | 7 | 8 | 9 | 10 | 11 | 12 | 13 | 14 |

The needs and demands of war were not always easy to cope with, 13
but in most cases the British people met them with stout hearts, broad 27
shoulders, and co-operation. The rationing of clothes brought on a 41
policy of mend and make do. Food rationing made cooking an ever more 55
difficult task and prompted the media to give out advice, hints, and 69
recipes. Those who had land, even a small plot in front of or behind 83
a house, dug victory gardens in which they grew fruits and vegetables. 97
When petrol became scarce, people took to bicycles, horses, or their 111
own feet to get about. 115

When the country fell short of war materials, it made a mass 128
appeal for anything that could be converted and used. The response 142
was phenomenal, and from then on, waste was looked upon as a mortal 156
sin. Few things were thrown away. Old blankets and bedding were 169
donated to bomb shelters. Kitchen scraps were set aside for making 183
into a brown soup, or mud pudding as it was called, to feed animals. 197
All paper and cardboard was collected for recycling. Animal bones 210
were saved to be made into glue. Scrap rubber in any form, even in 224
corsets, was given to make tires for military vehicles. 235

Any and all kinds of scrap metal were needed and salvage dumps 249
were set up for their collection. Aluminum pots and pans, old and new 263
and some still hot from the oven, were donated for the building of 276
spitfires, hurricanes, and other aircraft. Tin foil, tin cans, tire 290
rims, and even thimbles were collected. All kinds of plain and ornate 304
wrought iron fencing, freshly removed from property perimeters, were 318
piled onto the scrap metal heaps. 325

The country had developed into a big national team that was dedi- 339
cated to sacrifice and hard work. In the midst of it all, sanity was 353
kept afloat, largely through the action of a good sense of humour. 366
Songs, jokes, wisecracks, and comic strips provided a lighter side to 380
the dangers and realities of war. Needed diversions were found, too, 394
in the music halls, movie houses, and pubs. 403

The war effort on the home front was not without some strife, 416
waste, unfairness, crime, and other taints that are always present 429
under any circumstances; but by far the vast majority of people gave 443
unstintingly their share of blood, toil, tears, and sweat. 455

| 1 | 2 | 3 | 4 | 5 | 6 | 7 | 8 | 9 | 10 | 11 | 12 | 13 | 14 |

Before you can begin to write a thing, you must have a clear 12 12
understanding of why you are writing; so collect all of the data you 26 26
will need for your letter. Then you must decide what you want to say 40 40
and how you are going to say it. Make a plan or outline of your 53 53
letter in point form. A plan can be a big help because it lets you 67 67
change your mind and add or delete items before you start to write or 81 81
dictate. Too, [1] if you were interrupted while you were writing and had 95 95
to come back to it at a later time, your thoughts would still be there 109 109
in point form and you could pick up right from where you left off. 122 122

Next, sort the points into a logical sequence. Then check the 136 136
points to be sure that you have not missed any. When you are writing 150 150
the letter from your plan, you will use paragraphs to group points 163 163
which relate to one main [2] idea. From your plan, you will soon see 176 176
which points belong together in one paragraph. Paragraphs make a 189 189
letter look nice, and they help to get the message across quickly. 202 202

As a rule, a business letter will have three or more paragraphs: 216 216
an opening one, one or more which contain the data, and a closing one. 230 230
Short paragraphs are easy to read and are more pleasing to the eye 243 243
than long ones. For this reason, it is good [3] practice to use fairly 257 257
short paragraphs in letter writing. Do not use a succession of two- 271 271
or three-line paragraphs, though; these do not look pleasing on the 285 285
page and force the reader to jump too quickly from one idea to the 299 299
next. 300 300

The opening paragraph should be short. It should tell the reader 314 314
the subject of the letter and the reason for writing. It should catch 328 328
the reader's attention and put him or her in the right frame of mind 342 342
for grasping the message. The closing paragraph is just as important, 356 356
if not more so. Its purpose is to convince the reader to take the 369 369
action you desire, or to inform him or her of what action is being 383 383
taken and what the next step will be. The middle paragraphs give the 397 397
information and the details. Each should contain just one main idea 411 411
and be no more than nine or ten lines long. [5] 420 420

When your letter is done, check it over to make sure that it is 434
clear and concise, complete and correct, and last but not least, that 448
it is courteous. 451

| 1 | 2 | 3 | 4 | 5 | 6 | 7 | 8 | 9 | 10 | 11 | 12 | 13 | 14 |

This was total war. All were in it – men, women, children, old 13
and young alike. This war was to be fought not only in the air, at 27
sea, and on the beaches and in the trenches of foreign lands, but on 41
the home ground as well. The home front was where some of the most 55
important battles were fought; if it failed, all could be lost. 68

The enemy thought this tiny country of Great Britain was an easy 82
mark, as had been several other countries before it; but Hitler had 96
not reckoned with the courage, resourcefulness, and determination of 110
his opponents. Although the odds were not in their favour, the 123
British aim was lofty – not mere survival, but victory. 134

On the home front, war became a fact of everyday life and every- 148
thing was geared towards it. Close to forty million gas masks were 162
issued in case the enemy resorted to chemical warfare. Many children 176
were evacuated from homes in prime target areas and were sent to safer 190
parts of the country. Food rations were imposed and nightly blackouts 204
were enforced. Basements and cellars in many buildings were taken 217
over for air raid shelters, and trenches for shelters were dug in 230
parks in the large towns. Medical and hospital services, rescue 243
teams, bomb disposal squads, and fire brigades were organized. 255

In open fields and parks, obstacles were placed to inhibit the 269
landing of enemy aircraft. To confuse the enemy should any of them 283
manage to land safely, signs telling distances and the names of towns 297
and villages were removed from roads, rail stations, and all other 310
display places. To augment the nation's food supply, gardens were 323
planted in golf courses, sports grounds, parks, city lots, and even in 337
reclaimed swamps. 340

Everyone was kept busy doing what she or he could to help the war 354
effort. Thousands went into offices and factories to carry on the 367
work left by those drawn into the armed forces. A number of people 381
acted as bomb spotters, blackout wardens, or members of the fire bri- 395
gade to put out fires started by the bombs. Many sewed and knitted 409
garments for the troops. Others worked in the shelters or did volun- 423
teer work where they were needed. People strove together in a cohe- 437
sive force, united in spirit and purpose. 445

| 1 | 2 | 3 | 4 | 5 | 6 | 7 | 8 | 9 | 10 | 11 | 12 | 13 | 14 |

On Time

88
GWPM

Boy, do I hate to get up in the morning. The trouble is I have | 13 | 13
to be at work by nine o'clock. Sometimes I get there by five after | 26 | 26
nine. Sometimes it's nine-thirty. I'm hardly ever on time but nobody | 40 | 40
says anything about it. I like my job. I am a transcription typist | 54 | 54
in a big office. My boss dictates her letters onto a tape; then I | 67 | 67
listen to her voice and type the letters. | 75 | 75

Well, this morning it's eight-thirty and I am still in bed.[1] Boy, | 89 | 89
I'm really going to be late today. I jump into my clothes and run a | 103 | 103
comb through my hair. Thank goodness my hair is short! I get into my | 117 | 117
car and drive – fast. I make good time, park the car in the lot, and | 131 | 131
dash into the office building. Everyone is working hard when I get | 144 | 144
in. A couple of the girls look up. When I say hi, I get a cool | 157 | 157
reception. I settle down at my desk. My boss is out, thank goodness. | 171 | 171
I turn on the transcriber[2] and hear my boss's voice on the tape. She | 185 | 185
tells me to type a letter to Ann Jones. Hey, that's me! She gives me | 199 | 199
the address – the whole works, just like a letter to someone I don't | 213 | 213
know. This is nuts. I type, and here is how it reads: | 224 | 224

"You have been working for this company for four months. During | 238 | 238
that time I have found you to be a willing, intelligent worker and a | 252 | 252
very fine typist. There is one serious problem, however.[3] You never | 266 | 266
come to work on time. Some days you are five minutes late. Sometimes | 280 | 280
you are as much as thirty minutes late. There are fifteen people | 293 | 293
working in this office. Fourteen of them get to work on time. You do | 307 | 307
not. I think we all feel irritated when we see you coming in late. | 321 | 321
You do not have special privileges here. I have heard the staff talk- | 335 | 335
ing about your lateness. One person suggested that maybe everybody | 349 | 349
should come in[4] late. If you don't have to be on time, why should | 362 | 362
they? I don't think you realize that your office friends resent you | 376 | 376
for coming in late. It is very bad for office morale. Besides, the | 390 | 390
company pays you for a full day, and you do not give it to us. In six | 404 | 404
weeks you will be eligible for a raise. If you can correct this bad | 418 | 418
work habit, I will recommend you for the raise. If you do not, I will | 432 | 432
have to fire you. Sincerely, Jane Dunn."[5] | 440 | 440

Boy, is my face red. I put the letter on my boss's desk. When | 454 |
she returns, she sees the letter and asks whether I have any ques- | 467 |
tions. I say no and she hands me a package. I open it. It's an | 480 |
alarm clock. "I will try hard, Mrs. Dunn," I say. "I just never | 493 |
realized that being on time was so important." | 502 |

| 1 | 2 | 3 | 4 | 5 | 6 | 7 | 8 | 9 | 10 | 11 | 12 | 13 | 14 |

Violin – History and Care

The excellence of the violin as we know it today was brought about through the changes and improvements made by countless people over a long stretch of time.

In the twelth century, a fiddle called the vielle was made. It had five strings and ranked as the most important stringed instrument of the time. Another forerunner was the tenor viol which had six strings but lacked the brilliance of tone and the versatility of the fiddle. For two hundred years, Cremona, a small town in Italy, reigned as the prime centre of violin making. Here, Nicolo Amati made instruments of such sweetness and tone that for some time it was thought they could not be excelled. As it turned out, his prize pupil began making a larger and flatter model which not only equalled the master's in tenderness but which had more volume and roundness of tone.

To this day, that student, Antonio Stradivari, is considered the master of violin makers. It is believed that during his lifetime, he made a thousand or so instruments, of which some four to six hundred still survive. Needless to say, each of these is a rare item and worth a fortune. While the violins of Stradivari are justly famous, a large number of concert players prefer to use those made by Joseph Guarnerius, a member of another family of violin makers from the same town.

The care of the violin should be a prime concern of the owner. Violins, and all stringed instruments for that matter, should not be exposed to extremes or large, rapid changes in temperature. Failure to observe this rule could result in such problems as cracks, open seams, or collapse of parts of the assembly. Because the glue in a violin softens in high heat, leaving a violin in a closed place like the trunk of a car in summer for even a short time can do damage. Also, transporting a violin in a car trunk in winter poses a threat, as does the unheated baggage hold of an aircraft. In fact, a maple back can crack if it is exposed to severe cold for just half an hour.

A fiddle should be cleaned regularly and checked for cracks or open seams. Any repairs should be done by a professional. With proper care, a violin will give years and years of service and then may be handed down to children as an heirloom.

| 1 | 2 | 3 | 4 | 5 | 6 | 7 | 8 | 9 | 10 | 11 | 12 | 13 | 14 |

92
GWPM

If you should ever come across a green giant of a plant with | 12
pretty flowers, it is more than likely that you are viewing kudzu. | 25
Kudzu is a vine that drapes its leaves over ordinary things until they | 39
look like spooky creatures. It will shroud anything in its path. It | 53
can cover an old junked car in a few weeks or an empty house in just | 67
one summer. Kudzu grows so fast that some people call it the mile-a- | 81
minute vine. Others say you can measure its growth in miles or kilo- | 95
metres per hour, just as you would measure the speed of a car. I have | 109
heard one tale which tells of a farmer who planted some kudzu behind | 123
his barn. The story says the kudzu grew so fast that it beat the | 136
farmer back to his house. I must admit that kudzu does grow fast, but | 150
not that fast. At most, a stem can grow about one foot or thirty | 163
centimetres per day. | 167

Kudzu did not always grow in North America. It came from Asia | 181
where it is used in many ways. The Japanese use the vines to make | 194
cloth, baskets, and paper. They make hay from the leaves. The | 207
Chinese grind up the vine's roots to make flour. | 217

Americans first saw kudzu at an exhibit over a hundred years ago. | 231
They liked the way it looked so much that they began to plant the vine | 245
to shade their porches from the hot summer sun. Farmers found that | 259
their animals liked to eat kudzu too; and when kudzu grew, it made the | 273
soil richer around its roots. Then someone found that the fast- | 286
growing plant helped keep the soil from washing away along new roads | 300
and highways. Kudzu was good for so many things that people began to | 314
call it the miracle vine. | 319

Kudzu grew especially well in the southern United States. There | 333
it grew, and grew, and grew. In fact, it grew too well. Now, most | 347
southern folks think kudzu is a curse. Foresters don't like the way | 361
it sneaks into forests and kills the trees by blocking out the sun- | 374
light. Farmers don't like the way it invades their fields and crowds | 388
their crops. Telephone companies don't like the way it sometimes | 401
pulls down their poles and wires with its heavy, grasping vines. | 414
Today, people no longer call kudzu a miracle vine. Instead, they call | 428
it a weed. But this fast-growing vine is neither all good nor all | 441
bad. Like so many other things in life, kudzu is a monster only when | 455
it gets out of control. | 460

| 1 | 2 | 3 | 4 | 5 | 6 | 7 | 8 | 9 | 10 | 11 | 12 | 13 | 14 |

Violin – First String

The violin is the best known and most widely used of all stringed | 13
instruments. This queen of instruments is also known as a fiddle. | 26
The violin section is the largest and most important part of an | 39
orchestra, and the lead violin player is the concert master and often | 53
the assistant conductor as well. | 59

Violins are made with great care. The wood used in them has an | 73
important influence on the tone produced and must be carefully sea- | 87
soned so that no part will warp. The seventy different pieces in each | 101
violin are shaped to fit together exactly. No nails, screws, or metal | 115
fasteners of any kind are used. All the parts are glued together with | 129
a special glue, and the finished body is carefully varnished. | 141

A violin has four strings which extend almost the length of the | 155
instrument from the tailpiece, which is secured to the body of the | 168
violin by the end pin; over a bridge, which supports the strings above | 182
the body; to the peg box, which contains the pegs, or pins, for tight- | 196
ening and loosening the strings. Attached to the tailpiece is a fine | 210
tuner, and this enables the violinist to achieve fine shades of tuning | 224
without using the pegs. The strings were formerly all made of catgut, | 238
which was most often the twisted intestines of sheep. Modern violins | 252
have metal strings, although the G string, the lowest one, is often | 266
catgut overwound with silver, copper, or aluminum wire. | 277

The violin is played with a bow, a long curved stick with about a | 291
hundred and fifty horsehairs stretched from one tip to an adjustable | 305
device called a frog at the other end. The hair is allowed to rest | 319
loosely when the bow is stored in the violin case. When the bow is to | 333
be used, however, the hairs are tightened to the desired tension for | 347
playing and are rubbed with rosin which coats the hairs and improves | 361
the resonance of the tone when the bow is drawn across the strings. | 375
Movement of the bow back and forth over the violin strings causes the | 389
strings to vibrate and give off sound. The violinist is able to pro- | 403
duce different tones or notes by depressing one or more strings with | 417
the fingers of one hand while using the other hand to stroke the | 430
strings with the bow. | 434

Most people tend to admire the finger dexterity of the violinist | 448
and do not realize that the art of the playing is in the bowing. | 461

| 1 | 2 | 3 | 4 | 5 | 6 | 7 | 8 | 9 | 10 | 11 | 12 | 13 | 14 |

Pygmalion

96

GWPM

The old Greek myths are full of unusual tales – of gods and men, of strange creatures, of heroes and adventure, and even of love. One of these tales is the story of a young sculptor named Pygmalion who despised women and vowed never to marry. Women, he believed, had faults too numerous to count. As a token of his scorn, he set about to sculpt his idea of the perfect woman. He devoted himself wholly to the task, and under his gifted hands, the statue took shape and daily became more beautiful. Day and night he worked until, at last, not a flaw could be found. His ivory maiden was lovely beyond compare and was so lifelike that she appeared to be alive and simply to have paused for a moment.

Soon after the work was completed, it became apparent that a strange thing had happened to Pygmalion. He had fallen deeply and madly in love with his creation. For some time, he pretended his statue really was alive. He spoke to her and pretended that she was too shy to reply. He kissed and caressed her. He brought her gifts of flowers and fruit, and pretended that she was pleased. At long last, he had to face the truth. He was in love with a lifeless piece of stone that could not return his love. The truth made him utterly wretched.

On the feast day of Venus, the goddess of love, Pygmalion was one of the thousands of unhappy lovers who came to the temple to ask for aid in their love affairs. Certain it was hopeless to ask for his heart's true desire, when it came his turn to pray, he asked only that he find a maiden like his ivory statue. The goddess looked with favour on Pygmalion, for she was aware of his sad plight. As a sign, she caused the flame on the altar in front of which he stood to flare up three times.

Pygmalion returned home in better spirits than he had for a long time, but still his heart was sad. Would he really find a maid, and if so, could she ever replace his beloved stone lady? He went in to his statue and touched her arms. They felt soft and warm, but surely he must be dreaming. He kissed her lips and could almost swear they mellowed under his. He clasped her body in his arms. Her cold stiffness vanished. She was alive! He looked into her face, and she smiled at him and blushed. Pygmalion called her Galatea. They were married soon after, and Venus, pleased with her good deed, was guest of honour at their wedding.

| 13 |
| 27 |
| 41 |
| 54 |
| 68 |
| 82 |
| 96 |
| 110 |
| 124 |
| 137 |
| 141 |
| 154 |
| 167 |
| 180 |
| 194 |
| 208 |
| 221 |
| 235 |
| 249 |
| 251 |
| 265 |
| 279 |
| 292 |
| 306 |
| 319 |
| 333 |
| 347 |
| 350 |
| 364 |
| 378 |
| 392 |
| 406 |
| 420 |
| 434 |
| 447 |
| 461 |
| 475 |
| 480 |

| 1 | 2 | 3 | 4 | 5 | 6 | 7 | 8 | 9 | 10 | 11 | 12 | 13 | 14 |

Typing vs. Keyboarding

The flood of computers into today's offices is giving new import | 13
to that most basic of office skills – typing. For years now, typing | 27
has been just a part of women's dead-end work. Now, experts are say- | 41
ing that in the next decade, typing will be one of the assets that | 54
will decide who will run the corporate race and who will falter at the | 68
takeoff. | 70

A recent study found that a lack of simple typing skill among | 93
bosses was a major obstacle in making offices computer-efficient. The | 107
advent of computers demands that bosses will have to write at least | 121
some letters and reports straight onto word processors, send memos by | 135
way of computer to destinations both inside and outside the firm, hold | 149
group meetings by computer link-ups, and use data stored in computers | 163
to file information and to form statistical charts and spread sheets. | 177
The managers who succeed will be the ones who are willing to use | 190
keyboards. | 192

The suggestion to a group of executives at a recent meeting that | 206
in the future they will be asked if they can type drew many laughs. | 220
In some ways, this made sense because at the moment most managers do | 234
not type; in fact, more than fifty per cent handwrite all or most of | 248
their correspondence. This fact undercuts the savings which a com- | 262
puterized office is designed to produce, savings which could greatly | 276
reduce the workload for managers and others. A manager using a com- | 290
puter can revise and restyle a document many times and still wind up | 304
with a perfect copy. | 308

The move is now on to persuade bosses to overcome their doubts | 322
and fears, and to learn typing. The thing to avoid at all costs is | 336
the suggestion that what a manager does on a computer is "typing." A | 350
brief survey showed that the word "keyboarding" seems to be preferred | 364
from a boss's point of view. As a word, keyboarding describes not | 377
just writing, but also the use of letters, numbers, codes, or special | 391
keys to call up data to the screen, create graphs, look at charts, and | 405
program the system itself. Reaction has been slow in the schools, but | 419
they are slowly catching on to the fact that typing – oops, keyboarding | 433
– is a must. | 436

| 1 | 2 | 3 | 4 | 5 | 6 | 7 | 8 | 9 | 10 | 11 | 12 | 13 | 14 |

WORDS

100
GWPM

It must have been late at night when I finally awoke, for the | 12
room was as black as could be. All of my limbs ached. I felt as | 25
though I had been the victim of a hard and powerful blow. How I had | 39
gotten here and for what purpose, I did not know. I yearned for some- | 53
thing or someone; yet I didn't know what, whom, or why. A feeling of | 67
loneliness crept over me, and then for some strange reason, I began to | 81
cry. A blinding light came on and a gigantic creature dressed in | 94
white came into view. I felt [1] helpless and scared. The creature | 107
walked over and stared down at me. Then it began making weird noises | 121
and distorting its face in the most peculiar manner. Somehow it | 134
seemed to relax me and I fell into a deep sleep. | 144

When morning came, I awoke more refreshed. Looking round me, I | 158
found that I was encaged in a glass cubicle which offered just enough | 172
room for my outstretched body. Now, I have always thought myself to | 186
be a gentle and harmless person, and so I found my imprisonment both [2] | 200
puzzling and disturbing. On glancing round the room, I saw that small | 214
glass cells were to be found everywhere I looked. As my eyes focussed | 228
I could see that each one held another unfortunate inmate like myself. | 242
There must have been thirty, all told. Further probing revealed a | 255
huge glass window in the wall directly facing me. What was this win- | 269
dow for? Was I on display in a zoo? As I pondered my plight, the | 282
door burst open and another creature, dressed in white and topped with | 296
brown fuzz, strode [3] in shouting in a strange tongue. As the creature | 310
made its rounds of the prisoners, I grew angry. I was getting hungry. | 324
Was there no food in this jail? What had we done to deserve this kind | 338
of treatment? As was my wont when I was upset, I began to cry. The | 352
white creature marched over to my cell and began to make gurgling | 365
sounds to me. I could not guess what it was trying to say, but a sud- | 379
den fatigue came over me and I fell asleep once more. | 390

I wakened up to find a host of faces peering [4] down at me through | 404
the great window. Creatures tapped on the pane and made outrageous | 417
faces. I spent three weeks in that terrible place. Thinking back | 430
now, a whole year later, I would never give up my luxurious crib here | 444
at home to return to my little cell there at the hospital. I know I | 458
would not want to endure those silly "people" again, looking down at | 472
me through that big glass window, tapping and making faces and dis- | 486
turbing my sleep – even if one of them did turn out to be my mother. [5] | 500

| 1 | 2 | 3 | 4 | 5 | 6 | 7 | 8 | 9 | 10 | 11 | 12 | 13 | 14 |

Titanic

	WORDS

It was a chilly April evening, but the sea was calm and the sky | 13
was full of bright shining stars. A couple of warnings about icebergs | 27
in the area had come in over the wireless, but the Titanic's radio | 40
operator was too busy to pay much attention. He had a raft of mes- | 54
sages from his passengers to transmit to their families and friends. | 68
In the crow's nest, the watch marvelled at the stillness of the night | 82
when suddenly an iceberg loomed up in front of him. He rang his warn- | 96
ing bell and phoned down to the bridge. The helmsman tried to change | 110
the ship's course, but it was too late. | 118

Most of those who felt the jolt attributed it to a variety of | 131
things – almost anything but an iceberg. It was some time before the | 145
extent of the damage could be ascertained and assessed. The captain | 159
learned that the ship had received a long gash in her side and water | 173
was pouring in. The first five watertight compartments were filling | 187
up fast. It was because of her fifteen watertight compartments that | 201
the Titanic was deemed unsinkable. She could float with some of her | 215
compartments flooded, but not with all of the first five. | 226

The captain ordered that distress signals be radioed out and that | 240
rockets be fired every five minutes in an attempt to alert the steam- | 254
er, Californian, sixteen kilometres away. He told the crew to lower | 268
the lifeboats and start loading the women and children into them. | 281
Replies started coming in on the wireless. The Carpathia was a hun- | 295
dred kilometres away and was on her way at full speed. No word was | 309
heard from the steamer that could still be seen on the horizon. The | 323
Californian's lone radio operator had finished his shift just ten | 336
minutes before the iceberg struck. | 343

It was hard at first to convince the passengers that they would | 357
be safer in the lifeboats than on this big, strong ship; and many | 370
women at first refused to get into the boats. Thus the first few | 383
lifeboats set off with considerably less than their full complement of | 397
people. When the last boat pulled away, just over 700 people out of a | 411
total of over 1 500 had escaped the sinking ship. Out in the boats, | 425
the occupants watched as the Titanic sank lower and lower in the | 438
water. They could see people still standing at the rails, and they | 452
could hear the band playing. Suddenly, the ship stood on end, then | 466
started to slip, picking up speed as she went down. Then she was | 479
gone. | 480

| 1 | 2 | 3 | 4 | 5 | 6 | 7 | 8 | 9 | 10 | 11 | 12 | 13 | 14 |

Renovation

28 GWPM

The room was small and certainly not designed with two boys in mind – especially two who fought constantly. The three-quarter bed they shared was a front line battle zone. Twin beds did little to improve matters; the bickering and fighting continued. The only solution seemed to be to give each boy his own room. There was just one problem: there was only one other bedroom, and it was ours. There were three ways to acquire a third bedroom: give up my hobby room, buy a larger house, or enlarge our present home. The more we thought about it, the more we liked the idea of expanding. Not only would we acquire another bedroom, but we would gain a larger master bedroom, more closet space, etc.

32 GWPM

We drew up a plan to expand the upstairs from half a storey to a full storey. We called in several contractors to price the job and learned we could hire a contractor to do the structural work and finish the outside; then we could finish the inside ourselves. Being reasonably handy people, we decided this option was tailor-made for us and we signed a contract. We managed to cram all of the bedroom furniture into the living and dining rooms, leaving a narrow passage that wound its way through the maze to the front entrance. Because of a chest of drawers in front of it, the door couldn't be opened, but we were able to shout through the door to direct callers to the rear entrance. In the midst of the furniture were two makeshift beds for the children, while we occupied the basement.

36 GWPM

After the workers removed the roof, we stood in our former bedroom looking up at the stars and praying that these people knew what they were doing. They did. The new roof was constructed and the outside was completed. Then it was our turn. We installed insulation between the wall studs; then we covered the walls and ceilings with a plastic vapour barrier. A drywall expert put up the walls and ceilings, and a plasterer taped, filled, and sanded the joints. All the while, we cleaned – before, during, and after each job. Painting was our next task, followed by installing wood trim. Then the broadloom was laid and the furniture was put in place.

Finally, it was finished and ready for habitation. What a pleasure it was to have bedrooms again. That evening, each boy settled happily and quietly in his own room. It had taken three months of chaos, but we had found peace at last.

| 1 | 2 | 3 | 4 | 5 | 6 | 7 | 8 | 9 | 10 | 11 | 12 | 13 | 14 |

Statues – Old and New

One of the largest of ancient statues on record was that of | 12
Apollo, the Greek god of the sun. This bronze statue was known as the | 26
Colossus of Rhodes; and at thirty-two metres tall, it surely was | 39
colossal. Although the statue was wrecked by an earthquake about | 52
sixty years after its completion, it had already been declared one of | 66
the wonders of the world. It is not known where in the city of Rhodes | 80
the statue stood, but one suggestion was the harbour. Thus the popu- | 94
lar picture is that of Apollo, with sun rays protruding above his | 107
head, holding aloft a burning torch, and straddling the harbour so | 120
that ships in full sail were able to pass between his legs and enter | 134
the safety of the harbour. | 139

It is highly unlikely that you would have failed to notice the | 153
similarities, except for the gender and stance of the figures, between | 167
the Colossus and another famous and much more recent statue which very | 181
well qualifies as a wonder of the world. It is quite probable that | 195
the Colossus inspired this later symbol of freedom, the Statue of | 208
Liberty. | 210

Facing out over the New York harbour, the Statue of Liberty is | 224
the figure of a woman draped in classical robes and wearing a crown | 238
from which seven spikes radiate. The broken shackles of slavery lie | 252
at her feet, in her left hand is a law book, and in her right hand she | 266
carries aloft a flaming torch. The figure is forty-six metres high to | 280
the tip of the torch and is made of large, hammered copper plates | 293
which have turned a rich shade of green from the weather. | 304

The statue was a gift from the people of France. It was built | 318
there, taken apart, and then shipped to New York where it was assem- | 332
bled. The statue is bolted to a great stone pedestal which is twenty- | 346
seven metres high. Thus the statue and base together reach a height | 360
of well over seventy metres. An elevator inside takes visitors to the | 374
top of the pedestal, from where they may climb a spiral staircase up | 388
through the hollow statue to the crown. Here, windows provide a mar- | 402
vellous view of the harbour. The statue, which is floodlit at night, | 416
is in full view of all watercraft which enter the harbour day or | 429
night; and for many people, it is an emotional and stirring sight. | 442

| 1 | 2 | 3 | 4 | 5 | 6 | 7 | 8 | 9 | 10 | 11 | 12 | 13 | 14 |

Baby Bonus

40 GWPM

When we arrived, Mrs. Nagle was sitting in a wheel chair under a big maple tree. Her hair was white now and cut quite short, but her face, although looking smaller and more delicate, had not changed at all; and you could tell by her twinkling eyes that her fine spirit and sense of humour were still intact. While my mother and Mrs. Nagle reminisced, I recalled my own memories.

When I was young, the Nagles came regularly to visit my parents. John Nagle was a quiet, pleasant man with a dry wit. He was tall, and I remember thinking that I had never seen anyone so thin. Kay Nagle was short and pretty with dark hair and eyes. I knew they had been friends of my parents since they were next-door neighbours before I was born. I also knew they had many, many children.

Kay was brought up on a farm north of Toronto. While in her early twenties, she moved to the city where she worked as a bookkeeper. She met and married John Nagle, a carpenter, and soon they were raising a family.

44 GWPM

With the onset of the Depression, John fell out of work and they joined the many other families on public relief. Their family continued to grow, and by 1935 the Nagles realized they had a chance to figure in a rather large legacy left by a bachelor lawyer who had died nine years before and bequeathed the bulk of his estate to the mother in Toronto who bore the greatest number of children in the ten-year period following his death. Kay entered her name as a candidate and quickly found herself engulfed in a whirl of publicity that was to continue for years. Newspapers vied for sole rights to her story, companies wanted her to endorse their products, and the city promised to bill for welfare monies paid out to winners. The family became the butt of praise, support, jokes, and threats.

When the ten years were up, Kay Nagle had borne ten children during the period, nine of whom were eligible according to the terms of the will. A year and a half later when the courts concluded the litigation, she was declared one of the four mothers who were entitled to share equally in the estate.

The sudden transition from welfare to wealth wrought many changes in the lives of the Nagles, but one thing it did not alter was their love of children. Mrs. Nagle went on to have three more for a total of fifteen. Most of them were present that day at the family reunion, paying tribute to this bubbly lady who had made it all possible.

| 1 | 2 | 3 | 4 | 5 | 6 | 7 | 8 | 9 | 10 | 11 | 12 | 13 | 14 |

Statues – Big and Beautiful

Of the millions of statues which have been built through the ages	13
to the present day, only a very select few have entered the realm of	27
wonders of the world. Because thousands of statues have been beauti-	41
ful works of art, designed and built with immense care and craftsman-	55
ship, it would seem impossible for a few to be widely acclaimed as	68
surpassing all others. What made these few so outstanding? A quick	82
study shows that they had one other thing in common besides beauty:	96
size. It would appear that these statues achieved their special	109
status, not only because they were beautiful, but also because they	123
were big.	125

Of the millions of statues which have been built through the ages
to the present day, only a very select few have entered the realm of
wonders of the world. Because thousands of statues have been beautiful works of art, designed and built with immense care and craftsmanship, it would seem impossible for a few to be widely acclaimed as
surpassing all others. What made these few so outstanding? A quick
study shows that they had one other thing in common besides beauty:
size. It would appear that these statues achieved their special
status, not only because they were beautiful, but also because they
were big.

One of the original wonders of the world, the Greek statue of the
god Zeus was said to be one of the most handsome statues ever made.
It was also over twelve metres high. The statue was carved out of
wood and the flesh parts were covered with sheets of ivory, the robes
were plates of solid gold, and the eyes were jewels. The figure sat
upon a throne that was gold-plated, engraved, and inlaid with ebony
and gems. A statue of such beauty and dimensions would be certain to
create a lasting impact. The statue was destroyed by fire a long time
ago, but written records attest to its merits.

Another beautiful and big statue is the Buddha of Kamakura in
Japan. Thirteen metres high, this bronze figure sits in a position of
meditation. Its eyes are gold and there is a silver bump in the middle of its forehead which denotes spiritual insight. The statue was
housed in a temple until the building was destroyed by an earthquake
and tidal wave. The statue survived and is now surrounded by a lovely
garden. Inside the figure are stairs which visitors may climb to the
shoulders where there is a small window looking out the back.

A much more recent statue built in this century is Christ of the
Andes in South America. It also is lovely, but not nearly as large as
the Buddha. It is only eight metres tall; however, because it is located in a pass that is more than sixty-one metres above sea level, it
is in a rather commanding position and is one of the highest statues
in the world. Crafted from bronze, it is a symbol of peace between
the two countries which border the pass in which it stands. Part of
its metal came from cannons that were melted down.

| 1 | 2 | 3 | 4 | 5 | 6 | 7 | 8 | 9 | 10 | 11 | 12 | 13 | 14 |

Garbage In, Garbage Out

48 GWPM   The saying "garbage in, garbage out" is used most often today in   14 14
reference to computers. It quite simply describes the fact that if   28 28
improper data is fed into a computer, then improper information will   42 42
come out.   44 44

Another place where this saying can be applied is in the matter   58 58
of eating habits. Good eating habits are becoming more and more dif-   72 72
ficult to acquire. Increasing dependence on fast foods has become a   86 86
way of life. To a great extent, this is to be expected. Our society   100 100
moves at a hectic pace. In most homes, both partners work. There is   114 114
neither the time nor the energy for spending hours in the kitchen.   128 128
What is too bad is that in taking the fast way out, we too often   141 141
sacrifice quality. Instead of reaching for an apple or a glass of   154 154
milk, we snatch a pop, a chocolate bar, white bread, or a hot dog –   168 168
the heavily refined foods that are loaded with salt and sugar. Not   182 182
only do they contain little of the food values our bodies require, but   196 196
they are loaded with chemical additives and preservatives with which   210 210
our bodies must contend. Some food producers even go so far as to wax   224 224
fresh foods, like apples and oranges, to give them a brighter, more   237 237
appealing look.   <u>240</u> 240

52 GWPM   Our bodies need an adequate supply of nutrients in order to nour-   14 254
ish, maintain, build, heal, fight infections, and remove wastes. The   28 268
body is a wonderful machine and is likely to withstand abuse much   41 281
longer than will a computer; but if the proper nutrients are not   54 294
forthcoming, sooner or later the body will react. Often it is some   68 308
time before the effects are actually felt, for the body has a way of   82 322
compensating for what it lacks.   88 328

Fortunately, there is hope on the horizon. More and more people   102 342
are learning about the importance of wholesome food. They are cutting   116 356
down on refined foods and are turning to natural foods instead – to   130 370
fresh fruits and vegetables, to nuts and whole grain products. They   144 384
are learning about the chemicals that are put in our food, and they   157 397
are checking food labels to find out what the ingredients are. Many   171 411
health food stores have sprung up and, as a result, a number of super-   185 425
markets are starting to stock some shelves with natural and more   198 438
nutritious products. But the biggest factor in keeping our bodies   211 451
healthy is us. What we buy at the store is what the grocers will keep   225 465
on their shelves. If we want to look and perform our best, then we   238 478
should do ourselves a favour and avoid the "garbage in" syndrome.   251 491
Otherwise, we become the "garbage out."   <u>260</u> <u>500</u>

| 1 | 2 | 3 | 4 | 5 | 6 | 7 | 8 | 9 | 10 | 11 | 12 | 13 | 14 |

Spring

Each year, I have been pained to notice that the approach of | 12
spring occasions a most distressing change in the conduct of many of | 26
my friends. Beside my house, I have an acquaintance who is a nature | 40
man. All through the winter he is fairly quiet and an agreeable | 53
friendly fellow, quite fit for general society. Spring, however, at | 67
once occasions in my nature friend a distressing disturbance. He | 80
seems suddenly to desire, at our every meeting, to make himself a | 93
channel of information between the animate world and me. From the | 106
moment that the snow begins to melt, he keeps me posted as to what the | 120
plants and the birds and the bees are doing. This is a class of in- | 134
formation which I do not want and which I cannot use, but I have to | 148
bear it. | 150

My nature friend passes me every morning with some new and bright | 164
piece of information, something he thinks so cheery that it irradiates | 178
his face. One day, he exclaims that he saw a finch; the next day, he | 192
noticed a scarlet tanager. What a tanager is I have never known; I | 206
hope I never shall. I cannot match my nature friend's information in | 220
any way. I know only two birds, the crow and the hen. I can tell | 233
them apart at once, either by their plumage or by their song. I can | 247
carry on a nature conversation up to the limit of the crow and the | 260
hen; beyond that, nothing. So for the first day or so in spring, I am | 274
able to say, "I saw a crow yesterday," or "I noticed a hen out walking | 289
this morning." Somehow, my crow and hen grow out of date awfully | 302
quickly and I never refer to them again; but my friend keeps up his | 316
information for weeks, running through a whole gamut of animals. I am | 330
aware that I ought long ago to have spoken out openly to my nature | 343
friend; but I have, I admit, the unfortunate and weak-minded disposi- | 357
tion that forces me to smile with hatred in my heart. | 368

I admit that I am the kind of person who would never notice an | 382
oriole building a nest unless it came and built it in my hat. There | 396
are other people like me, too. There are signs of spring that every | 410
sensible person like us respects and recognizes. We see the oyster | 424
disappear from the club menu and know that winter is passing. We | 437
notice the asparagus appear in the local supermarket and the price of | 451
produce begin to drop, and we realize the season is advancing. These | 465
are the signs of spring that any person can appreciate. | 476

| 1 | 2 | 3 | 4 | 5 | 6 | 7 | 8 | 9 | 10 | 11 | 12 | 13 | 14 |

56
GWPM

Proficiency at the keyboard may be defined as speed, plus accur- 13 13
acy, plus thinking responses. The quickest route to proficiency is 26 26
through a daily session of concentrated drilling in which the drills 40 40
are ones that meet your personal drill needs. 49 49

Do not be surprised if you encounter times in your drill program 63 63
when progress seems to have come to a standstill or even to have taken 77 77
a step backwards. Your speed may reach a plateau, or maintaining 90 90
accuracy may become a problem. These periods are only temporary, so 104 104
do not get discouraged. Keep a positive frame of mind at all times. 118 118

When you are checking your drill work, be sure to proofread very 132 132
carefully. Good proofreading is important in any aspect of keyboard- 146 146
ing, and drill is no exception. Without good proofreading, you will 160 160
not have a true picture of your accuracy and will proceed to work on 174 174
drills that are not appropriate for you. Here are a few things you 187 187
should not do when proofreading. First, do not assume that you have 201 201
no errors because you did not feel a misstroke while you were key- 214 214
boarding. Do not just scan your typing looking for non-words. A word 228 228
may contain an error but still be a word. For example, you might type 242 242
"were" instead of the word "where." Also do not simply look at words 256 256
with no regard for their logic within the context of the sentence or 270 270
paragraph. There could be a word or a line missing. 280 280

Now let's look at some of the things you should do. Do read your 294
typing for logical meaning. Do read what has actually been typed, not 308
what you know it should say. Do check for obvious spacing or align- 322
ment errors and do circle errors to make them easier to see and count. 336
With good proofreading, you will know where your accuracy stands. 349

If maintaining reasonable accuracy becomes a problem, use an 362
error analysis chart to help you analyze your errors and to find out 376
what corrective steps to take or drills to do. Typing by letter re- 390
sponse – that is, where you say each and every character and space as 404
you keyboard – can also help you to acquire accuracy. This forces you 418
to pay attention to your stroking and the letters you are typing. If 432
accuracy is good but speed is a problem, you should forgo accuracy for 446
a short period of time so that all effort can be put into increasing 460
speed. 461

| 1 | 2 | 3 | 4 | 5 | 6 | 7 | 8 | 9 | 10 | 11 | 12 | 13 | 14 |

Mr. Smith came down to Mariposa and bought out the inside of what   13
had been the Royal Hotel. By the inside of a hotel is meant every-   27
thing except the four walls of it – the fittings, the furniture, the   41
bar, Billy the desk clerk, the three dining room helpers, and above   55
all the licence granted for the sale of intoxicating liquors.   67

From the first, Mr. Smith was a wild success as a hotel manager.   81
He had all the qualifications. He weighed 127 kg. He could haul two   96
drunken men out of the bar, each by the scruff of the neck, without   110
the faintest anger or excitement. He carried money enough in his   123
trouser pockets to open a bank, and spent it on anything, bet it on   137
anything, and gave it away in handfuls. He was never drunk, and, as a   151
point of chivalry to his customers, never quite sober.   162

Everyone was welcome at the hotel who cared to come in. Anybody   176
who didn't like it could leave. Drinks of all kinds cost five cents,   190
or six for a quarter. Meals and bed were practically free. For any   204
persons foolish enough to approach the desk and pay for them, Mr.   217
Smith charged according to the expressions on their faces.   229

At first, the loafers and the shanty men settled on the place in   243
a deluge, but they were not the trade Mr. Smith wanted. He knew how   257
to discourage them. An army of char people turned into the hotel and   271
scrubbed it from top to bottom. A vacuum cleaner, the first seen in   285
Mariposa, hissed and screamed in the corridors. Forty fancy beds were   299
imported from the city. A bartender with a starched jacket and waist-   313
coat was put behind the bar. The loafers were put out of business.   327
The place had become too classy for them.   335

To encourage the high-class trade, Mr. Smith set himself to dress   349
the part. He wore wide-cut coats of filmy serge, light as gossamer;   363
chequered waistcoats with a different pattern for every day in the   376
week; fedora hats light as autumn leaves; and ties of saffron and   389
myrtle green with a diamond pin the size of a hazelnut. On his fin-   403
gers there were as many gems as would grace a native prince of India.   417
Across his waistcoat lay a gold watch chain in huge square links, and   431
in his pocket, a gold watch that weighed more than half a kilogram and   445
marked minutes, seconds, and quarter seconds. Just to look at Josh   459
Smith's watch brought at least ten customers to the bar every evening.   473

| 1 | 2 | 3 | 4 | 5 | 6 | 7 | 8 | 9 | 10 | 11 | 12 | 13 | 14 |

WORDS

60
GWPM

The difference between the price of a new car and a used one, plus the difference in the rate of depreciation, can make the purchase of a good used car instead of a new one quite appealing. Choosing a used car, however, can be somewhat risky. Unless you are an automobile expert, you could wind up just inheriting someone else's problems. But do not feel discouraged; there are a number of checks you can make when looking into a prospective purchase that will help to keep risks to a minimum.

When phoning about a used car for sale, as well as asking the usual questions about make, model, price, condition, and special features which you may be seeking, inquire about the paint. Is it still the original? If not and it was recently painted, there is a strong possibility that the new paint job was done to conceal rust or body work. When you are satisfied that the car sounds promising, you will, of course, go to see it. When you do, be sure to check under floor mats (both inside the car and in the trunk or hatch) for moisture or holes indicating advanced rusting in the underbody. Look inside front and rear windows for water stains caused by leaky windows. Try out the horn, radio, windshield washers and wipers, and all lights. Open and close all doors (including the one on the glove compartment) and windows to ensure that they function properly. The cleanliness and condition of the interior and trunk are often indicators of how well the car has been maintained.

Now for the test drive! Notice the efficiency, or lack of it, of the start-up. As you are driving, listen for unfamiliar noises and check for the car's ease of handling. Travelling at about 50 km/h on a straight stretch of road, loosen your grip on the steering wheel and notice whether the car continues in a straight line or veers off to the right or left. If the car veers, it may have had front-end damage which causes it to lose its alignment. Ask about it. If possible, take to the highway for part of the test. Accelerate to the highway speed limit and watch out for vibrations caused by improper wheel balance. Finally, if you feel satisfied that this is the car for you, make your offer right then and there, for a good used car sells quickly. If you have any doubts, bow out.

| 1 | 2 | 3 | 4 | 5 | 6 | 7 | 8 | 9 | 10 | 11 | 12 | 13 | 14 |

Skiing

Skiing is one of those activities which, unless mastered when young, is probably best left alone. Why on earth, then, would a normal, rational person over thirty consider taking it up? Looking back, I realize that two forces were at work which caused me to abandon my better judgement and head for the hills. Firstly, the Canadian winter! I had been living in Canada for fourteen years and had been miserable for the three months of each winter. That totalled nearly four years of misery, which I finally decided was simply too much. It was definitely time to do something constructive.

The second force at work was pressure from family and friends who had been saying for years that one has to get out and enjoy the snow and the invigorating temperatures. These were the same people who had persuaded me to try ice skating. After skating had been painfully eliminated, they began to talk of skiing. "Snow is much more forgiving than ice; the ski is much broader than the skate and not as high off the ground," they said.

The trouble was they neglected to tell me that the beginner slopes are mountains and the runs are almost vertical. No one mentioned that to get to the top, one uses a hoisting device which has no patience with, or sympathy for, beginners. Even the clothing was a challenge. In magazines and on TV one sees the beautiful people schussing down, always smiling and thoroughly enjoying themselves. One thing is sure: they are not wearing my boots. The designers of my boots had absolutely no regard for the shape and the anatomy of the human foot. My foot and ankle were held rigidly together as though there were no ankle joint at all. The boot buckles bore an uncanny resemblance to mousetraps and were just as hazardous to fingers.

I persevered. I fell down so often I lost count. I fell off the lift going up. I fell getting off at the top. When I looked down the hill and saw how far and how steep it was, I nearly fell over from shock. For some reason, I could not make a left turn going down. I'm sure I collided with every tree on my right-hand side. Getting up after a fall was a ten-minute manoeuvre. I had snow down my back, in my socks, inside my gloves. My glasses kept steaming up and my cap kept falling off. Still I persevered. Finally the great moment came when I made a complete run without a single fall. It was wonderful! I began to talk about skiing vacations – the Laurentians, Vermont, maybe even the Swiss Alps. I had joined the ranks of skiers.

| 1 | 2 | 3 | 4 | 5 | 6 | 7 | 8 | 9 | 10 | 11 | 12 | 13 | 14 |

64
GWPM

It used to be that the roles of husband and wife were quite   12   12
clearly defined. The husband had the overall responsibility for the   26   26
family's well-being. He was the breadwinner, the person who went out 40   40
to work every day. The wife usually did not go to work. She stayed   54   54
at home and was responsible for things inside the [1]home – cooking, 67   67
cleaning, bearing children and attending to them. All this began to   81   81
change a few decades ago.   86   86

As the cost of living increased, a number of wives found it   99   99
necessary to go to work in order to make ends meet. More and more   112   112
women chose or were forced to continue to work after they married and 126   126
while the [2]children were growing up. Before long, it became clear that 140   140
wives could not handle the double workload and that husbands would   153   153
have to pitch in and help. As a result, many home duties became   166   166
shared tasks. In time, better jobs began to open up for women, and   180   180
many females moved into positions that gave them more money[3] and pres- 194   194
tige. At home, the male/female roles continued to evolve so that,   208   208
today, equal-sharing roles are common.   216   216

A few families have gone a step further and opted for a reversal   230   230
of traditional roles. In this situation, the wife is the financial   244   244
provider while the husband stays home and takes on the functions[4] and 258   258
duties that used to belong to the wife. There is, however, one func- 272   272
tion that he cannot take over, that of child bearing. In the human,   286   286
this is the sole domain of the female. There is at least one animal   300   300
species, however, in which the male does bear the young. The one that 314   314
comes to mind is the sea horse.[5]   320   320

Swimming along in an upright position and looking for all the   333
world like a carved chess piece, the sea horse is the steed of many a 347
child's dream. Not only is the appearance and swimming style of this 361
fish unusual, but so is its method of bearing its young. Contrary to 375
accepted practice, it is the male, not the female, that gives birth to 389
the little sea colts. The female places her eggs in a pouch on the   403
belly of the male. The eggs are fertilized in the pouch and are nour- 417
ished there. When the colts are ready to be born, father attaches   430
himself by his tail to a sea plant. He experiences the pangs of   443
childbirth and soon the baby colts, looking just like dad, are ejected 457
from the pouch. The newborn do not stay around long, but soon strike 471
out to make their own way in the big wide sea.   480

| 1 | 2 | 3 | 4 | 5 | 6 | 7 | 8 | 9 | 10 | 11 | 12 | 13 | 14 |

Sheep Farming

Running a sheep farm is not an easy business. It requires know-how and hard work. Australia and New Zealand are two countries famous for sheep raising and their sheep products are exported to countries throughout the world. Most farms raise several breeds of sheep – some for wool, some for mutton, and some for breeding – and the different groups are usually kept separate.

Lambing is a busy but exciting time on a sheep farm. There may be a few hundred pregnant ewes waiting to give birth at approximately the same time. A week or so before the lambs are due, the ewes are mustered with the assistance of sheep dogs (not the big, shaggy creatures that we are familiar with) which respond with efficient obedience to their master's whistles and signals. The ewes are given shots to protect them and their newborn from disease. Also, they are clipped around the udders and tails to eliminate tags of dirty wool where the babies will nurse. In a week or two, there are soft white lambs everywhere. As with fully grown sheep, great care is taken with the lamb's nutrition and physical condition. As the lambs grow, their coats become thicker and warmer. Lambs being raised for wool will likely be in their second year before they are sheared along with the older animals.

Shearing is an important event. On a large farm, a team of shearers is usually hired to undertake the job, which often takes days. An expert shearer operates at lightning speed and is capable of shearing a sheep in less than three minutes. The main fleece is removed from the sheep's back in one piece and might weigh from three to five kilograms. The fleeces are packed very tightly into huge sacks, each weighing two to three hundred kilograms when full. They will be used not only for wool, but also for their grease which will be extracted and refined into lanolin, the base of most cosmetics and skin creams.

After each animal is shorn, it is whisked into the pen of its shearer. When each pen is full, the sheep are released one at a time so that they can be counted, for a shearer is paid according to the number of sheep shorn. Considerably lighter now, the newly shorn sheep runs from the pen, leaping into the air just as frisky as a lamb.

| 1 | 2 | 3 | 4 | 5 | 6 | 7 | 8 | 9 | 10 | 11 | 12 | 13 | 14 |

13
27
41
55
69
76
90
104
118
132
146
160
173
187
201
215
229
242
256
259
272
285
299
312
326
339
353
367
381
383
396
410
424
437
450
451

WORDS

68
GWPM

It is interesting to note how a name from the pages of history 14 14 can evoke an instant picture in people's minds. Too often, though, 28 28 the picture has lost the historic significance of the person or the 42 42 event and, instead, has latched onto the specific feature which origi- 56 56 nally fired the imagination and made the name memorable. For example, 70 70 at mention of the name Lady Godiva, most people will automatically 84 84 conjure up the portrait of a naked lady riding a horse through the 97 97 streets. What many people either don't know or tend to forget is the 111 111 reason for that famous journey. Let me make it clear here and now 124 124 that it was not, as is often inferred, the act of a naughty lady. 137 137 Rather, it was the fulfillment of a deal that would bring much relief 151 151 to the poor in the region in which she lived. 160 160

Lady Godiva, the wife of an earl, was a beautiful and devout 173 173 woman. She gave her support to many churches and she helped to estab- 187 187 lish a monastery. Her heart went out to the people of Coventry who 201 201 toiled long and hard, only to have their rewards eaten up by heavy 214 214 taxes. She appealed constantly to her husband, the earl, to relieve 228 228 the people of their tax burden. Finally, tired of listening to her 242 242 constant pleas, he retorted that he would comply with her request if 256 256 she would condescend to ride nude through the town. It is quite like- 270 270 ly that the earl believed his gentle, pious wife would not deign to 284 284 expose herself in such a fashion, and would thus be forced to retreat 298 298 and refrain from nagging him further. If that was his intent, his 311 311 ploy was doomed to failure, for he was dealing with a woman of great 325 325 courage, strong will, and bold determination. Godiva accepted his 338 338 challenge. 340 340

On the day appointed, with only her long hair to cover her body, 354 Godiva mounted her horse and rode through the streets. Some accounts 368 say that all of the townsfolk were instructed to stay indoors and to 382 keep their windows shut during the time of the ride. It is also said 396 that a man by the name of Tom was caught looking out through the shut- 410 ters. This "peeping tom" was, it is told, immediately struck with 424 blindness. 426

The earl kept his side of the bargain and eliminated most of the 440 taxes in the area, and, as a result, the populace enjoyed a long 453 period of comfort and prosperity. Now and then, a festival is still 467 held to honour Lady Godiva and her noble deed. 476

| 1 | 2 | 3 | 4 | 5 | 6 | 7 | 8 | 9 | 10 | 11 | 12 | 13 | 14 |

Last week we received from the minister of education a letter in | 13

which we were asked whether it would be possible to arrange for a | 26

group of five or six persons to tour our school next month. The group | 40

would include three or four visitors from other countries who will be | 54

travelling our country from east to west and visiting many schools | 67

along the way to get a firsthand picture of our educational system. I | 81

propose that we arrange a tour along the following lines. | 92

First of all we will need a tour guide, and I suggest that Mrs. | 106

Chang would be an excellent choice. The tour would begin at nine in | 120

the morning in the reception area where Mrs. Chang would welcome the | 134

guests. She would give the visitors a brief history of our school, a | 148

rundown on student numbers, the types of programs we offer, the system | 162

under which we operate, etc. | 168

The group would then be taken to the electronics room where the | 182

teacher in charge would show some of our equipment and explain how the | 196

program operates. Then the tour would proceed to the typing workshop | 210

where one of the instructors on duty would describe the operation of | 224

the workshop and provide such information as textbooks in use, speed | 238

requirements, etc. A look at the practice office might also be in | 251

order, as well as an outline of when and for how long students work in | 265

the office and the kinds of duties that are performed there. | 277

The next stop would be the word processing centre for information | 291

on the set-up of the course, its duration, success of our graduates, | 304

etc. A demonstration of our equipment would be given, at the end of | 318

which a cartoon picture calendar would be printed out and a copy pre- | 332

sented to each guest. The group would then carry on to the computer | 346

centre. If there are enough terminals free at the time, the visitors | 360

could try a few hands-on activities. | 367

After a brief look at our resource and audio/visual centre, the | 381

group would be conducted to the lounge where they would be served cof- | 395

fee. You and I and other personnel would meet them there. I suspect | 409

that it would be near noon before this gathering would disperse, and I | 423

suggest that you and I take our guests to the staff dining room for | 437

lunch. | 438

Does this plan meet with your approval? Please let me know as | 452

soon as possible so that I can conclude the arrangements and confirm | 466

them with the minister. | 471

| 1 | 2 | 3 | 4 | 5 | 6 | 7 | 8 | 9 | 10 | 11 | 12 | 13 | 14 |

WORDS

72

GWPM

Billy Bishop was a mother's boy. He spoke with a lisp and was called a sissy by his classmates. He was a rotten student. He cut classes to play pool. His report cards were terrible. His principal didn't think he would amount to much. The one thing he was good at was fighting.

Billy had learned to ride early and well, and he was a crack shot with a rifle.[1] At the start of World War I, Billy joined up. He hated the military camp with its mud everywhere. Standing on the parade ground one day, he gazed up into the sky and saw a cleansing sight: a trim little fighter plane zooming out of the clouds. Then and there, Billy made up his mind to fight the war in the air.

Learning to fly was not the breeze that[2] Billy had envisioned. As a pilot he never could manage a decent take-off or landing. On his solo, he pancaked his training plane. In the air, he handled his plane like a spirited steed. But he had an advantage: he couldn't miss with a machine gun. He was so deadly accurate he could shoot down enemy pilots before they knew he was behind them. He developed[3] the quick, darting attack as the key element of his personal style.

One day, after destroying one enemy plane and forcing down two more, Billy ran headlong into the Red Baron. With the odds five to two in his favour, the Baron was out for blood. As the seven planes swirled and crisscrossed in the air, the Baron poured a stream of bullets at Billy.[4] One entered the fold of Billy's flying coat; another pierced his instrument panel. Billy lost his temper and charged. Black smoke poured from the Baron's plane. For a moment, Billy thought he had him, but the Baron had merely used an old escape trick. He dove over twelve hundred metres, flattened out, waggled his wings and was gone. They never met again.[5]

Billy was sure that if he could reach the enemy airfields, unseen, at first morning light, he could launch himself into reckless attack before the enemy could recover from the shock. He started flying alone.

By the end of the war, Billy Bishop had won every cross, medal, and honour available to him. He had shot down seventy-two enemy planes confirmed. Counting the many hits made alone, far behind enemy lines where no allied witness could spot and confirm the wreckage, the real total, however, was certainly more than a hundred. Billy Bishop, the Lone Hawk, had become the world's greatest living air ace.

| 1 | 2 | 3 | 4 | 5 | 6 | 7 | 8 | 9 | 10 | 11 | 12 | 13 | 14 |

13	13
26	26
40	40
53	53
56	56
70	70
84	84
97	97
111	111
125	125
135	135
149	149
163	163
176	176
189	189
202	202
216	216
230	230
243	243
257	257
271	271
284	284
297	297
310	310
324	324
338	338
352	352
360	360
	374
	388
	401
	404
	418
	431
	445
	459
	473
	485

Robots

They're called the steel collar workers. To some people, they   13
are the stuff of which great science fiction is made. To others, they   27
are nothing more than fancy screwdrivers. For yet others, they repre-   41
sent the fearful push of technology to replace the human hand with a   55
metal claw. Robots. They don't look anything like the famous ones in   69
the movies. Few of them even have a head. Instead, they're more apt   83
to be just a mechanized arm with a metal gripper at the end that forms   97
a "hand." With that hand, robots can perform many different tasks,   111
from grasping and moving an object to feeling its contours.   123

A large number of robots are being used in industry. While the   137
robot is quite expensive to buy, it can quickly pay for itself because   151
at certain jobs it can work faster and better than a human, thus   164
boosting productivity and lowering production costs. Even as you read   178
this, robots are working away at what were once exclusively human   191
jobs: welding and painting cars, mining coal, moving hazardous sub-   205
stances, building stoves, and even washing windows and shearing sheep.   219
In some places, the steel collar brigade is working round the clock to   233
build other robots.   237

Unlike people, robots don't take coffee breaks, lunch breaks,   250
sick days or vacations. They don't need sleep and they don't collect   264
a pay cheque. A robot can work twenty-four hours a day in unpleasant   278
surroundings and it will never threaten to quit or to go on strike.   292
In short, a robot can do the dull and sometimes dangerous work that   306
humans will not or should not do. In fact, the term robot comes from   320
a word which means forced labour.   327

Smart robots depend on computer technology to help them see and   341
feel. A robot compares what it sees and feels with information in its   355
computer memory bank to decide which pre-programmed course to follow.   369
Robots are learning to do things humans could never hope to do, such   383
as "see" infra-red light and "hear" ultrasonic sound. They cannot   397
think for themselves, though. They can only respond to things in ways   411
that have been programmed into them; and while robots can be taught to   425
program other robots, only humans can conceive and map out these   438
programs.   440

In spite of the human qualities of feeling and emotion portrayed   454
by robots on the movie screens, these are only products of the human   468
imagination. The robot has a cold, steel heart.   478

| 1 | 2 | 3 | 4 | 5 | 6 | 7 | 8 | 9 | 10 | 11 | 12 | 13 | 14 |

Nullarbor Plain

76
GWPM

The Nullarbor Plain is noted for containing the longest straight stretch of railway line in the world – over three hundred kilometres without a curve. I had often thought I would like to take the journey by train across the plain to Perth, a distance of more than five thousand kilometres. The opportunity finally came when I learned that Trevor, an old friend who was born in Perth,[1] wanted to visit his home town. Trevor had lung cancer and was keen to see his birthplace once again before he died, but he did not want to travel alone. I offered to make the trip with him.

The morning we departed Melbourne, we were given a rousing send-off by family and friends. Our first stop was at Adelaide, and after a hearty lunch in the station restaurant, we[2] began the long journey across the Nullarbor Plain. Nullarbor, which is Latin for "no trees," proved to be an apt name, for the only vegetation we could see was just low scrub. We did, however, manage to catch sight of several bright, colourful, and noisy parrots, as well as a few kangaroos and other animals, which broke the monotony of the landscape. The four-day trip was a[3] mini-holiday in itself. Excellent food was served, live entertainment was provided in the lounge car, and there were stops in several towns along the way. We particularly enjoyed the singsongs we had around the piano, and we joined in with great gusto and enthusiasm.

At last we arrived in Perth, a city of great beauty and one in which many architectural styles exist side by[4] side. It also contains many lovely parks; in fact, even its freeways are landscaped. Perth is probably the most isolated city of its size in the world. Located on the banks of the Swan River and blessed with mild winters, warm dry summers, and many sunny days, Perth is a city where beaches and boats play an important part in its way of life. Sailing is a regular pastime.[5]

Our ten-day visit was over before we knew it, and our parting from Trevor's family and the friends we had made was touching. We began the long trek back to Melbourne, a tired but satisfied pair. We had each fulfilled a wish.

| 1 | 2 | 3 | 4 | 5 | 6 | 7 | 8 | 9 | 10 | 11 | 12 | 13 | 14 |

Revolution

We learned that a rising had taken place led by rebels who prom-	13
ised the nation a new era of freedom. The armed forces in the south	27
refused to move against the rebels. The air force, too, refused to	41
act, but in any case its planes were out of action for lack of fuel,	55
for the government treasury was empty. It was clear that the presi-	69
dent had no choice but to resign. A military cabinet was set up under	83
General Ponce.	86

I had never witnessed a revolution before so I, a young univer- 100
sity student at the time, went to the town square to see what was 113
happening. A large crowd had gathered before the palace. By the time 127
I arrived, Ponce was haranguing the crowd in an attempt to make as 150
much political gain for himself as he could, although with little 163
apparent success. Then, pointing to his uniform, he offered this to 177
his listeners as evidence of his devotion to the country. One of his 191
supporters cried out in his favour, but was met with a stony silence. 205

At this precise moment, a senorita standing near me had the 218
embarrassing misfortune to discover that the elastic of her panties 232
had given way. However, with great presence of mind, she marked time 246
till her feet were free and then walked quickly away. Spotting the 260
garment at his feet, a bystander picked them up and, hurling them into 274
the air, yelled in Spanish, "Long live the panties!" Immediately the 289
plaza echoed with an affirmative chorus. The panties proved to be 302
more meaningful to them than a cartload of Ponces. His star, which 315
gave such good promise of rising only a short time before, now plum- 329
metted to earth. I never heard of him again. 338

A few moments later, the crowd surged towards the mansion of the 352
ministry. At the entrance, a guard was on duty. The guard, evidently 366
deciding that discretion was the better part of valour, promptly took 380
to directing the traffic flow, keeping the invading tide to the right 394
of the entrance so as to facilitate the exit on his left of the loot- 408
ers and their booty. 412

The next attack was made on the residence of the president. 425
Following the crowd, I tried to approach the house, but just as I came 439
to the corner a shot rang out. Now a mob was surging around at the 452
entrance and some students were pushing their way through bearing the 466
body of one of their number who had been wounded. Having no desire to 480
end up in a like manner, I decided to go home while the going was 493
good. I had had enough revolution for one day. 502

| 1 | 2 | 3 | 4 | 5 | 6 | 7 | 8 | 9 | 10 | 11 | 12 | 13 | 14 |

Potatoes

80 GWPM

Not only are potatoes cheap, but they are good for us. They are 13 13
a low-calorie food that fills us up, not out – unless, of course, we 27 27
dress them up with butter and sour cream. Spuds are a good source of 41 41
vitamin C and thiamin, as well as iron and potassium. How much of 54 54
these nutrients is available to the eater depends on how the potato is 68 68
cooked. Because most of the nutrients are close to the skin,[1] it is 81 81
best to cook and serve potatoes in their skins. Potatoes being boiled 95 95
should be cooked in as little water as possible. Potatoes are ex- 108 108
tremely versatile. They may be cooked and served in a variety of 121 121
ways. They may be baked, boiled, roasted, or fried. They may be 134 134
served stuffed, mashed, scalloped, in stews, in soups, in pies, etc. 148 148

Canadians are one of the potato's biggest fans, consuming[2] about 162 162
seventy-five kilograms per person per year. Canada grows over fifty 176 176
varieties of spuds. 180 180

Potatoes will grow almost anywhere if they are planted in a rich, 194 194
acid soil with good drainage, in a place where they will receive lots 208 208
of sunshine. Pieces of potato, each containing at least one eye (a 221 221
small depression from which sprouts will grow), are used as seed. 234 234
When they are planted, the sprouts[3] from each eye produce a bright 247 247
green, leafy plant above the earth and clusters of potato tubers 260 260
below. Farmers mound up earth, straw, or leaves around the plants to 274 274
protect the tubers developing close to the surface. 284 284

In many areas, two crops can be planted: one in early spring as 298 298
soon as the frost is out of the ground, and another in summer after 312 312
the early crop has been harvested.[4] Harvesting of the tubers can be 326 326
started when the potato flowers are in bloom, about eight weeks after 340 340
planting. These first young spuds are the "new" potatoes that we so 354 354
highly prize. Potatoes left in the ground will have grown to full 367 367
size by the time the plant withers and dies down. The late spud crop, 381 381
harvested in the fall, may be washed and stored in a cool, dark place 395 395
for use over the winter.[5] 400 400

Although potatoes are native to South America where they grow 413
high up in the Andes Mountains, they are grown in many other parts of 427
the world as well and have become a staple food in a number of 440
countries. 442

| 1 | 2 | 3 | 4 | 5 | 6 | 7 | 8 | 9 | 10 | 11 | 12 | 13 | 14 |

When listing time frames on your resume, just the years are quite	13
enough. If you worked somewhere from March to August of the same	26
year, just enter the year. Don't clutter the document. An employer	50
who wants more details will ask for them.	58

When listing time frames on your resume, just the years are quite enough. If you worked somewhere from March to August of the same year, just enter the year. Don't clutter the document. An employer who wants more details will ask for them.

When giving your education, you must decide which is more important and therefore should be highlighted – the schools you attended or the credits you received. The same applies to work experience. Which information is going to do the most to sell you – the positions you have held or the name of the firms for which you worked? It will all depend on your situation and the job you are after. You may also want to give a brief description of your jobs, projects you were involved in, things you were responsible for, etc. If you have been out of the work force for periods of time as a homemaker, don't hesitate to include this in your work data.

By now, you are sure to be onto the second page of your resume. Be sure to put your name, as well as the page number, at the top of the second and any subsequent pages. Otherwise, if the pages get separated, no one will know to whose resume they belong.

Often the next items covered are interests, hobbies, and/or social activities. Sometimes one of these might warrant being listed near the beginning on the first page. For instance, if you were applying for a job with a computer firm and one of your hobbies is micro computers, that information could stand you in good stead as an opener on the first page. Do not underestimate the value of social or community work you may have done. Be sure to mention any, plus any positions you may have held in clubs or groups. These show that you are willing to get involved and that you have been held in high enough esteem by your peers to be chosen to fill a higher position.

Likely the last topic in your resume will be references. Some people list them; others state they are available on request. Take your pick. If you have a good letter of reference on hand, though, attach it to the resume.

Finally, the set-up of your resume is very important. Keep in mind that often resumes are just scanned and only the most interesting ones are read completely. So keep your resume short and set up in such a way that the major information stands out clearly and is easy to follow.

| 1 | 2 | 3 | 4 | 5 | 6 | 7 | 8 | 9 | 10 | 11 | 12 | 13 | 14 |

WORDS

84
GWPM

The first Olympic games were held in Olympia, Greece, hundreds of   13   13
years before Christ. The most important contest at those games was   27   27
the stadion. This was a short foot race in which contestants ran from   41   41
one end of the stadium to the other. In the beginning, the games   54   54
lasted one day, but as more events were added, the festival was ex-   68   68
tended to five days, with the main contests taking place on the third   82   82
day. Sports like running, long jump, leaping, wrestling, boxing,   95   95
javelin throwing, and chariot racing were popular. The rules and 108 108
regulations for the various contests appear to have been somewhat 121 121
different from the ones we follow. The naked wrestlers were doused 135 135
with oil to make holds more difficult, and it was common for boxers to 149 149
have ears torn off during the games. In another event, everything but 163 163
biting was permitted. 167 167

The fifth day of the games was a day of parades and banquets, a 181 181
day when the victors were crowned with garlands of olive branches 194 194
picked from a sacred tree. The name of each winner, his father, and 208 208
his country was loudly proclaimed. Winners were highly honoured. 221 221
They received many presents, songs were written and sung about them, 235 235
and statues were erected to them. 242 242

At first, only free-born Greeks were allowed to compete in the 256 256
games, but as Roman influence increased, other athletes were allowed 270 270
to take part. Even slaves, trained by their wealthy owners, competed. 284 284
Gradually, the character of the games changed – for the worse. To 298 298
claim the honour of nurturing winners, cities bought top athletes. 311 311
Slaves who had been promised their freedom if they won were caught 324 324
cheating. Gladiators fought to the death, and wild animals were 337 337
introduced into the fighting arena. When the emperor Nero decided he 351 351
would compete in a chariot race, all the other racers, afraid of what 365 365
he might do to them if they beat him, withdrew from the race. Al- 378 378
though Nero's performance didn't quite set the world on fire, needless 392 392
to say he won the race. At last in the year 393, a Christian emperor 407 407
banned the games, putting an end to the slaughter and bloodshed. 420 420

The Olympic games were reborn through the efforts of a French 433
baron, and the first games as we know them took place in Athens in 446
1896 with thirteen countries taking part. Today, athletes from almost 460
all of the civilized world compete, and the Olympics have become a 473
symbol of international goodwill. 480

| 1 | 2 | 3 | 4 | 5 | 6 | 7 | 8 | 9 | 10 | 11 | 12 | 13 | 14 |

Resume Planning

In your search for a job, your resume can be a highly influential
factor. Even if you were never to hand out one single copy, just the
writing and preparation of the resume is rewarding in itself. Why?
Because it forces you to clarify in your own mind what you have to
offer a future employer. The very nature of the resume requires you
to collect and condense a wealth of information about yourself. It
compels you to study your past and pull out your worthwhile experiences and successes, and the skills you have had to use or develop as
a result. It is important to note here that you must not confine your
search to previous jobs you have held, but you should draw on social
and home experiences too.

It will help if you can get hold of several good resumes that can
serve as guides and give you some ideas. Do not, however, fall into
the trap of thinking that the pattern and format of a resume are
carved in stone. This is not the case. A resume is a flexible document and must be designed to set off YOUR best features, to put YOUR
best foot forward. Start off your resume with your name, address, and
telephone number. Remember that YOU are what this resume is all
about; therefore your name is the most important thing on the page
and should be the most prominent.

You may then wish to state what type of job you are seeking and
perhaps what your goals are. If so, keep it brief. Many resumes
today tend to omit such personal data as age and marital status; however, if you feel that this kind of information will advance your
cause, for goodness' sake, put it in. For example, if a want ad calls
for a person within a certain age group and you are within the range,
then tell them your age. Of course, if you don't fall within the age
group, then bypass that information. If an ad mentions that a job
involves travel and you are single, that fact may indicate your freedom to travel. If you think it has a bearing, include it; otherwise
leave it out.

Most resumes then move on to the topic of education, followed by
work experience. Feel free to reverse this order without blinking an
eye. It may well be that your work experience is far more impressive
than your education. If so, list it first. You want to impress the
reader as soon as possible so that he or she will not lose interest
and stop reading. It is also beneficial to get as many goodies as
possible on the first page where it counts the most.

| 1 | 2 | 3 | 4 | 5 | 6 | 7 | 8 | 9 | 10 | 11 | 12 | 13 | 14 |

Disaster

This story describes but one of many natural disasters which have   13   13
struck an area of the globe that seems prone to such catastrophes.   27   27
The place is a valley high up in the Andes Mountains where the highest   41   41
peak rises to a height of over seven thousand metres above sea level.   55   55
Towards six o'clock in the evening, the clouds that had enshrouded the   69   69
summit dispersed. The view of the peak, which is never more beautiful   83   83
than at this time of the [1] day when its vast snowclad slopes are en-   96   96
livened by the warm tints of the setting sun, was magnificent.   109   109

Suddenly, the scene changed. Thousands of tonnes of solid ice   123   123
broke off from the northern peak and came hurtling down the mountain-   137   137
side. Clouds of snow and ice blotted out the enchanting scene of a   151   151
few moments ago. An ever louder roar accompanied the cloud in its mad   165   165
downward career. Gathering volume and ferocity as it [2] descended, it   179   179
carried everything before it. Two and a half million tonnes of rock   193   193
and ice had split off from the summit to leave a scar and a trail more   207   207
than nine kilometres long.   213   213

In the first village in its path, it was just at the time of the   227   227
evening meal and all of the inhabitants were either in their homes or   241   241
hastening to be there before dusk. Only two minutes elapsed between   255   255
the first warning of trouble and the arrival [3] of the avalanche. Per-   269   269
haps it was fortunate that the victims were unaware of their impending   283   283
doom till the moment it struck them, for there was no possible way of   297   297
escape. Two hundred homes and nine hundred people were wiped out in   311   311
an instant. There were only eight survivors.   320   320

Sweeping along at three hundred kilometres per hour to the next   334   334
village, the avalanche swallowed up another four hundred people. It   348   348
left no survivors in [4] its wake nor any trace of the village. With a   362   362
sickening roar, the avalanche raced on to engulf the third and largest   376   376
village. Half of the town was wiped out and a thousand souls were   389   389
lost. Within a matter of minutes, all the villages in the path of the   403   403
avalanche between the summit and the river had been erased from the   417   417
face of the earth, leaving nothing more than a scar of torn earth that   431   431
was four kilometres deep to tell the tale. [5]   440   440

When the avalanche reached the river, the sudden rise in the   453
water level sent a wall of water ten metres high racing down the val-   467
ley to the sea. Bridges, farms and villages along the way disappeared   481
in a trice. The flood reached the ocean and was borne out to sea.   494

| 1 | 2 | 3 | 4 | 5 | 6 | 7 | 8 | 9 | 10 | 11 | 12 | 13 | 14 |

Why on earth would anyone in his or her right mind elect to write   13
about a subject like rags? What bright, witty, enlightening, or even   27
vaguely interesting things could one possibly say or tell about rags?   41
That is precisely what I asked myself right after I chose that topic.   55
However, I figured that all things have their role in history and   68
deserve to be mentioned somewhere, and surely rags should not be an   82
exception. For that reason, I now present an expose on rags.   94

Since the beginning of history, the extent to which people made   108
use of rags has tended to rise or fall according to the tides of' pros-   122
perity. In our throw-away age of affluence and consumer goods, rags   136
have a very small part to play. In fact, most people today have   149
little use or regard for rags and are likely to sentence them pretty   163
quickly to the garbage can. This was not the case in pioneer days.   177
Then, there were only limited resources with which to equip homes and   191
make them comfortable; and so it was essential that every resource be   205
used to its utmost. One of these resources was rags.   216

Every rag or scrap of useable material from torn or worn cloth   230
items was salvaged for further service. Some pieces were suitable for   244
employment as dusters or cleaning cloths. Some went into the making   258
and stuffing of rag dolls. Others were fashioned into dolls' clothes.   272
Often, strips of rags were used for tying plants to stakes in the gar-   286
den. Rags functioned as a beauty tool, too, for strips of rags often   300
served as hair curlers. Probably the most famous use of rags was in   314
the making of patchwork quilts. Rags, cut into patches of the desired   328
shapes and sizes, were fitted and stitched together to form an outer   342
cover of a quilt.   345

Another common use for rags was in the making of rugs. There   358
were hooked rugs made from short lengths of rag which were hooked into   372
canvas. There were braided rugs made from long rag strips sewn end to   386
end to form three very long pieces. These were braided together, just   400
as one would braid hair. The braid was then stitched into a coil   413
shape, forming a circular rug. Woven rugs or mats were also popular.   427
For these, lengths of rag were tied side by side across a wooden   440
frame. Other strips were then woven under and over them, and the ends   454
were bound to produce the finished mat.   462

It appears that rags have had a notable history after all – of   476
cleanliness, warmth, comfort, amusement, and beauty. That's quite an   490
achievement for something as humble as a few scraps of cloth.   502

| 1 | 2 | 3 | 4 | 5 | 6 | 7 | 8 | 9 | 10 | 11 | 12 | 13 | 14 |

92
GWPM

Writing a collection of stories is really very easy. You have 13
just to sit at the typewriter and type all those wonderful notions and 27
ideas that are swirling around in your head. Normally, this works 40
well, but I must admit there are times when you just stare at the 53
machine for hours, your mind a complete void, until tiny drops of 66
perspiration start running down your face and your fingers become 79
stiff from being poised so long in position ready to strike. 91

At [1] this point, you realize that you need a little diversion and 105
then the thoughts will flow. So you make yourself a cup of tea; you 119
leaf through a few magazines; you tidy up the kitchen. That should do 133
it, and you plunk yourself down again in front of the typewriter. Not 147
a word nor even a letter appears on the paper. You cannot think of a 161
solitary thing to say. Usually your fingers stumble all over each 174
other in their rush to record your thoughts and words, but not today. 188
All you can do is stare. Today you are Ms. Blank from Empty City, and 203
your brain has turned to mush. Your confidence has exited through the 217
back door and panic has entered through the front. 227

You try a few more change-of-pace tactics. You put some clothes 241
into the washing machine, listen to some music, and have another cup 255
of tea. It doesn't work. Nothing you do is setting the wheels in 268
motion. Gradually it occurs to you that your talent has up and de- 282
serted you, leaving you dumb and stupid. The gift is gone and you 295
will probably never write again. All you feel now is terror. You 308
check out the folders of interesting clippings you have been saving 322
over the years, your books of famous quotations, also the Bible. 335
Nothing twigs even a glimmer of a story in your mental mush. The end 349
has come. Your career is over. You've failed. Everyone and every- 363
thing is against you. Even your typewriter, for so long your obedient 377
helpmate, is laughing at you; and you deserve it, you dull, stupid, 391
untalented author. You may as well be dead. At least that would give 405
someone else something to write about. 413

So you go to bed hoping you may never wake up. You toss and turn 427
and finally slumber begins to settle. Then it hits you – the next 440
story. You scramble out of bed and rush downstairs to your beloved 454
typewriter and start to write. 460

| 1 | 2 | 3 | 4 | 5 | 6 | 7 | 8 | 9 | 10 | 11 | 12 | 13 | 14 |

Quilting

Quilting of covers for beds began in North America not long after | 13
the arrival of early settlers. Because of the nature of pioneer life, | 27
there was little with which to decorate a home. Probably as a result | 41
of this, quilts were seen as a way to brighten and decorate at least | 55
one part of the home – the bedroom. | 62

Because so much work was required to make a quilt, and at night | 76
there was only the dim light of candles and coal oil lamps to work by, | 90
quilting bees soon became a way to finish a quilt quickly in the day- | 104
light. Bees also served as a form of social intercourse. A quilting | 118
bee was often held at the same time as a barn raising. A bride-to-be | 132
would have prepared a few quilt tops before the bee, and, with one or | 146
two quilting frames and about ten pairs of hands around each frame, a | 160
quilt could be finished in a day. | 167

The most common quilts were the patchwork quilt and the applique | 181
quilt. A patchwork quilt was just that: an assemblage of bits and | 195
pieces of material left over from other projects, as well as pieces | 209
cut from the usable portions of worn-out clothing. When one could | 222
afford to buy material especially for quilting, intricate patterns and | 236
colour schemes were often produced. Most patterns had names and often | 250
more than one. Many of the names, such as Jacob's ladder, had origins | 264
in the Bible. One of the most unique forms of patchwork quilting was | 278
the crazy quilt. This was an arrangement of squares of odd-shaped | 291
scraps of fabric. These were outlined with embroidery stitches, with | 305
dozens of different stitches and colours of thread being used. | 317

Applique quilts tended to be mainly decorative, as the overall | 331
patterns depended on colour schemes that were well thought out and on | 345
patterns that were accurately cut. As a rule, this meant the material | 359
was bought especially for the project. In most cases, the result was | 373
considered to be one's best quilt. | 380

A recent and widespread interest in quilting has occurred, with | 394
many persons and groups re-creating the patterns of traditional | 407
quilts, but also adding many bold new patterns and techniques. Some | 421
are such lovely works of art that what once was used to decorate beds | 435
and bedrooms can now be found adorning walls in any room in the house. | 449

| 1 | 2 | 3 | 4 | 5 | 6 | 7 | 8 | 9 | 10 | 11 | 12 | 13 | 14 |

WORDS

96
GWPM

It was a moment of joy and triumph for Morgan Robertson when he 13
learned that his latest novel, FUTILITY, had been accepted by a pub- 27
lishing house. After a long and difficult struggle, his determination 41
and hard work had paid off. It was a thrilling story he had written, 55
a wild tale he had concocted about a passenger liner that was larger 69
and more luxurious than any that had, as yet, been built. She was a 82
huge, triple-screw vessel that could travel at twenty-four knots. The¹ 96
finest design and workmanship had gone into her making. Her interior 110
was a showcase of glamour and opulence. She could accommodate three 124
thousand people, although the lifeboats strapped to her side had room 138
for only a small fraction of that number. This was not viewed as 151
cause for concern because the liner was unsinkable. When Robertson's 165
ship set sail on her maiden voyage, she was filled with rich and prom- 179
inent people. Nothing was too good for these passengers, and the² 192
staff catered to their every whim. They were treated to the best of 206
food and liquor, both of which they consumed in huge amounts. Gam- 219
bling, games, sports, and music were provided for their entertainment. 233
Nothing had been overlooked in the way of comfort and amusements. 246

The liner had been at sea a few days when the first ice floes 259
appeared. The floes were widely scattered, but they added an inter- 273
esting new element to the seascape and, for a brief while, were a 286
topic of conversation.³ According to Robertson's yarn, it was a chilly 300
night that April when his ship hit a great iceberg. The lifeboats 313
were launched but there were not nearly enough to go around. The 326
unsinkable ship went down with most of its passengers and crew on 339
board. 340

Little did Morgan Robertson know that this novel, published in 353
1898, was almost prophetic, and that fourteen years later his story 366
would be enacted live and for real. The similarities between his tale 380
and the later event⁴ are uncanny. The two ships were of similar size, 394
mass, and speed. They each had about the same passenger capacity. 407
Both were luxury liners on their maiden journeys and had many well- 421
to-do passengers on board. Neither ship had nearly enough lifeboats 435
for the number of people on board, but then both ships were labelled 449
unsinkable. Both vessels struck an iceberg and sank on a cold April 463
night. Robertson had named his fictional liner the Titan; the real 476
ship was the Titanic.⁵ 480

| 1 | 2 | 3 | 4 | 5 | 6 | 7 | 8 | 9 | 10 | 11 | 12 | 13 | 14 |

Quicksand

The perils of being ensnared in this natural deathtrap have been | 13
portrayed so frequently and with such suspense and gruesome reality in | 27
movies and novels that many of us have a tendency to tremble at the | 41
very word, quicksand. The instant vision of a person sinking help- | 55
lessly to his or her death is made even more horrible by the knowledge | 69
that the trap is so well camouflaged that the victim is taken by com- | 83
plete surprise. | 86

On top, the quicksand may look as solid and safe as concrete, but | 100
throw a rock into it and the caked surface crumbles, and the quicksand | 114
quivers and seems almost alive as it devours the object. Why is this | 128
sand so different from most sand which is quite capable of supporting | 142
things? Through a series of experiments, it was learned that the sand | 156
is plain ordinary sand, but what makes the difference is water flowing | 170
up like a spring from the bottom, forcing the grains slightly apart, | 184
and making the sand mass swell. | 190

Although quicksand pits exist in many parts of the world, they | 204
have not been the cause of nearly as many deaths as entertainers would | 218
have us believe. Depending on the speed of the upwelling water and | 232
the texture of the sand, the speed with which a human would sink | 245
varies – from immediately, to slowly enough to allow a person to turn | 259
after a few steps and get out. | 265

When it comes to quicksand, the wisest course is to avoid walking | 279
in areas that are suspected of containing quicksand pits. Should you | 293
happen to step into one, however, you have a good chance of escape if | 307
you follow these rules. The most important is don't panic. Panic and | 321
struggle are the worst reactions to the situation. They will stir up | 335
the quicksand pot and sink you all the faster. | 344

Immediately warn any companions of the danger, both to prevent | 358
their entrapment and so that they will be able to assist you. Discard | 372
any heavy items on you that might weigh you down. Slowly lie on your | 386
back with your arms spread wide. Relax your body, and your legs and | 400
feet should rise to the surface so that you are afloat. Because | 413
quicksand is heavier than water, you should be able to float on it | 426
readily. Have your companions extend a long branch or other lifeline | 440
which you can hold onto while they tow you to safety. If you can't | 454
reach the lifeline or you are alone, very gently paddle or squirm your | 468
way to firm ground. | 472

| 1 | 2 | 3 | 4 | 5 | 6 | 7 | 8 | 9 | 10 | 11 | 12 | 13 | 14 |

Of the many materials with which nature has provided us, wood 12
must be the most wonderful and the most useful. Our pioneer fore- 25
fathers would never have survived without it. With it, they acquired 39
such necessities as shelter, warmth, tools, and fire over which to 52
cook their food. 55

To some extent, wood has since been replaced by other materials. 69
For the most part, gas, oil, and electricity have replaced it as fuel. 83
Aluminum has replaced it as home siding. Plastic and chrome steel 96
have replaced it in some types of furniture. In spite of all this, we 110
still put wood to abundant use. Everywhere we look, we see wood in 124
some form or another. It may be the framework of a doorway, the fence 138
around a garden, crutches that are helping someone to walk, the bowl 152
in which a salad is served, the letter opener on a desk, or the cross 166
on the wall of a church. Wood has made fortunes for many and is a 179
sought-after commodity in the world trading market. Countries with 193
large preserves of trees are deemed wealthy indeed. 203

Each wood has its own unique character – its own grain, its own 217
colour, its own smell. Its value is measured by its strength, the 230
texture of its grain, and its versatility. Some woods are better for 244
certain uses than others. Most softwoods come from evergreen trees 258
(also called conifers because of the cones in which their seeds are 273
formed). These include fir, pine, cypress, hemlock, and spruce. 287
Softwoods are commonly used for building materials and for the produc- 301
tion of pulp and paper. Hardwoods are usually derived from deciduous 315
trees – that is, trees that shed their leaves each autumn. Hardwoods 329
like cherry, birch, walnut, oak, and mahogany are popular in furniture 343
making. Solid hardwoods have become so expensive that today most 356
pieces of furniture are made from pressed board, rather than solid 369
wood, which is covered with a wood veneer to provide the wood grain. 383
Pressed board is composed of sawdust and wood chips pressed together 397
into sheets or boards. Wood veneer is a very thin sheet of natural 411
wood. 412

Almost everyone has an affiliation with wood. Some love to whit- 426
tle it, some build with it, some admire its handsome grains, sculptors 440
carve it, many folks rock in chairs made from it, and sometimes chil- 454
dren even get paddled with a stick of it. For many people, one of the 468
most pleasant associations with wood is watching it crackle and burn 482
in a fireplace, breathing in its scent, and basking in its light, 496
warmth, and comfort. 500

| 1 | 2 | 3 | 4 | 5 | 6 | 7 | 8 | 9 | 10 | 11 | 12 | 13 | 14 |

Property for Sale

I have been in touch with the owners of the property about which you inquired. They have informed me that they have listed the property with a real estate agent and it will be coming onto the market in two weeks. The owners are a retired couple who have decided that the upkeep and maintenance of a house is too much for them and they are now seeking a suitable apartment.

This home is clean, compact, and well maintained. It is a frame bungalow with white aluminum siding and a painted front with wooden shutters. It was recently caulked and has a new front storm door. The front verandah and stairs have wrought iron railings which have been freshly painted. A new roof was installed three years ago. The house contains a living room, a separate dining room, a kitchen, a four-piece bathroom, and two bedrooms. The floors in the living area are hardwood and the walls are plaster. The kitchen is small but modern with lots of cupboard space. The living and dining rooms are broadloomed, and the owners are willing to leave all blinds and curtains on the windows.

The full basement is poured concrete. It has a high ceiling and could be finished as a recreation room or a separate apartment. The house has a large-capacity water heater, copper piping throughout, and a new forced-air gas furnace that was installed two years ago. Taxes and the cost of heating are reasonable.

The size of the lot is ten metres by forty metres. Behind the house is a large, fenced yard that contains a hedge across the back, two mature trees, a garden, and a flagstone patio. The front of the house is nicely landscaped with flowers and shrubs, and there is a hedge down one side and across the front. The house uses city water and is fronted by a paved street with curbs, sidewalk, and sewers. Schools, shopping, bus transportation, and the highway are all close at hand.

Although this charming place does not have parking facilities on the premises, parking is available nearby. The asking price of this property is within the range you quoted me. If you are interested in viewing it, please contact me as soon as possible. I do not believe it will be on the market for long.

| 1 | 2 | 3 | 4 | 5 | 6 | 7 | 8 | 9 | 10 | 11 | 12 | 13 | 14 |

WORDS column:
13
27
41
55
69
76
90
104
117
131
145
158
172
185
199
213
217
231
245
259
273
281
295
309
323
336
350
364
378
380
394
408
422
436
443

Bionics

Although the word bionics was coined in this century, the idea   13
goes back a few thousand years. The word was formed from the Greek   27
words bios, which means life, and ics, which means to have the nature   41
of. Bionics covers a wide range of equipment that functions in place   55
of living parts. These range from prosthetic parts, such as dentures   69
and limbs which are worn outside the body, to internal replacement   83
parts like synthetic arteries, to machines like the kidney machine   96
that takes on the function of an organ.   104

One of the earliest bionic devices was false teeth, an item with   118
which we are all familiar. In ancient Egypt, missing teeth were re-   132
placed by carved bone or ivory attached with fine wire. False teeth   146
have continued to be made and worn down through the ages, but it was   160
not until the development of the technique of using moulds from which   174
the plates could be designed that dentures became comfortable to wear.   188

Peg legs and hooks are bionic parts which were used for hundreds   202
of years and even into recent times to replace lost legs and arms.   215
These are probably best known through the literary characters of the   229
pirate Long John Silver, who lost his leg in a duel and replaced it   243
with a peg leg, and Captain Hook, whose hand was bitten off by a croc-   257
odile and replaced by a hook. It's certain that neither of these   270
bionic parts was of much use for fine manipulations, but at least they   284
could carry out some functions.   290

In the last few decades, bionics has taken giant steps forward.   304
With the knowledge from research in almost every field – from animal   318
studies to miracle fibres to electronics – all kinds of bionic parts   332
have been devised. Many people are walking around today with a bionic   346
device – perhaps a lens implanted in the eye, a heart valve in the   359
heart, a pacemaker, a synthetic hip joint, an artificial vein, or a   373
bionic ankle. Peg legs and hooks have been replaced by limbs that   386
look real and are electrically connected to the wearer's muscles so   400
that they can be made to respond almost like the real things. Some   413
even provide more strength than a normal limb. Work is currently well   427
under way to produce bionic blood, eyes, livers, ears, hearts, etc.   441

The world has come a long way since Long John Silver and Captain   455
Hook. Now it's only a matter of time till the six-million-dollar man   469
becomes a fact, instead of just a fantasy.   478

| 1 | 2 | 3 | 4 | 5 | 6 | 7 | 8 | 9 | 10 | 11 | 12 | 13 | 14 |

Potholes

We get them every spring. As soon as the snow melts and the | 12
earth begins to thaw, you start to hit them as you are driving inno- | 26
cently along. Plunk! There go the new shocks you had installed last | 40
year. Plunk! That's another one you must remember to drive around or | 54
over, but not into, next time. After a while, you begin to feel like | 68
an inebriated driver wheeling in and out like that, but what else can | 82
you do when you're running an obstacle course? | 91

Potholes, the scourge of northern winters, are caused by water | 105
getting under roads and causing erosion. Although most roads are | 118
covered with asphalt, water still manages to get below. Side ditches | 132
provide a ready access for water. Traffic heavier than a street was | 146
built for may cause the street to crack, providing a passage for | 159
water. Improper grading may allow water to sit in pools for extended | 173
periods, giving the water time to penetrate the road surface. If | 186
cracks and minor holes in a road are not mended, they develop into | 200
bigger cracks and holes. Add to all this the constant freezing and | 214
thawing during winter, and in spring the potholes open their gaping | 228
mouths. | 229

How subject a road is to potholes depends to a great extent on | 243
its construction. A light duty road may have a few centimetres of | 256
asphalt on a shallow sand and gravel base. Often, it will have | 269
ditches. This type of street can be fairly prone to potholes. | 282

Some medium duty roads are built with a thick layer of asphalt on | 296
a deep sand and gravel base, which gives good durability and is fairly | 310
easy to dig up, if need be, to install services. Others are con- | 323
structed with the quantities reversed – a deep layer of asphalt on top | 337
and a shallow sand and gravel base. This combination gives very good | 351
durability and saves on maintenance. | 358

The road that is the most durable, however, is the heavy duty or | 372
industrial road. This consists of a thin topping of asphalt on a | 385
thick concrete base. Now, if all our roads could have this type of | 399
construction, we should have few pothole problems. As luck would have | 413
it, however, concrete is expensive and these roads are difficult and | 427
costly to dig up to install services. We must not feel discouraged, | 441
though; new formulas and materials are being tried, and perhaps soon | 455
we will have roads that are free of potholes. In the meantime, you'd | 469
better check your shocks and alignment; spring is just around the | 482
corner. | 483

| 1 | 2 | 3 | 4 | 5 | 6 | 7 | 8 | 9 | 10 | 11 | 12 | 13 | 14 |

Bluenose

Right up to the last lap of the race, the pair of graceful fish- | 13
ing schooners, their white sails billowing in the wind, had been rid- | 27
ing the waves almost bow to bow. Now, on the last stretch they turned | 41
to windward and a surprising thing happened. While the American | 54
defender Elsie struggled against the strong blow, Canada's Bluenose | 68
charged ahead with her prow held high and proud. As she glided to the | 82
finish line, the triumphant winner of the Fishermen's Cup, a great | 95
roar went up from the jubilant crowd on shore. After the disgrace of | 109
the previous year's defeat, the town of Lunenburg's faith and pride | 123
had been restored. The news was flashed across the country and around | 137
the world, and the Bluenose was on her way to becoming the best-known | 151
sailing vessel of this century. | 157

While the Bluenose was under construction, Captain Angus Walters | 171
hovered about the shipyard like an expectant father. On checking the | 185
framed hull and finding it allowed only a hundred and fifty centi- | 198
metres of headroom, he growled that his crew were not a bunch of midg- | 212
ets. The bow was raised forty-five centimetres, giving it an elegant | 226
and distinctive look. | 230

To both seagoers and landspeople, the sight of the Bluenose was | 244
enough to take one's breath away. Riding at anchor with her tall | 257
masts bare, her long plunging lines and the defiant lift of her bow | 271
gave her the air of speed. Under full canvas with the breeze whis- | 285
tling merrily through her rigging, one would swear she surged with | 298
sheer joy. Even in high winds and rough seas, she bore on as though | 312
there was nothing that could stop or hurt her – and nothing did. It | 326
did not seem to matter whether the Bluenose was fishing or racing, | 339
every fibre of her make-up seemed to come alive. When Walters was at | 353
the wheel, he always talked to his ship, and the crew were certain | 366
that she heard and responded to his commands. | 375

Right through those final years of sail, the famous windjammer | 388
was acknowledged as Queen of the North Atlantic fishing fleets. She | 402
held the record for the largest single catch of fish, and her racing | 416
feats were the inspiration for songs, pictures, books, and poems. Her | 430
home country honoured her with a stamp, and her portrait can still be | 444
seen on Canadian dimes. The lofty clipper provided a fitting and | 457
exciting end to the romantic era of wooden ships, billowing sails, and | 471
lusty fishermen. | 474

| 1 | 2 | 3 | 4 | 5 | 6 | 7 | 8 | 9 | 10 | 11 | 12 | 13 | 14 |

Pets

I never could understand why so many people kept pets around the house. Somehow pets just didn't fit into my scheme of things. Now don't get me wrong; I love animals – cats, dogs, you name it – as long as they're someone else's. I just always figured that children to cook for, to clean for, to nurture, to discipline, and to cherish were quite enough for me. Neither did I want a pet interfering with our freedom to pack up and get away for a weekend or a vacation when we felt like it. We didn't do that very often, mind you, but I liked the feeling that we were unfettered and could if we decided to.

My husband didn't quite agree with me, though. He believed in the old theory that every boy should have a dog. I think he meant that every man should have a dog. Anyhow – you guessed it – one day he appeared in the kitchen with a little collie pup. The boys were ecstatic, so what could I say? Actually, after that cute little mutt chewed up my sweater, created odours in the basement, and did his business all over my garden, I found quite a bit to say. The problem was that both my husband and I worked all day, and that poor wee animal was left all by himself. That was okay in the summertime when he could stay outdoors, but what about the wintertime when he would be cooped up alone in his kennel in the basement? It took some persuading, but my husband was finally convinced that the dog would be better off with a family that could give it the attention it needed. In a few weeks, it was returned to the pound.

Oh, I know pets can also be fun and interesting. My mother used to have a pet parrot that had spent some time on a merchant ship. It had quite a patter. Its favourite was, "Pretty Polly, pretty dear, all the way from Kashmir. Fetch me a pint of beer quick, quick, quick." Imagine all the effort, at least in those days, that went into training a bird to say that. It's much easier now I discovered when I was visiting relatives last week. They bought a parrot not long ago and they showed me a stereo record that teaches birds how to talk – in fourteen easy lessons. It contains fourteen short phrases, each of which is repeated over and over and over again for three or four minutes. It must be pretty boring for the bird, but I must admit it's closer to my idea of pet ownership. You just turn on the record and leave.

| 1 | 2 | 3 | 4 | 5 | 6 | 7 | 8 | 9 | 10 | 11 | 12 | 13 | 14 |

WORDS
13
27
41
54
68
82
96
109
121
135
148
162
176
190
203
217
231
245
259
273
287
301
309
323
337
351
364
377
391
404
418
432
446
460
474
476

With the Fishermen's Cup in the permanent possession of the | 12
Bluenose and the era of windships drawing to a close, Walters was | 25
asked to race once more. After much thought, he agreed. | 36

In spite of a fresh overhaul, new paint, and sparkling white | 49
sails, it was obvious the champion was old and tired after seventeen | 63
years of weathering the rigours of working the fishing grounds – and | 77
the first of the five meets proved it. The younger American schooner | 91
established a lead in the first round and held onto it to the finish. | 105
In the second race, Bluenose found her speed and won. Under light | 119
winds in the third of the series, she won again. In the fourth meet, | 133
her backstay parted and the challenger darted ahead to take the race. | 147
With the competition in a two-two tie, the fifth and final race would | 161
decide the victor. | 165

Sailing well in a light breeze, the Bluenose took an early lead | 179
and held onto it. With the finish line almost in sight, suddenly her | 193
topsail halyard block gave way. With no time for repairs and her | 206
opponent bearing down on her, Walters pleaded with his beloved vessel, | 220
"Just one more time." Like an old war horse with a new surge of ener- | 235
gy, Bluenose gathered every breath of wind into her sails and crossed | 249
the finish line with less than three minutes to spare. For a moment, | 263
the crowd of Americans on shore stood in awed silence; then a loud | 276
roar of applause and cheering filled the air. There was no doubt that | 290
this was a true champion. | 295

After Walters retired from the sea, the Bluenose lay idle for | 308
several years, losing money. No longer able to afford her, he finally | 322
sold her to a freighting firm. After four years of lugging molasses, | 336
bananas, sugar, and tobacco, the Bluenose struck a coral reef off the | 350
coast of Haiti and sank. | 355

Some years later, a brewery company built a full-scale replica, | 369
Bluenose II, and invited the seamen from the original ship as guests | 383
on her first sailing trial. Soon after the cruise got under way, | 396
Walters was asked to try her out. Holding the wheel in his gnarled | 409
old hands, he cocked his head to one side and seemed to be listening | 423
for a long-lost voice. After the trip, the old hands agreed she was a | 437
fine vessel, but there was only one Bluenose and there'll never be | 450
another like her. | 454

| 1 | 2 | 3 | 4 | 5 | 6 | 7 | 8 | 9 | 10 | 11 | 12 | 13 | 14 |

Parachuting the First Time

I cannot think of another feeling that can match the thrill and | 13
excitement of diving out of an airplane at eight hundred metres. I | 27
cannot begin to explain the thoughts and emotions that ran through my | 41
mind when I leaped from that Cessna plane. | 49

The training took about six hours to complete. The first three | 63
hours consisted of classroom work during which we were given instruc- | 77
tions. We watched slides and films, did exercises, and then were | 90
tested. We broke for lunch, but were so excited that we could hardly | 104
eat. All we could think and talk about was the jump and how nervous | 118
we were. After lunch, we engaged in the practical training. Dangling | 132
from a hoist, we practised our emergency procedures. From high plat- | 146
forms, we made mock jumps onto foam mattresses and mock landings onto | 160
gravel until we were tired and sore all over. | 169

Finally, our training was over. As I was being placed in my | 182
equipment, my aches and fatigue were forgotten. Instead, I was begin- | 196
ning to feel edgy and scared. What if my chute didn't open? I kept | 210
running the procedures over and over in my head: "Arch thousand, two | 225
thousand, three thousand, four thousand, five thousand, check thou- | 239
sand. On last count, check chute. If it didn't open, immediately | 252
punch the emergency chute; then pull the ripcord. Remain calm. If | 266
the main chute opened only partially, place left arm over the emer- | 280
gency chute to prevent it from releasing right away, look at the | 293
chute, and pull the ripcord. Place right hand inside the chute con- | 307
tainer, catch the chute and throw it away as far as I can so that it | 321
won't go straight up and get twisted in the main chute. Arch thousand | 335
...." | 336

We climbed into the Cessna plane and took off. The only way out | 350
now was down and that was where I was headed. The four of us took our | 364
jumping positions. I was the second in line. At the jump master's | 378
command, the first jumper disembarked. Then it was my turn. The mas- | 392
ter said "Go," and I jumped. All of my fears vanished in an instant | 407
in my amazement at what I was doing. I seemed to be falling forever | 421
as I watched that patched quilt below getting closer and closer. | 434
Actually, forever lasted only three seconds, and suddenly I felt as | 448
light as a feather and I knew my chute had opened. The thrill and | 461
excitement overtook me and all sense of time and reality was lost as I | 475
floated down to earth. | 479

| 1 | 2 | 3 | 4 | 5 | 6 | 7 | 8 | 9 | 10 | 11 | 12 | 13 | 14 |

Break-in

We were probably rather smug about the fact that in the twenty 13
years we had lived in our home, we had never had a break-in. A break- 27
in was one of those things that happened to other people, but not to 41
us – at least not until about eleven o'clock one morning last year 54
when a young man came knocking at our front door. 64

Down in the recreation room, my teenage son Greg was annoyed that 78
his guitar practice was being disturbed, but he went upstairs and 91
looked out the window to see who was there. A chap was standing at 105
the door, while another appeared to be waiting at the sidewalk. When 119
the latter fellow shouted to his friend to knock louder, Greg became 133
suspicious and decided not to answer the door. 152

In a few minutes, there was a noise, at the rear entrance this 166
time; and Greg rushed to the kitchen window to investigate. Just as 180
he got there, he heard the sound of breaking glass, then the back door 194
opening. Grabbing the nearest weapon at hand, a frying pan, Greg ran 208
shouting and threatening to the back door. Well, the would-be bur- 222
glars were so startled, they took off at a gallop – out the door and 236
down the driveway with Greg in pursuit, shouting and brandishing his 250
frying pan. 252

As the burglars fled down the street, Greg hurried back to the 266
house and telephoned the police. In a matter of minutes, four cruis- 280
ers had arrived and sealed off the immediate area. After a quick 293
briefing, Greg and two policemen set off for a cruise of the neigh- 307
bourhood. They drove up one street and down the other, but the bur- 321
glars were nowhere in sight. Finally giving up, the cruiser headed 335
home. They were almost there when Greg spotted a couple of figures 349
that looked awfully familiar. The cruiser halted immediately and the 363
police were out of the car in a flash. A short chase and a tussle 376
later, they had their men. A search at the police station produced 390
gold chains and other small wares from the pockets of the two sus- 403
pects. It was obvious their burgling had been more successful earlier 417
in the morning. 420

Greg arrived home from the police station a hero that day. Not 434
only had his surprise tactics scared the burglars off, but he had been 448
involved in their apprehension. It was certainly a day of excitement, 462
drama, luck, and pride. 467

| 1 | 2 | 3 | 4 | 5 | 6 | 7 | 8 | 9 | 10 | 11 | 12 | 13 | 14 |

Parachute Training

Parachute jumping is often considered to be a very risky business, and the thought of it tends to invoke fear in the minds of most people. Parachuting is not nearly as difficult or as dangerous as it would at first appear, and the number of accidents is fewer than one might suppose. The major concern of non-jumpers is that the parachute may not open. In fact, this rarely happens. Jumpers are equipped with two chutes – the main parachute backpack and an emergency or reserve chute in a front pack. Both chutes have been packed with care by qualified riggers, and the chances that one or both of them will malfunction are slim.

The key to successful jumping lies in having the right equipment and knowing and following the safety procedures. In most cases, the fee for a first-time parachute jump will cover everything a jumper needs: the use of equipment, the training, the plane ride, and supervision of the jump by a qualified master. The equipment most often includes a jumpsuit, helmet, goggles, gloves, boots, and of course, the parachutes. The training time varies from school to school, but will likely be from three to twelve hours long.

Classroom instruction and films are followed by mock practice jumps and landings from platforms and/or other structures. The jump or exit from a plane is important and is made by springing up and out from the door at the go command. Right away, the jumper must assume a stable, face to earth, falling position. This involves a hard arch with head up, knees slightly bent, and arms and legs spread-eagled. As the parachute opens and fills with air, the jumper will slowly be pulled into a more upright position in which he or she can clasp the suspension lines. As with skiers, the parachutist has to learn how to fall correctly so that the shock will be distributed evenly over the body. The jumper must then get to his or her feet quickly, run to the chute canopy and collapse it before the wind catches it and drags it and the jumper along the ground.

The first few jumps made by a beginner will be static line jumps, in which the main chute is opened automatically at a proper distance from the plane by a line attached to the chute pack and to the plane. A jumper may then engage in freefall jumps, in which it is the jumper who opens the main chute by pulling a ripcord. To this may be added manoeuvres such as turning, rolling, looping, and aiming to land at a certain target, such as a small disk.

| 1 | 2 | 3 | 4 | 5 | 6 | 7 | 8 | 9 | 10 | 11 | 12 | 13 | 14 |

Brownbagging

It may be that an American president was the first executive to | 13
give brownbagging a touch of class. True, a chef cooked, assembled | 27
and packed the gourmet delights in the wicker basket and the presi- | 41
dent's wife carried it to her husband's private office and laid out | 55
its yummy contents, complete with silver service and linen napkin; but | 69
despite the grand style, it was still brownbagging. The habit has | 82
since caught on with a number of Canadian executives in the top and | 96
middle management groups who were quick to see its merits. | 108

Brownbagging is a good way to avoid lining up every day for the | 122
business lunch at which you often eat too much and feel obliged to run | 136
or jog it off at night, and drink too much causing you to be in a dull | 150
stupor at the afternoon meeting with your superior and the person who | 164
has an eye on your job. Brownbagging is also a time saver and a money | 178
saver. | 179

It is important, however, to brownbag it in the right way. Some | 193
executives restrict themselves to a piece of fruit and a slice of | 206
cheese; then they take a brisk walk and return to the office looking | 220
slim, but bored. Others throw together a peanut butter or ham sand- | 234
wich which they sneak into the office concealed in their briefcases | 248
and gulp down when no one is around. This kind of brownbagging is | 261
bad, bad; it can cause indigestion, gas, heartburn, and perhaps even | 275
ulcers. | 277

Good brownbagging involves a bit of planning, shopping, and a lot | 291
of self-indulgence. If you're a sandwich toter, liven it up with | 304
fillings like asparagus or lobster with mayonnaise, pate with slivers | 318
of cucumber, or cream cheese topped with slices of smoked salmon. At | 332
least one side dish to go along with the sandwich is a must to dispel | 346
thoughts of the packed lunches we used to take to school and to add a | 360
touch of sparkle and glamour. If you live in the city, there's no | 373
need to go to a lot of fuss making up your own. Chances are you will | 387
find there are many specialty take-out places that offer all kinds of | 401
delectable things, like quiche, croissants, exotic salads, stuffed | 414
tomatoes, fresh fruit tarts or pecan pie. | 422

With lunches like these, you won't have to sneak your noon-day | 436
meal any more; you'll be the envy of the whole office staff. Not only | 450
that, but you'll feel relaxed and satisfied and ready to tackle the | 464
rest of the day. So if you're going to brownbag it, do it in style. | 478
Give it a real touch of class. | 484

| 1 | 2 | 3 | 4 | 5 | 6 | 7 | 8 | 9 | 10 | 11 | 12 | 13 | 14 |

Parachute Jumping

It's gratifying to note the important role played by women in the | 13
development of parachuting, or sky diving as it is also known. Under | 27
daring conditions, the first female jumper made about forty jumps from | 41
balloons. She was the first person on record to steer her descent | 54
toward a specific drop zone. | 60

Another female sky diver was the first person to come up with the | 74
idea of packing the chute in a bag and stowing the suspension lines in | 88
a way that prevented them from becoming tangled during the drop. When | 102
the jump was made, the lines strung out first in an orderly way, fol- | 116
lowed by the chute. This same woman was one of the first people to do | 130
a double jump. Two chutes were used in this jump. The first chute | 144
opened and the jumper cut it away. Then a second chute opened, which | 158
the jumper used to complete the descent. | 166

It was a female, too, who was the first person to do a freefall | 180
jump. In this jump, the skydiver is not attached in any way to the | 194
plane. After the exit, the jumper freefalls for a few seconds until | 208
clear of the plane, then pulls a ripcord which releases the chute from | 222
the backpack. | 225

In the first part of this century, the airplane was a wondrous | 239
thing, and stunt fliers were common attractions at fairs and carni- | 253
vals. As interest began to wane, parachutists came on the scene and, | 267
with all kinds of crazy antics, kept public interest high. | 279

World War I prompted a look at the parachute as a possible tool | 293
of war, but it was really in World War II that the parachute took its | 307
place in the war game. Not only did it save the lives of hundreds of | 321
pilots and other war personnel, but it was used as a means of dropping | 335
supplies, equipment, jeeps, and troops. After the war, parachutes | 348
were put to other uses. The Russians landed a spacecraft, by para- | 362
chute, on the planet Venus. The Americans used a huge chute to lower | 376
the Gemini space capsule to its water landing, and three giant chutes | 390
to land the Apollo spacemen on their return from the first moon trip. | 404

Parachuting as a sport continued to develop and it branched into | 418
new areas like parasailing. The latter sport looks like a great deal | 432
of fun and more suitable to the less daring of us. The parachute is | 446
tied to the back of a vehicle – a car, boat, or even a snowmobile – | 460
and is towed. The wind created by the moving vehicle fills the chute | 474
with air so that it rises by itself, carrying its human passenger | 487
aloft. | 488

| 1 | 2 | 3 | 4 | 5 | 6 | 7 | 8 | 9 | 10 | 11 | 12 | 13 | 14 |

Burglars

By the time you have finished typing this page, one or more homes	13
or apartments in this country will have been struck by burglars. In	27
most of these cases, the break-ins will have occurred when the homes	41
were unoccupied. One of the ways, then, in which you can deter bur-	55
glars is to ensure that your residence always has a lived-in look.	68
You can do this by eliminating the clues that tell a burglar the home	82
is empty.	84

By the time you have finished typing this page, one or more homes or apartments in this country will have been struck by burglars. In most of these cases, the break-ins will have occurred when the homes were unoccupied. One of the ways, then, in which you can deter burglars is to ensure that your residence always has a lived-in look. You can do this by eliminating the clues that tell a burglar the home is empty.

If you are going to be away for a few days or a few weeks, stop all deliveries, such as the newspaper. Arrange for someone to pick up your mail, handbills, etc.; mow the lawn; shovel the snow; and check your home regularly. Home timers attached to lights in various locations throughout the house will help to make the place look occupied. Even better are programmable timers which will turn lights on and off more than once during the evening. Outside lights at entrances would also help to discourage would-be burglars who prefer to work in the dark. Be sure to use a timer, however; outside lights left on all day are a good indicator that the folks are away.

Home timers can also be used to turn radios and televisions on and off. The sound will help to reinforce the illusion that someone is home. Pull some, but not all, window shades and leave blinds slightly open. Be sure to lock all doors and windows, including those in the basement, the second floor, and the garage. If possible, leave a car parked in the driveway.

If, when you return, you notice any evidence of a break-in, do not enter. The burglar, who could be armed, may still be inside. Get to a telephone and call the police at once. If, in spite of all your efforts, your home is robbed, you will be required to itemize the things that are missing, not only for the police but for your insurance company as well. It is important, then, that you have available a list of all your expensive items, along with models, serial numbers, dates of purchase, costs, and, if possible, pictures. Keep this data tucked away in a safe place, such as in a safety deposit box.

Last, but not least, to help you and the police to identify your property should it be recovered after a theft, have all of your valuables marked with your personal identification. This can be engraved onto metal objects or marked with an indelible marker on other materials. In many places, the marking tools may be borrowed free of charge from the local police department.

| 1 | 2 | 3 | 4 | 5 | 6 | 7 | 8 | 9 | 10 | 11 | 12 | 13 | 14 |

Parachute History

There's an old saying that what goes up must come down – and one way to come down is by parachute. The parachute dates back some hundreds of years. It is believed the Chinese tried using parasols as parachutes way back in the thirteenth century. However, the first known parachute design was drawn by Leonardo da Vinci. His chute was a large linen pyramid. It had five suspension cords, one hanging from each of the four corners and one from the apex down through the middle of the chute. The cords, or lines, were brought together some distance below the chute and were connected to a bar from which the jumper hung by his or her hands.

It was another hundred years or more before people were reported to be jumping themselves or dropping animals from high points, such as the tops of towers. The sport did not arouse much interest, though, until the advent of hot-air balloons made it possible for humans to ascend high enough to make use of parachutes. The chute was fastened high up on the balloon, with its lines connected to the jumper, who waited in the balloon's basket until the right moment to exit. The tug of the jumper's body as he or she fell wrenched the chute free of the balloon. Parachuting became a sensation all over Europe and drew large crowds at exhibitions and fairs. Feats like jumping from burning balloons, landing in the water, and performing tricks on a trapeze bar while descending, made for thrills and excitement.

When airplanes came into being, there was great interest on the part of jumpers in parachuting from moving planes. Pilots, however, had misgivings; they were afraid the sudden shift as someone jumped would cause the plane to go out of control. The fear proved unfounded and parachuting began a new stage in its history.

One of the problems with jumping from a plane was that the chute was attached to the aircraft and opened immediately upon the jumper's exit. This meant that it could easily get caught on the plane. A device called the static line was devised. This line was connected to the aircraft and to the bag containing the parachute, which the jumper now carried. With this set-up, the parachute was not released until the jumper had fallen far enough to fully extend the static line, by which time he or she was clear of the plane. Then the pull of the jumper tugged the chute right out of its bag attached to the line, and jumper and chute went sailing down to earth.

| 13 |
| 27 |
| 41 |
| 54 |
| 68 |
| 82 |
| 96 |
| 109 |
| 123 |
| 129 |
| 143 |
| 157 |
| 171 |
| 185 |
| 199 |
| 213 |
| 227 |
| 241 |
| 255 |
| 269 |
| 283 |
| 294 |
| 308 |
| 322 |
| 336 |
| 350 |
| 360 |
| 374 |
| 388 |
| 401 |
| 415 |
| 429 |
| 443 |
| 457 |
| 470 |
| 484 |
| 493 |

| 1 | 2 | 3 | 4 | 5 | 6 | 7 | 8 | 9 | 10 | 11 | 12 | 13 | 14 |

Caves Below

The world holds many natural wonders both on the ground and in | 13
the sea, but some of the most beautiful of all are found in caves | 26
beneath the earth. The natural splendour of caves has oft been | 39
described as fairylands and wonderlands, but sometimes even these | 52
words do not do them justice. These underground worlds of endless | 65
passages, vast halls, gleaming walls, swift rivers, cascading water- | 79
falls, crystal lakes, and unbelievable formations seldom fail to cast | 93
their magic spell on anyone who sees them for the first time. | 105

A cave can best be defined as a natural underground cavity that | 119
is large enough for a human to enter. It may be a single cavity or a | 133
group of cavities called a cave system. Some caves have been formed | 147
by the flow of volcanic lava, some by ocean waves hurtling rocks and | 161
gravel against cliffs, some by the frequent bombardment of rock by | 174
high-speed winds carrying grit and sand, and some by ice; but most | 187
caves have been formed by the continuous action of acid water on lime- | 201
stone rock. | 203

Like the cave of Tom Sawyer, a limestone cave is made up of a | 216
maze of shafts, passages, and chambers. The outer area of a cave, | 229
where light still penetrates, is known as the twilight zone. Inside | 243
the cave proper, there is no light, no reflections, no distant glows, | 257
just total darkness. In some caves, the only noise is the constant | 271
dripping of water, the roar of a raging river, or the thunder of a | 284
teaming waterfall. In others, there is no sound at all. The presence | 298
of so much moisture in a cave creates a constant high humidity. | 311
Often, too, there is almost a complete lack of air currents so that | 325
the cave temperature remains constant and moderate in spite of exter- | 339
nal weather changes. | 343

Probably the most spectacular feature of many caves is the vari- | 357
ety of glistening white formations that have developed in them. Some | 371
hang from the ceilings like great icycles or rise up from the floor | 385
like dunce caps. Some hang in sheets like curtains or are shaped like | 399
flowers or sparkling jewels. | 405

Caves in all their glorious beauty can be viewed in many places | 419
throughout the world where they have been lit up and transformed into | 433
dazzling tourist showcases. | 438

| 1 | 2 | 3 | 4 | 5 | 6 | 7 | 8 | 9 | 10 | 11 | 12 | 13 | 14 |

Orpheus was said to have been more than mortal, having been born 13
of one of the Muses. He learned to play the lyre, and he played and 27
sang so beautifully that he charmed everyone who heard. Such was the 41
power of his music that no one and nothing could resist or refuse him. 55

Orpheus fell in love with a beautiful maiden called Eurydice and 69
in time they were married. Shortly after the wedding, the bride was 83
walking in a meadow when she was bitten by a viper and died. Orpheus 97
was beside himself with grief; not even his music comforted him. 110
Unable to endure it longer, he made a bold decision. He would venture 124
down into the underworld and use his music to charm Pluto, king of the 138
dead, and persuade him to allow Eurydice to return to the living. 151

He found the cave which led to the kingdom of the dead and fol- 165
lowed its path into the depths, playing and singing as he strode. 178
Eventually he came to a river and, with his refrain, charmed the boat- 192
man into rowing him across. On the other side, he encountered the 205
three-headed dog that guarded the gates of the underworld realm, but 219
his music so entranced the animal that it permitted him to pass. 232

Orpheus continued to play as he wandered and all of the dead that 246
he passed stopped to listen. Finally, he found himself before the 259
king and queen, and through words and music he pleaded his case. His 273
sweet and mournful melody cast such a spell that he "drew iron tears 287
down Pluto's cheek, and made hell grant what love did seek." Orpheus 301
was given permission to take his wife back to the world of the living, 315
but only on condition that he precede her all the way and not look 328
back at her until they had reached the upper world. Orpheus agreed 342
and started on the journey. 347

As Orpheus travelled, he could detect no sound behind him and he 361
longed to turn around and ensure that his beloved was following. At 375
last he reached the cave entrance. He stepped into the sunshine and 389
turned around. It was too soon, for Eurydice was still in the cave. 403
He heard a soft farewell as she faded into the darkness. Orpheus ran 417
into the cave to follow but she had disappeared. He continued on 430
until he reached the river, but this time the boatman was immune to 444
his entreaties. Orpheus returned to the earth alone. A heartbroken 458
man, he forsook the company of humans and became a sad and lonely 471
wanderer. 473

| | 1 | 2 | 3 | 4 | 5 | 6 | 7 | 8 | 9 | 10 | 11 | 12 | 13 | 14 | |

Caves From Limestone

It may sound too simple to be true, but the fact of the matter is | 13
that most of the caves that exist in the world today were hollowed out | 27
over eons of time by the actions of three elements: carbon dioxide, | 41
water, and limestone. Even as you are reading, these elements are at | 55
work enlarging existing caves and forming new ones, perhaps below your | 69
very feet. The process is lengthy but simple. | 78

Large amounts of carbon dioxide are present in the soil as a re- | 92
sult of the decay of plants and other organic matter. As water seeps | 106
through the soil, it picks up the carbon dioxide and they join forces | 120
to make carbonic acid. This acid water carries on down and slowly | 133
makes its way through the joints and cracks in the limestone rock | 146
below. Now limestone is mainly a mineral called calcite which breaks | 160
down in the presence of carbonic acid. As a result, as the water | 173
passes, it dissolves some of the limestone and carries it along in | 186
solution. This slow but constant action enlarges the cracks in the | 200
rock. Some grow bigger than others and are able to take in more water | 214
and grow still faster. The water in these large channels becomes tur- | 228
bulent and robs the water from the small ones. The motion and the | 241
increase in water speeds up the dissolving action in the large chan- | 255
nels, rivers may enter and help with their enlargement, and the chan- | 269
nels grow into cave passages. | 275

What is perhaps most appealing about caves is their strange land- | 289
scape formations. The interesting thing is that these formations are | 303
the result of the reversal of the cave-forming process. As the caves | 317
grow and the water level drops, large air spaces develop into which | 331
the water solution seeping down through the rock begins to drip. The | 345
air contains much less carbon dioxide than the water, which causes the | 359
carbon dioxide to leave the water in favour of the air. This loss | 372
permits calcite to come out of its water solution and be deposited. | 386
Ever so slowly, the deposits grow and take on a variety of shapes. | 399
The best known are the stalactites that hang from the ceilings of | 412
caves and the stalagmites that have built up from the ground. It's | 426
easy to remember which of these are which if you notice the "c" for | 440
ceiling in stalactite and the "g" for ground in stalagmite. | 452

The amazing sizes and shapes of caverns and their formations have | 466
inspired such names as Giant Dome, Hall of the Thirteen, the Big Room, | 480
Bamboo Grove, Frozen Fountain, Leaning Tower of Pisa, Bridal Veil, | 494
Jewel Cave, and Paradise. | 499

| 1 | 2 | 3 | 4 | 5 | 6 | 7 | 8 | 9 | 10 | 11 | 12 | 13 | 14 |

Opera

An opera company on tour was in need of chorus singers, musi- | 13
cians, and extras. I was young, fancy free, bone idle, and without | 27
funds. The company was offering good pay and I managed to get a part | 41
in most of the operas it was playing. All went well until Carmen, | 54
which, apart from its musical merit and popularity, contains a glori- | 68
ous amount of wine drinking. The stage director, who was a great | 81
admirer of the grape, did not believe his cast should be fobbed off | 95
with coloured water, so in the tavern scene, the actors were divided | 109
into four labels. The principals drank fine vintage wine in elegant | 123
glasses; the chorus, a light table wine in tumblers; the supers, the | 137
cheapest wine on the market, generously laced with the best tap water | 151
available; and the waiters, lashings of all three. I was a waiter. | 165

From the very first performance, everyone developed a passion for | 179
the grape. There was something heady about drinking wine in front of | 193
a packed audience, especially as the issue was free. The principals | 207
had to spend a lot of their energy during that scene wrestling their | 221
vintage away from the chorus, who were trying to prevent all their | 234
table wine being swiped by the supers, who were attempting, without | 248
much success, to stop the waiters from drinking all three. By the | 262
time the dancers came on, Carmen was as merry as could be, with a | 275
vivacity that was unequalled. | 281

Needless to say, things got out of hand, for the waiters were the | 295
only ones who had legitimate excuses to keep popping on and off stage | 309
and getting at the bottle store. This was our undoing. We never had | 323
a rehearsal; we had been marched around the stage before the curtain | 337
went up and given brief verbal instructions. They would have been | 350
difficult to follow as it was, but with three free wines around, none | 364
of the waiters had any intention of following them. We just wandered | 378
around the stage drinking, until one teenage lad feel backwards off | 392
his chair in the middle of the Torreador song. I thought it added to | 406
the general gaiety, but the singer was hopping mad – so mad that when | 420
he tried to down his vintage at the end, it spluttered all over his | 434
shirt. I did not let him have any more; but before the curtain came | 448
down, the wine store had run dry anyway. | 456

The stage director had a few words to say before sacking the lot | 470
of us. He did relent, however, and I got my job back as a waiter, but | 484
there was never the same run on the raspberry syrup that replaced | 497
those dark, succulent, grape juices. | 504

| 1 | 2 | 3 | 4 | 5 | 6 | 7 | 8 | 9 | 10 | 11 | 12 | 13 | 14 |

Caves Have Life

In view of the conditions of cave living, the variety of life 12
found in caves is quite surprising. Caves do offer a constant, moder- 26
ate climate, but it is in a world of total blackness. Many animals, 40
like bears, moths, owls, frogs, snakes, and even humans, may shelter 54
in a cave entrance or in the twilight zone where there is light, but 68
seldom will they venture into the black depths beyond. 79

There are some animals, however, that can find their way in the 93
dark. The best known are bats which use sonar sounding to navigate in 107
darkness. Some bats use caves just for winter hibernation. For 120
others, caves are daytime resting places. At dusk, they leave their 134
caves en masse, sometimes looking from a distance like a dense cloud 148
of smoke. They forage for food, usually insects or fruit, and return 162
to their caves at dawn. 167

Two birds which nest in caves also appear to have sonar vision, 181
although not as highly developed as the bat's. These are the oil bird 195
and the salangane, a type of swallow. The nest of the latter is built 209
with spittle secreted from under the bird's tongue, and is the main 223
ingredient in the well-known Chinese dish, bird's nest soup. Another 237
animal which manages to travel in the dark is the pack rat, but this 251
creature relies on memory and its own scent markers for navigation. 265
None of these animals, however, can be considered true cave creatures, 279
for they live outside as well as inside caves. 288

True troglobites spend their entire lives in caves. Their total 302
population is normally quite small, mainly due to the keen competition 316
for a meagre food supply. Without light, the only plant life in caves 330
is fungi and bacteria which provide some food, and, of course, some 344
cave animals feed on their neighbours. Most of the food, however, is 358
brought in from the outside, either via flowing water which contains 372
plant debris or other food, or by animals, like bats, which occupy the 386
caves and leave organic matter behind. Among the many troglobites are 400
cave forms of fish, flatworms, spiders, crayfish, shrimps, and sala- 414
manders. They tend to be small, white, and blind. Some have only 427
vestiges of eyes, and others have no eyes at all. Their sense organs, 441
however, are extremely well developed and they survive by hearing, 454
smell and touch. 457

| 1 | 2 | 3 | 4 | 5 | 6 | 7 | 8 | 9 | 10 | 11 | 12 | 13 | 14 |

Nature Was First Again

More of nature's scientific ingenuity can be seen in the built-in 13
parachute of the flying squirrel which makes the rodent appear to be 27
flying. When the squirrel jumps from tree to tree, it spreads its 40
legs wide which, in turn, spread out a special membrane that runs 53
along either side of its body. This forms a parachute which enables 67
the squirrel to glide some distance before it lands. 77

When it comes to dams, the beaver is a skillful engineer. The 91
beaver starts its dam with stones and then builds it up with sticks, 105
sod, mud, and water weeds. Not only does the dam provide a pond in 119
which the beaver can lodge, but it also helps to control spring 132
flooding. 134

Another builder is the mallee fowl. This bird builds an incuba- 148
tor for its eggs and then uses its long tongue as a thermometer to 161
test the temperature. The incubator is a large pit dug up to a metre 175
into the ground and filled with organic matter, like twigs and leaves, 189
which is then covered with a high mound of loose sand. The organic 203
matter decays and gives off heat, and it is into this compost heap 216
that the female mallee lays her eggs. The male bird checks the tem- 230
perature often and adds or removes sand as needed to keep the incu- 244
bator at the correct heat. 249

Snowshoes are worn by a number of animals. The polar bear wears 263
his snowshoes all year round. They are, of course, his big furry feet 277
with the non-skid soles. These enable this great, half-tonne animal 291
to traverse ice that is too thin to support a human. The fly, too, 305
has special feet but for a different reason. Glands in the pads of 319
its feet secrete small amounts of liquid glue which enable the insect 333
to walk on ceilings. 337

One of the reasons for the penguin's survival in polar regions is 351
its internal heat-exchange system which maintains two internal body 365
temperatures. Its inner body is kept at normal, while its extremities 379
run at a temperature close to that of the outside air. The bird's 392
veins and arteries are so entwined that warm blood flowing to the 405
extremities is cooled, and cold blood coming from the extremities to 419
the inner body is warmed. 424

There are some fish, like the electric eel, that have their own 438
power plants which can generate electricity. The eel's power house is 452
located along most of the length of its sides and can produce a strong 466
current that is capable of dealing a stunning blow. 476

| 1 | 2 | 3 | 4 | 5 | 6 | 7 | 8 | 9 | 10 | 11 | 12 | 13 | 14 |

Caving (alias Spelunking)

Have you ever secretly thought that some day you would like to | 13
engage in a really daring sport, something that would test your stam- | 27
ina and courage, that would offer excitement and adventure, perhaps | 41
even give you the thrill of discovery? For myself, I could not imag- | 55
ine doing such a thing, but I know there are a lot of people who not | 69
only dream of adventure, they get right out there and do something | 82
about it. Why, the news is full of the daring exploits of people like | 96
mountain climbers, deep sea divers, and spelunkers. Actually, I | 109
haven't seen too many stories about spelunkers, but I just thought I | 123
would throw that in. Oh, you've never heard of a spelunker? Well, a | 137
spelunker is another name for a caver, one who explores caves for the | 151
sport of it. | 153

I have explored a few caves and I love it. Of course, my idea of | 167
caving may be a little different from that of true spelunkers. I | 180
rather like the smooth paths, stairways, bridges, elevators, and | 193
superb lighting found in commercial caves. True cavers, however, go | 207
in more for dangling in mid-air on ropes over plunging rock caverns, | 221
crawling on their bellies through mud in low tunnels, squeezing | 234
through tiny openings not designed for their girth, swimming and wad- | 248
ing in cold water, or climbing strong waterfalls. This kind of caving | 262
is a real challenge but it takes a lot of skill and experience. If | 276
you think you'd like to try it, let me give you some advice. | 288

Start with a nice, easy cave where you can build up some experi- | 301
ence. Having the right equipment is a must, and the most important is | 315
light – not just one light source, but several in case of failures. | 329
Most cavers use a headlamp attached to a hard hat as their main light | 343
source. A map if there is one available, a compass, drinking water, | 357
some energy food, a watch, and a long rope would also be useful. | 370
Caves are cool, damp, and dirty so warm clothing, stout boots, and | 383
tough gloves would be in order. Caves do contain hazards, so never go | 397
caving alone. Also, let someone on the outside know where you are | 410
going and when you expect to return. Always stay within the bounds of | 424
your proven strength and endurance. Lastly, observe the rules of | 437
conservation. A cave is a closed and fragile environment that took | 451
perhaps millions of years to develop. Leave it just as it was when | 465
you arrived; the next spelunker wants to enjoy it too. | 476

| 1 | 2 | 3 | 4 | 5 | 6 | 7 | 8 | 9 | 10 | 11 | 12 | 13 | 14 |

In the field of scientific discovery, it is nearly always nature   13
that has led the way. Take radar, for instance. The bat was using   27
radar long before we discovered it. The bat has so little eyesight   41
that it depends on its radar to guide its flight. As the bat flies,   55
it emits short, sharp cries at a frequency that is far beyond the   68
limit of human hearing. When these ultrasonic waves bounce off ob-   82
jects, the bat hears the echoes and is able to assess the position and   96
distance of objects in its path.   102

Jet propulsion is another of nature's inventions and has been the   116
squid's method of travel for thousands of years. The squid takes   129
water into its mantle cavity and squirts it out through a siphon. This   143
propels the squid backwards or forwards like a rocket. The squid is   157
also a living kaleidoscope. When angered, it turns crimson red; when   171
frightened, it becomes pale. It changes colour by opening or closing   185
the many tiny colour cells on its body.   193

Suction cups are a common tool of many sea creatures, like   206
snails, who use them to cling to plants, rocks, and sometimes other   220
animals. The hollow fangs of a viper work like a hypodermic needle to   234
discharge poison into its prey. Bees, like humans, are fond of air-   248
conditioned comfort. When it becomes too hot in the hive, they fan   262
their wings so that a cross draught is created which expels hot air   276
out of the hive and draws cooler air in.   284

Like a tiny helicopter, the hummingbird hovers over blossoms   297
while it eats. It rotates its wings in their sockets while flapping   311
them rapidly. The forward and backward propelling beats counteract   325
each other so that the bird remains stationary in mid-air. Also, the   339
hummingbird has a tongue that is similar to a soda straw and works   352
like a suction pump as it sucks up nectar and tiny insects from   365
flowers.   367

Snorkels are used by small water scorpions foraging for food at   381
the bottom of shallow water. The snorkel, a lengthy tube attached to   395
the insect's breathing organ in its tail, is raised to the surface to   409
supply the scorpion with oxygen. Another insect, a type of beetle,   423
solves the air supply problem by stretching up its wings and envelop-   437
ing a pocket of air. With this air tank on its back, it dives to the   451
bottom of the water to search for food. When the air grows stale, the   465
beetle surfaces and renews its supply.   473

| 1 | 2 | 3 | 4 | 5 | 6 | 7 | 8 | 9 | 10 | 11 | 12 | 13 | 14 |

Country Mouse

The little country mouse prepared her nest in a field of wheat · 13
and, in due course, six tiny pink babies were born. As the wheat · 26
matured, the baby mice also grew. Mother mouse told her youngsters · 40
that the wheat was almost ready for cutting, and before that happened · 54
they would have to vacate the field or be cut to pieces by the · 67
combine. · 69

One day while mother mouse was foraging for food, the young mice · 83
overheard the farmer and his son as they walked in the field discuss- · 97
ing the harvest. The farmer was telling his son that he expected the · 111
neighbours to come the following day to assist in harvesting the · 124
wheat. The mice were very excited and impatient as they awaited · 137
their mother's return. At last she arrived and they stumbled over · 151
each other in their haste to recount what they had heard. When they · 165
had finished, mother mouse did not appear at all concerned and in- · 179
formed her children that there was no need to relocate yet. The · 192
following day, the young mice were alert for signs of harvesting, but · 206
the day passed and the wheat continued to stand uncut – much to the · 220
relief of the young mice. · 225

The farmer and his son strolled through the field again. The · 238
young mice strained to listen and overheard the farmer comment that he · 252
had invited his relatives to assist with the harvesting the next day. · 266
The youngsters were very worried and anxious, and when their mother · 280
got home they related the latest revelation. Again, mother mouse took · 294
the news calmly and assured her offspring that they were in no danger. · 308
Mother mouse was right, for the relatives did not arrive and the wheat · 322
did not get cut. · 325

Once more, the farmer and his son appeared in the field. As they · 339
passed by, the little mice overheard the farmer inform his son that · 353
because his neighbours and relatives had failed him, it looked as · 366
though they would have to harvest the wheat themselves the following · 380
day. The young mice were in a panic and relayed the conversation to · 394
their mother. This time, mother mouse replied, "Now, my children, we · 408
will prepare to move to safer quarters before morning, for when the · 422
farmer decides to do the work himself, it will get done." The family · 436
moved immediately, and the following day the wheat was harvested. · 449

| 1 | 2 | 3 | 4 | 5 | 6 | 7 | 8 | 9 | 10 | 11 | 12 | 13 | 14 |

Musical Training

All children at birth have the potential to produce beautiful music. Using the same method by which children learn their mother tongue, we can help them to develop an amazing ability in the field of music. From birth to about three months of age, babies the world over make the same infant sounds. At about three months, they start to discard those sounds they do not hear around them, and imitate those they do hear. By the time children reach six months, a trained linguist can tell what language they are getting ready to speak. A child who lives in silence has no sounds to imitate and does not learn to talk. Sounds must be heard and absorbed in order to feed them back.

Music education also begins at birth; and some people believe even a few months before birth. Too many parents wait for their children to reach a level of maturity before starting them on music lessons. They do not realize that precious time is slipping away during which the children are slowly losing their natural musical ability. When the children do not do well at their lessons, the parents conclude they were born without musical talent.

An ear for music is not innate, but can be acquired by listening. The earlier this listening is begun, the more effective it will be. So, treat your newborn to a daily bath of music. Infants exposed to good quality music will gradually learn and be able to recognize the pieces, and will develop an ear for music. Just as infants absorb speech patterns in preparation for the day they will start to form words, so they will absorb music and be ready for lessons around the age of three years.

It is a good idea for a parent to attend the music lessons with the child and to practise with the child on a daily basis. This should be a happy time for both parent and child. If the parent cannot play the chosen instrument, he or she can learn the basics of it and, by so doing, will understand some of the problems the child may encounter. Parental support and encouragement during these sessions is important. The parent needs to find things to praise and learn to give correction in a positive way. The child who is shown respect and approval for work well done, and who is allowed to feel the glow of success after each accomplishment, will gain self-esteem and respond with a keen desire to learn and to reach his or her full musical potential.

| 1 | 2 | 3 | 4 | 5 | 6 | 7 | 8 | 9 | 10 | 11 | 12 | 13 | 14 |

WORDS

12
25
39
53
66
80
94
108
122
136
149
163
177
191
205
219
228
242
256
270
284
298
312
326
330
344
357
371
385
399
413
427
441
455
469
482
484

Cruising used to be only for those who knew they had good sea 12
legs and for those who were willing to find out. Although many people 26
thought of a cruise as the ultimate vacation, when the choice came, 40
often the cruise was bypassed in favour of dry land. After all, who 54
wanted to work hard all year to earn a few weeks' holiday and then 67
take a chance on having to spend it seasick on a boat? Now, all that 81
has changed. Seasick pills have almost eliminated that bane of sail- 95
ing, and cruises have reached a new peak in popularity. 106

Cruise ships are virtual pleasure resorts afloat, and all kinds 120
of fun and games await their passengers. It seems that food is a 133
star attraction on these floating spas. It is available in great 146
abundance and variety. With breakfast, lunch, dinner, morning and 159
afternoon snacks, and sumptuous midnight buffets being offered, almost 173
any time is mealtime and anything from fresh fruit to lobster may be 187
served. 189

All the tasty temptations can play havoc with one's diet, but 202
exercise classes and lots of activities are provided to help compen- 216
sate. Tennis courts, shuffleboard, a swimming pool, and other facili- 230
ties are available to the sports enthusiast. Even the golfer can keep 244
his hand in at the driving range, although it is suggested that golf- 258
ers do not attempt to retrieve their balls; it's a long way down to 272
the ocean floor. The sundeck is a popular spot for sunbathing and 285
reading. In the evenings, entertainment and dancing are the order of 299
the night. Talent shows, costume parties, and other special attrac- 313
tions are common too. For those who like to try their luck at the 326
tables or slot machines, a casino is usually available. Cruise ships 340
stop at several ports at which passengers may go ashore for sightsee- 354
ing and shopping. These stops are an important feature of a cruise 368
and add a nice change of scene and pace. 376

Movies have so often depicted a cruise ship as the place where 390
boy meets girl that many folks have developed the notion that it is a 404
great man-woman meeting place. Sad to say, the records show that wom- 418
en guests far outnumber the men. This may be quite satisfactory from 432
the man's point of view, but it clearly indicates that the woman who 446
is seeking romance on a ship is more than likely to be disappointed. 460

| 1 | 2 | 3 | 4 | 5 | 6 | 7 | 8 | 9 | 10 | 11 | 12 | 13 | 14 |

Mother's Day

As a special surprise for Mother's Day, we hired an automobile to take Mother for a beautiful drive in the country. Mother hardly ever has a treat like that because she is busy in the house nearly all the time. It occurred to Father that a better idea would be to take Mother fishing. Father said if you are going fishing, there is a definite purpose to the trip which heightens the enjoyment. Father had just purchased a new rod the previous day and said Mother could use it if she wanted to.

We got everything arranged, and Mother prepared a picnic lunch although we were expecting a big dinner on our return. When the motor car arrived, there hardly seemed as much room as we had supposed, probably because we hadn't reckoned on Father's fishing gear; and it was obvious we couldn't all get in. Father said he could just as easily stay home. He said we should forget that he hadn't had a holiday for three years; he wanted us to go ahead and have a wonderful day. Of course, we all felt we couldn't let Father stay home, especially as we knew he would make trouble if he did. The two girls would gladly have remained behind and prepared the dinner, only it seemed a pity on such a lovely day; but they both agreed that if Mother said the word, they'd gladly stay. Will and I would have dropped out, but we would have been useless getting dinner.

Finally, it was decided that Mother would stay home and have a lovely restful day around the house, and get the dinner. Anyway, it was slightly chilly outdoors and Father declared he would never forgive himself if he dragged Mother round the country and she caught a severe cold, when she might have been enjoying a beautiful rest. So we drove away while Mother watched us from the verandah.

We had the loveliest day you could possibly imagine, and Father caught such big specimens he felt certain Mother couldn't have landed them anyhow. Will and I fished too, and the girls met two handsome young gentlemen and chatted and had a splendid time. It was late when we returned, but Mother had the dinner ready and we sat down to the grandest meal. When dinner was over, we all wanted to clear up and wash the dishes, only Mother said she would really rather do it herself; so we could hardly argue. When we kissed Mother goodnight, she said it had been a wonderful day.

| | 1 | 2 | 3 | 4 | 5 | 6 | 7 | 8 | 9 | 10 | 11 | 12 | 13 | 14 | |

The customs of various peoples down through the ages are truly   13
amazing. Some of the most interesting to ponder are those that were   27
allowed to develop even though they inflicted extreme discomfort,   40
pain, and/or disfigurement on the human beings involved. One of these   54
was a custom prevalent for many years in China where tiny feet on   67
women were thought to be a most desirable attribute and the very foun-   81
dation of a woman's beauty. To acquire these dainty tootsies, the   94
feet of female children of the ruling class were tightly bound from   108
the time they were babies until their growing years were over. Some-   122
how they learned to walk on these little supports, but their steps   135
were difficult and faltering. In spite of the pain and discomfort,   149
the ladies were proud of their tiny feet. They clad them in pretty   163
slippers made of satin and adorned with gold and silver designs, and   177
seldom missed a chance to show off their dainty feet, or "golden   190
lilies" as they were termed, below their long robes.   201

Tattooing was another painful custom of old. For a long time, it   215
was common in some American Indian tribes where often both sexes went   229
under the needle. Normally females had just a few designs on the face   243
and sometimes on the wrists, fingers, and legs; but males often had   257
extensive work done on chest, back, arms, and hands. As well as being   271
a very painful operation, tattooing was a long and tedious process   284
that could take two or three days of constant work to complete.   297

In Africa, many tribes had practices which did much to alter   310
their physical appearance. In some groups, members wore bones or   323
strips of wood or other material through their pierced noses. Others   337
wore such large, heavy earrings dangling from the upper, as well as   350
the lower, part of the ear that the ears were severely and permanently   364
stretched out of shape. In many African cultures, body scarring was a   378
matter of course, and so were some surgical procedures. The latter   392
were carried out with no anaesthetic and with tools that were not   405
sterile, and many deaths from infection occurred. One tribe is well   419
known for its habit of stretching the lips with the use of wooden   432
plates until they extended out like a duck's bill, sometimes jutting   446
out as much as sixteen centimetres.   453

It is likely we will never know just how or why these odd customs   467
ever got started, but we do know that without them, this timed writing   481
would not have been possible.   487

| 1 | 2 | 3 | 4 | 5 | 6 | 7 | 8 | 9 | 10 | 11 | 12 | 13 | 14 |

Martha's Job Interview

Martha's thoughts were interrupted when the receptionist gave her | 13
a job application form to fill out. Having left her resume in her | 26
other purse, Martha filled out the form as best she could. She was | 40
then asked to do a ten-minute speed test. Ten minutes? Why, at | 53
school she had never been given more than a five-minute test. Martha | 67
looked with horror at the old manual typewriter. After the test, she | 81
was given some shorthand dictation. She got down as much as she | 94
could; after all, it was very fast and contained a lot of long words | 108
which she had never heard before. | 115

When Martha had finished typing her notes, the receptionist | 128
offered her a cup of coffee. Martha eagerly accepted. Just as she | 142
was settling down to drink her coffee, the personnel manager emerged | 156
from his office and asked Martha to come in. Forgetting the broken | 170
heel on her shoe, Martha jumped up and lost her balance. The coffee | 184
cup in her hand fell forward, spilling coffee all over the manager. | 198
While he was away wiping off his clothes, Martha waited in his office. | 212
Nothing was going right for her today, but surely her test results | 225
would be good in spite of that dreadful old typewriter. | 236

The manager returned with Martha's graded tests and partially | 249
completed application form. Looking at her tests upside down on the | 263
desk, Martha could see that she had scored fifteen net words per min- | 277
ute on the timing. The transcription appeared to contain a number of | 291
spelling errors, and the marker had noted that the letter just did not | 305
make sense. | 307

Thinking that he might soothe this angry girl, the manager began, | 321
"You seem to have had a few problems this morning. I'm sorry about | 335
the typewriter; our electric one is out ...." but he got no further. | 349
Martha could not contain her feelings any longer, and she gave a full | 363
account of all her troubles and their causes down to the very last | 376
detail. She was especially eloquent about that ancient typewriter. | 390
Then she launched her sales pitch, giving reasons why she should be- | 404
come the secretary to the junior executive. | 413

When Martha finally stopped talking, the manager looked into her | 427
make-up streaked face. "You're not going to believe this, Martha," he | 442
said, "but ...." What do YOU think he said? | 452

| 1 | 2 | 3 | 4 | 5 | 6 | 7 | 8 | 9 | 10 | 11 | 12 | 13 | 14 |

Whenever my children and I get into a discussion and I endeavour | 13
to compare their circumstances to mine when I was their age, they | 26
always remind me that those days were different. When I stop to think | 40
about it, many things then were different. | 48

Throughout the Depression, during which our family grew to eight | 62
people, we lived in a rented, three-room cottage. The woodstove was | 76
in the basement and that was where Mother did her cooking and then | 89
carried the food upstairs to the kitchen table. | 98

Like so many other men, my father was on public relief. Until | 112
the food voucher system came in, the men on welfare went to a downtown | 126
warehouse to pick up their relief food. There was a variety of goods | 140
available, but each family was allowed only a limited quantity of each | 154
item. It wasn't long before the men started trading items among them- | 168
selves – perhaps a can of beans for a jar of peanut butter – so that | 182
each took home a better supply of the things his family used. Each | 196
morning, Dad walked downtown to the employment office. Sometimes he | 210
would be sent out on a job shovelling snow, delivering coal, painting, | 224
or doing odd jobs and, if he were lucky, would earn a few dollars. | 237
Once he came home with three chairs instead of money because the | 250
employer claimed to have no money with which to pay him. | 261

Our landlady was an elderly widow who lived with her son in the | 275
country. They raised hens and when she came to collect the rent, she | 289
sometimes brought us a freshly-killed chicken. We children had lots | 303
of fun plucking it. | 307

During the war, everyone had to observe the blackouts. All | 320
streetlights were out and there could be no light showing from homes | 334
or buildings. Wardens patrolled the streets to ensure that darkness | 348
prevailed, and as soon as ours had passed, we would peep out beneath | 362
the blinds and watch him disappear out of sight. Then, with a little | 376
coaxing, my older sister would entrance us with one of her wonderful | 390
tales. | 391

Of course there were no televisions in those days. The old floor | 405
radio was our indoor family entertainment and we children sat around | 419
it on the floor and listened to mystery shows like The Shadow. On | 433
Saturday afternoons, we were allowed to go to the cinema, a small | 446
local one that we dubbed Dutchy's Palace. Admission was all of five | 460
cents. En route we passed under a railway bridge where we picked up | 474
bits of tar to chew along the way. | 481

| 1 | 2 | 3 | 4 | 5 | 6 | 7 | 8 | 9 | 10 | 11 | 12 | 13 | 14 |

Martha Seeks Employment

Martha had been looking for a job since graduating from college three months before. Not one of her many interviews had resulted in even a nibble of a job offer. She was not worried; sooner or later, an employer would realize her worth. All she had to do was find the right employer.

Martha glanced through the want ads to see whether there were any new jobs since yesterday. There it was – the perfect opportunity for her: "Wanted immediately. Secretary for junior executive. Recent graduate preferred. Good shorthand, typing, and machine transcription skills. Some knowledge of word processing would be an asset." Without a doubt, this was the job for Martha. Martha called the number shown in the ad and arranged an interview for eleven the next morning. That task out of the way, she made arrangements for the rest of the day. She planned on cycling, dinner, roller skating, and a party afterwards.

It was three in the morning when Martha finally climbed into bed. At ten, she awoke with a start. Why, she had to be at that interview at eleven. She dressed quickly and raced out of the house towards the bus stop. She was almost there when the bus trundled past. Oh no, that meant a twenty minute wait for the next bus. While Martha waited, a sudden downpour drenched her to the skin. She had not brought her raincoat, and had lost her mother's only umbrella two weeks ago. She was so upset, she did not notice the delivery van driving close to the curb until it had spattered mud all over her legs and skirt. Martha wiped off the mud as best she could until, at last, the bus arrived and she hopped on.

It was only a ten-minute ride to Martha's destination, but to her it seemed like hours. She stepped off the bus and as she walked away, the heel of her shoe caught in a grill in the sidewalk, and the heel snapped off. Martha hobbled on to the office building and got into the elevator. The elevator had started to ascend before Martha noticed that it did not go all the way up to the floor she wanted. Back to the main floor she had to go to catch the right elevator. Some thirty minutes after her scheduled appointment, Martha hurried into the personnel office. The manager was interviewing another job applicant. Martha sat in the waiting room and fumed about her bad luck.

| 13 |
| 27 |
| 41 |
| 55 |
| 58 |
| 72 |
| 86 |
| 100 |
| 114 |
| 128 |
| 142 |
| 156 |
| 170 |
| 183 |
| 185 |
| 199 |
| 213 |
| 227 |
| 241 |
| 255 |
| 269 |
| 283 |
| 297 |
| 310 |
| 323 |
| 328 |
| 342 |
| 356 |
| 370 |
| 384 |
| 398 |
| 412 |
| 425 |
| 439 |
| 453 |
| 467 |

| 1 | 2 | 3 | 4 | 5 | 6 | 7 | 8 | 9 | 10 | 11 | 12 | 13 | 14 |

Different Times

During the war, Remembrance Day held special meaning, for every- · 13
one had a son, father, husband, brother, or friend fighting overseas. · 27
I can remember quite clearly the siren sounding all over the city at · 41
eleven o'clock in the morning on Remembrance Day, and every vehicle on · 55
the road and every person on the street came to a standstill for the · 69
two minutes of silent remembrance. · 76

The war was well along before my father finally found permanent, · 90
full-time work. Just before I turned seven, we moved into our own · 103
house and, shortly after, our first telephone was installed. It · 116
became my job to go to the store every day after school. Because we · 130
had no ice box, it was necessary to shop for perishables on a daily · 144
basis. Milk and bread were delivered to the door, but meat and fresh · 158
produce were purchased from the corner store. In the summertime, our · 172
milk was kept cold by standing the bottle in the kitchen sink under a · 186
constant drizzle from the cold water tap. · 194

Old clothes and other items for which we no longer had any use · 208
were kept in a rag basket in the basement. When the ragman came driv- · 222
ing his horse and wagon up the lane behind our house and ringing his · 236
bell, my mother would take out the rag basket and sell him the con- · 250
tents for a quarter, or sometimes even a dollar or two. · 261

Although we sometimes managed to excel in some subjects, for the · 275
most part we children tolerated school as a necessary nuisance. Most · 289
of our efforts were expended at recess time on games like volleyball, · 303
rounders, and ledgers, and I especially liked to play alleys in the · 317
snow in winter. Rounders is similar to baseball except that the ball · 331
is larger and softer, and there is no pitcher. Instead, the person · 345
who is up throws the ball into the air, hits it with the hand, and · 358
then runs the bases. Ledgers was usually played with a tennis ball · 371
and involved throwing the ball overhand to strike the flat surface of · 385
the slanted concrete ledge on the wall of the school so that the ball · 399
bounced into the air and was caught. Often on the way to or from · 412
school, we would hitch a ride with the local breadman or milkman in · 426
his horse and wagon. We were always delighted when he allowed us a · 440
turn at the reins. · 444

| 1 | 2 | 3 | 4 | 5 | 6 | 7 | 8 | 9 | 10 | 11 | 12 | 13 | 14 |

Lightning is a flash of light in the sky caused by an electrical	13
current. The flash is really a huge spark, something like that pro-	27
duced by the spark plugs of a car. When a thundercloud becomes	40
charged, it has great electrical potential which is in proportion to	54
the number of water droplets it contains. A huge spark may result	68
when two clouds of opposite charges come near each other. When the	82
electrical potential of a cloud is great enough, it can overcome the	96
resistance of the air which is between it and the earth and normally	110
insulates the earth, and a lightning flash occurs.	120

As a lightning flash streaks through the sky, it heats the air, causing molecules of air to expand and fly about in all directions. As these molecules seek more room, they collide violently with cooler air. This sets up a great air wave which gives off the sound we call thunder. Primitive people had their own ideas about what caused thunder. Some thought it was the gods roaring in anger.

Because light travels faster than sound, we see the lightning before we hear the thunder. Since we know that sound travels about one kilometre in three seconds, by counting the seconds between the lightning flash and the sound of the thunderclap we can tell how far away from us the lightning struck. If the thunder followed in thirty seconds, we would know the lightning hit about ten kilometres away.

Although the loud noise made by thunder frightens many people, it can do us no harm. The lightning which accompanies it, however, may cause property damage and loss of life. Lightning chooses the easiest path between the clouds and the ground, even though this may not be the shortest path. Steel buildings, tall trees, power lines, and telephone poles are all good conductors of lightning. If a building is properly grounded, the electricity flows through it into the ground without causing any damage.

It is wise to take certain safety precautions during a thunder storm. Since lightning often strikes chimneys, stay away from open fireplaces. Do not decide to take a bath or stand near a metal object. If it is necessary to be out of doors, stay away from lone trees, wire fences, and open fields where you are the tallest object around – for you could become a lightning rod. Take shelter, if possible, in dense woods, a cave, or at the foot of a cliff. If you are caught in the open, the safest thing to do is lie down.

| 134 |
| 148 |
| 162 |
| 176 |
| 190 |
| 200 |
| 213 |
| 227 |
| 241 |
| 255 |
| 269 |
| 283 |
| 297 |
| 311 |
| 325 |
| 339 |
| 352 |
| 366 |
| 380 |
| 385 |
| 399 |
| 413 |
| 427 |
| 440 |
| 454 |
| 468 |
| 482 |
| 493 |

| 1 | 2 | 3 | 4 | 5 | 6 | 7 | 8 | 9 | 10 | 11 | 12 | 13 | 14 |

Different Ways

Every summer, we spent a week or so visiting our former landlady.	13
We loved the change from the city – picking apples and cherries, feed-	27
ing the hens and trying to gather the eggs without getting pecked,	40
investigating the woods across the road and bringing back toads. We	54
were longing for a pet, and I adopted one of the hens as my favourite.	68
There was a big old cat called Jack on the premises, but he permitted	82
no one near him except his owners. When the cat's food was ready,	95
Mrs. Marks would stand at the open door and sharpen her long carving	109
knife. The sound would bring the cat running for his dinner.	121

Each bedroom in the old farmhouse was equipped with a wash basin 135
and pitcher for bathing, and we slept in the biggest, softest feather 149
bed you could ever imagine. We never had to be asked twice to pump 163
water at the old hand pump outside the kitchen door, and of course we 177
pumped far more than was needed. Somehow we didn't have the same 190
enthusiasm for the outhouse facilities, but we became adept at holding 204
our breath and at closing the door quickly in an attempt to keep the 218
flies out. 220

Our modes of transportation at that time were our legs, public 234
transit, and bicycle. Even Dad had his bicycle which he rode to and 248
from work every spring, summer, and autumn workday for over fifteen 262
years. Eventually my brothers taught him to drive, and in 1958 he 276
bought his first car. It was his pride and joy, and every night he 290
dusted and polished it until it gleamed. That car represented the 304
culmination of a lifetime of hard work and the beginning of a more 318
leisurely future. 321

Yes, many things were different then. We certainly did not have 335
the affluence that we enjoy now. We were perhaps more independent at 349
an earlier age. We did not have the gadgetry and conveniences that 363
are now widely prevalent, nor did we have the influence of television 377
on our lives. But were people and values really so different? We 390
were brought up to believe in kindness, honesty, hard work, fair play, 404
respect for other people and their property, and respect for our- 417
selves. Aren't those values still applicable today? I think so, and 431
I believe our children will too when their sons and daughters inform 445
them that things were different way back then. 454

| 1 | 2 | 3 | 4 | 5 | 6 | 7 | 8 | 9 | 10 | 11 | 12 | 13 | 14 |

It all started nearly a hundred years ago when a trio of men · 13
filled a pan with gravel from a creek, washed it out, and stared down · 27
at gold. Unknown to them at the time, they had just discovered one of · 41
the world's largest deposits of free gold. Excitedly, they checked · 55
out more of the creek to confirm their find. Before long, their · 68
claims were staked and they were hurrying off to the registry office · 82
to file them. · 85

The word spread like wildfire, and prospectors from across the · 99
valleys and up and down the rivers converged on Bonanza Creek. In a · 113
short time, almost all of the creek area had been staked and the · 126
claims recorded. Just a few miles north of the strike at the junction · 140
of the Yukon and Klondike Rivers, a supply store was built and the · 153
area was named Dawson City. · 159

It was nearly a year before news of the strike hit the outside · 173
world, but when it did it came at a time of economic depression and · 187
unemployment. Fortune seekers of all kinds from all over the world · 200
began to pore in – prospectors, doctors, lawyers, bankers, gamblers, · 214
thieves, people of good and ill repute. Most came by steamer to · 227
Alaska, then travelled on foot over a high and treacherous pass into · 241
Canada. Here, those that survived the storms and blizzards stopped to · 255
fell trees and construct scows which they used to traverse the lakes · 269
and streams to the Yukon River, then down the river nearly nine hun- · 283
dred kilometres to the gold fields. The whole journey was long and · 297
full of hardships and hazards, and many gold rushers died along the · 311
way from accidents, sickness, and exposure. Only one in four made it. · 325

In Dawson City, tents, log cabins, shacks, stores, hotels, dance · 339
halls, and saloons sprang up along the muddy roads. This was a wild · 353
and wide-open town, ripe for the picking by the many toughs, con men, · 367
professional gamblers, and easy women who moved in. Most of the · 380
action centred in the saloons where all of the vices were at work to · 394
relieve the miners of their newly-acquired wealth, and many a hard- · 408
earned fortune was lost on the turn of a roulette wheel or the deal of · 422
a card. Money went out also on food, lodgings, and supplies. Fresh · 436
food was scarce and prices were exorbitant. Within just a few years, · 450
Dawson grew from one shack to over twenty thousand people. By that · 464
time, most of the placer gold which could be mined by crude methods · 477
had been extracted. Soon, the hordes of people moved on, many to · 490
Alaska, and Dawson was reduced to a skeleton of two thousand people. · 504

| 1 | 2 | 3 | 4 | 5 | 6 | 7 | 8 | 9 | 10 | 11 | 12 | 13 | 14 |

Language is the vital tool by which we are able to think, read, 13
write, speak, understand, and learn. For most of us, that language is 27
English. 29

In the past fifteen hundred years, English has made tremendous 43
strides. From a few thousand words spoken by a few hundred thousand 57
people on a small island, it has grown to a million or so words spoken 71
by over 250 million people in every corner of the globe. This is more 85
than double the number who communicate in the next most widely spoken 99
tongue, French. 102

One of the intriguing sides of English is where it came from and 116
how it developed. Its evolution is commonly broken into three peri- 130
ods. The first of these is known as Old English. It dates back to 144
the rough and tumble Anglo-Saxons who invaded and settled in England 158
after driving the native peoples into the north and west of the 171
island. Their language, Englisc, was complex. Its pronunciation was 185
quite different from ours; and its nouns, adjectives, and verbs had an 199
array of endings, called inflections, which showed the function of the 213
words in a sentence. 217

The language reigned supreme for some six hundred years until the 231
country was conquered by the French Normans, one of the most cultured 245
people of the time, who set up their royal court in England. For 258
quite a number of years, the new reign saw two distinct languages 271
being spoken: French by the ruling class and English by the working 285
mass. 286

In time, the rulers began to learn English to enable them to 299
improve their dealings with the bulk of the people. This set the 312
stage for the Middle English period, during which the language under- 326
went a great many changes. A lot of the older words fell out of use. 340
Because the complicated word endings were difficult to learn, many of 354
them were dropped and more importance was placed on the order of words 368
in the sentence. A large number of French words were absorbed into 382
the language, not so much to replace English words, as to add to them. 396
This brought new colour and dimension to the language and greatly 409
enriched it. As the years went by and more and more Normans took up 423
English, their mother tongue was abandoned and English became the one, 437
official tongue. 440

| 1 | 2 | 3 | 4 | 5 | 6 | 7 | 8 | 9 | 10 | 11 | 12 | 13 | 14 |

It happened that the king's chief butler and baker were in the | 13
same prison as Joseph. There, they each had a dream and described | 26
it to Joseph. He interpreted their dreams saying that in three days | 40
the butler would be restored to his former position, but the baker | 53
would be executed. In three days' time, the events occurred just as | 67
foretold. | 69

Two years later, the king had a dream but no one could explain | 83
its meaning. The butler remembered Joseph, who was called before the | 97
king. Joseph listened to the king's dream and then unfolded its | 110
meaning. For seven years, Egypt would have bountiful crops and great | 124
prosperity. This would be followed by seven years of drought and | 137
famine. The king was impressed and he appointed Joseph to rule over | 151
his dominion and prepare it to withstand the famine. | 161

Joseph governed wisely, and during the seven prosperous years | 174
laid up great stores in preparation for the lean years. Then the hard | 188
times began. As the famine worsened, people arrived from near and far | 202
to purchase food from Joseph. One day, ten men knelt in front of him, | 216
and when they lifted their faces he knew they were his brothers; but | 230
they did not recognize him. Joseph dealt roughly with them, bound one | 244
up and sent the rest back to their homeland with supplies and instruc- | 258
tions not to return unless they brought their youngest brother. The | 272
brothers returned to their father's house and related everything that | 286
had happened, and when they opened their sacks of provisions they | 299
found their money resting on the top, and they were afraid. | 311

When their corn was almost gone, their father sent them again to | 325
Egypt to buy stores, and after much persuasion he allowed the youngest | 339
to go too. They came again to Joseph and he was overjoyed to see his | 353
young brother. He returned the captive brother to them, feasted them, | 367
and sent them off with their goods. Again, their money was returned, | 381
but this time he also planted his silver cup in his young brother's | 395
sack. After they were gone, he sent servants to overtake them and | 408
find the cup, and they all returned to Joseph's house. | 419

Joseph declared he would retain the young lad as his servant | 432
because he had stolen the cup, but an older brother offered to serve | 446
in his place, lest their father die of sorrow at the loss of the boy. | 460
Joseph could contain himself no longer and he revealed himself to them | 474
and there was much crying and kissing. He sent for his father and all | 488
of his family, and they came and dwelled in the land of Egypt. | 500

| 1 | 2 | 3 | 4 | 5 | 6 | 7 | 8 | 9 | 10 | 11 | 12 | 13 | 14 |

The Middle English period saw a great evolution in the English	13
language. From the Old English were retained the short, homey words	27
which form the basis of the tongue today. Man, foot, wife, sun,	40
night, heart, mother, and good are but a few. Of the vast number of	54
words injected from the French, many had to do with the arts, fine	67
living, government, law, property, and war. These included words such	81
as dance, council, judge, rent, parliament, and armour. Often words	95
from both sources, even though they held the same meaning, persisted –	109
the Old English as the common form and the French as the more literary	123
form. Examples of these are begin and commence, work and labour, meet	137
and assemble, hit and assault, need and require, and clothes and	150
garments.	152
The next important event which was to greatly affect the language	166
came about shortly before the start of the sixteenth century. The	179
event was the start-up of the first printing press in England. At	192
that time, the language was in rough shape with many dialects and no	206
standards for grammar or spelling. Words were spelled the way they	220
sounded to the writer. As a result, the same words were found spelled	234
perhaps half a dozen ways. The printers set about to rectify the	247
situation by setting up some standards. This marks the beginning of	261
the period we term Modern English.	268
For the most part, the setting of standards was a good thing, but	282
it did have its adverse effects. One of these had to do with spell-	296
ing. While spelling was becoming constant, pronunciations continued	310
to change. This produced words like knight, knit, gnaw, wrong,	323
wrench, and write, which contain silent letters that used to be	336
sounded but the sounds were eventually dropped.	345
Throughout the Modern English period, which extends to this day,	359
the English language has continued to expand. Shakespeare was, per-	373
haps, the biggest single contributor. He was a great language innova-	387
tor who did not hesitate to switch words from one part of speech to	401
another, to accept and use new words from any source, and to coin his	415
own new words and phrases as he required them.	424
Trade, travel, and classical learning have added a host of new	438
words, many taken from other languages all over the world. From poli-	452
tics, war, industry, and science have come many more. A vast number	466
of words have evolved in this century alone, and more are yet to come.	480

| 1 | 2 | 3 | 4 | 5 | 6 | 7 | 8 | 9 | 10 | 11 | 12 | 13 | 14 |

Joseph was the second youngest of twelve sons. His father's | 12
favourite child, he always wore the beautiful coat of many colours his | 26
father had made for him. His ten older brothers were jealous and | 39
hated him. | 41

Joseph was a dreamer and he was in the habit of telling his | 54
brothers his dreams. One night he dreamt he had grain growing tall | 68
and straight in a field. His brothers had grain growing there, too, | 82
but their grain was bowed down before his grain. On another occasion | 96
he dreamt that the sun and moon and eleven stars paid homage to him. | 110
When he told these dreams to his brothers, they became angry and swore | 124
the day would never come that they would bow themselves before Joseph. | 138

When Joseph was seventeen, his older brothers were far off in the | 152
country feeding their father's flock. They were gone for some time | 166
and their father began to worry. He sent Joseph to find them, learn | 180
what progress they were making, and report back to him. Joseph set | 194
off, and after making inquiries along the way, headed for his broth- | 208
ers' camp. The brothers saw Joseph in the distance and recognized him | 222
by his colourful coat. They decided this was an opportune time to rid | 236
themselves of this boy whom they hated, and when he entered their camp | 250
they seized him, tore off his coat, and threw him into a pit. | 262

While deliberating how to kill him, a company of merchants hap- | 276
pened to be passing by, and the brothers saw a way of disposing of the | 290
boy without having his blood on their consciences. They sold Joseph | 304
to the merchants for twenty pieces of silver and congratulated them- | 318
selves on having found such a simple solution to their problem. Then | 332
they dipped Joseph's coat in goat's blood and took it home to their | 346
father. Jacob, thinking that his beloved son was dead, was beside | 359
himself with grief and mourned for days, and none of his family could | 373
comfort him. | 375

The merchants journeyed into Egypt where they sold Joseph to a | 389
high-ranking official. Joseph was put to work and was so successful | 403
at everything he undertook that eventually he was made overseer of all | 417
his master owned. The master's wife had eyes for Joseph and she tried | 431
to attract his interest, but he would have none of it. It chanced one | 445
day that they were alone in the house and the mistress caught the edge | 459
of his garment to flirt with him, but he ran away leaving his cloth | 473
behind. She was so enraged by his rejection that she falsely accused | 487
him of misbehaviour and her husband clapped him in prison. | 499

| 1 | 2 | 3 | 4 | 5 | 6 | 7 | 8 | 9 | 10 | 11 | 12 | 13 | 14 |

Eskimo Art

Canadian Eskimo art as a part of the world art scene is still
fairly new. It began some thirty years ago when the federal government took steps to establish a cottage craft industry that would help
to relieve a highly welfare way of life. A southern artist was hired
to get the program under way.

Two modes of expression soon came to the fore: lithograph and
sculpture. Prints, at first, were made from stencils cut from dried
sealskins, but the true lithograph, or stone-cut print, was soon
favoured. Attempts at etching did not meet with wide-spread success,
although the technique was mastered by a few artists who made changes
such as hacking copper plates with an axe, rather than using the more
common tools, which produced some highly effective results.

Sculpture is practised by most of the artists. Whalebone, tusk,
caribou antler, and types of soft stone are the chief materials used.
The tools used are simple and few. Gross carving is begun with hack-
saws or hatchets, followed by a progression of files or rasps and then
sandpaper of ever finer grades to achieve a fine polish. An amazingly
wide range of work is produced – from the most simple or primitive to
the most fragile and fine – which rivals the sculpture produced by
more advanced and more complex means.

Some remarkable traits could soon be seen in Eskimo art. Not
only was the work of specific artists easy to recognize, but communities were often just as individual. With prints, the locale of the
artist could be determined by the theme, as well as by the style used.
With sculpture, until recent years, the place where a piece was made
was known by the kind of material used – such as bone versus stone, or
by the kind of stone – as well as by the theme of the work.

The results of the program went far beyond all hopes and expecta-
tions. Eskimo art in general, and a number of artists in particular,
is now recognized and acclaimed by the worldwide art community.

The end or decline of Eskimo art had been prophesied almost from
the start, but still it persists. What is astounding is the variation
still produced on what could be termed the old themes. What's more,
an evolution can be seen in both the prints and in the sculptures as
more exposure to southern culture and technology occurs. Perhaps the
purely Canadian art that has been so long sought after may be found in
the work of these, one of Canada's first native peoples.

| 1 | 2 | 3 | 4 | 5 | 6 | 7 | 8 | 9 | 10 | 11 | 12 | 13 | 14 |

Once I might have taken my pen in hand to write about humour with 13
the confident air of a known professional. But that time is past. 26
Such claim as I had has been taken from me. In fact, I stand un- 39
masked. A reviewer writing in a literary journal, the very name of 53
which is enough to put contradiction to sleep, has said of my writing 67
that there is little in my humour but a rather ingenious mixture of 81
hyperbole and myosis. 85

The man was right. How he stumbled upon this trade secret, I do 99
not know; but I am willing to admit, since the truth is out, that it 113
has long been my custom in preparing an article of a humorous nature 127
to go down to the cellar and mix up two litres of myosis with half a 141
litre of hyperbole. If I want to give the article a more literary 154
flavour, I find it well to add in a cup of paresis. The whole thing 168
is amazingly simple. 172

I only mention the foregoing by way of introduction and to dispel 186
any idea that I am conceited enough to write about humour with any 199
professional authority. All that I dare claim is that I have as much 213
sense of humour as other people. Oddly enough, I notice that everyone 227
else makes this same claim. People will admit, if need be, that 240
their sight is poor, that they cannot swim, or that they shoot badly 254
with a rifle; but to question their sense of humour is to give them a 268
mortal affront. 271

The other day, a friend of mine admitted that he never goes to 285
the opera; then he added with an air of pride that he has absolutely 299
no ear for music. He went on to say that he can't tell one tune from 313
another and can't tell whether someone is tuning a violin or playing a 327
sonata. He seemed to get prouder and prouder over each item of his 341
own deficiency. He ended by saying that he had a dog at his house 354
that had a far better ear for music than he had. 364

When he had finished, I made what I thought a harmless comment to 378
the effect that I supposed his sense of humour was deficient in the 392
same way since the two often go hand in hand. In a moment, my friend 406
was livid with rage. He lashed out with a defense of his sense of 419
humour, and from that turned to bitter personal attack on mine. He 433
said that my sense of humour seemed to have withered altogether. With 447
that, still quivering with indignation, he left me. 457

| 1 | 2 | 3 | 4 | 5 | 6 | 7 | 8 | 9 | 10 | 11 | 12 | 13 | 14 |

Exercise Needed

"Exercise should be a must for all office workers." This strong | 14
statement was made by a well-known doctor at a meeting held in | 27
Calgary. His comment was met with quick support from all of his | 40
colleagues, one of whom went so far as to say that it is the place of | 54
all employers to make sure that employees do, in fact, exercise. At | 68
first, you may think that this suggestion is extreme, but when you | 81
hear some of the facts about worker absence, you may change your mind. | 95

Studies have shown that the worker who exercises on a regular | 108
basis or is active in sports is seldom absent from work. The studies | 122
show further that the fit employee is a much more productive staff | 135
member. With these facts before you, you may want to consider start- | 149
ing an exercise program for the staff in your office. We offer just | 163
such a program. It has been adopted by more than five hundred firms | 177
across the country, and in all cases, attendance at work has shown a | 191
major improvement. The details of the program are fully explained in | 205
the attached brochure, but let me summarize them for you. | 216

First of all, a trained fitness expert will come to your office | 230
to discuss how an exercise program would best fit into your office | 244
routine. It would require setting aside ten minutes a day for exer- | 258
cises right at the work station. A pamphlet describing the exercises | 272
would be handed out to each employee for previewing. A few days | 285
later, the expert would return to your office to conduct the first | 299
ten-minute exercises to taped music and instructions. A volunteer | 312
from among your workers would then be called for. This person would | 326
take on the task of setting up and starting the tape each day at the | 340
appointed time. If you wish, this role may be rotated each week or | 354
each month among the people involved. | 361

Also, a one-hour class would be arranged for one day a week at a | 375
suitable location, either on your premises or in our gym, for all | 388
those interested. A more rigorous program can be set up for anyone | 402
wishing it, but for this, a medical check-up would be required. We | 415
know you will be amazed at the pep, drive, and increased feeling of | 429
well-being that our program will induce in your workers. Stress is | 442
reduced and attendance improves. | 448

Our fitness expert will call you next week to arrange an appoint- | 462
ment that will start your workers on the right road to fitness. | 475

| 1 | 2 | 3 | 4 | 5 | 6 | 7 | 8 | 9 | 10 | 11 | 12 | 13 | 14 |

Last week, I attended open house at my daughter's school. During | 13
my visit, I was greatly impressed with all of the modern tools and | 26
equipment which today's students have at their disposal. I couldn't | 40
help but reminisce about facilities in my old school some fifty years | 54
ago when one of my favourite subjects was Household Science. | 66

There was a house located on our school premises which had been | 80
remodelled to serve the Household Science classes. On the main floor | 94
of the house, the living room and kitchen had been combined to make | 108
one large area for cooking. In this area was the teacher's demonstra- | 122
tion table, around which the work areas for the students were arranged | 136
in a circle. Each girl had her own supply cupboard and her own Bunsen | 150
burner for cooking, and she learned to produce individual portions of | 164
basic recipes. In a corner of the room were an ice box, a large stove | 178
for baking, and a double sink where two or three girls would be de- | 192
tailed for clean-up after each class. | 199

Also on the main floor was a dining room containing a mahogany | 213
dining suite which we dusted with tender loving care. Here, we | 226
learned how to set a table, how to serve a meal, and how to eat and | 240
behave with good manners at the table. | 248

Upstairs was a furnished bedroom in which we learned the art of | 262
making a bed. The wall between the other two bedrooms had been re- | 276
moved to make a large, bright sewing room. This housed several large | 290
work tables and a number of treadle sewing machines. It was in this | 304
room that we learned the intricacies of making a nainsook slip and | 317
other garments. | 320

In the basement were cement washtubs and scrub boards on which we | 334
washed our dirty tea towels, then hung them on a clotheshorse to dry. | 348
In an effort to teach us thrift, even paper towels were washed, hung | 362
to dry, and reused. | 366

Through the years, Household Science went through a few name | 379
changes, which included Home Economics and Family Studies. Its male | 393
counterpart, Manual Training, also took on new names like Shop and | 406
Industrial Arts. It never occurred to anyone when I was young that a | 420
boy might benefit from taking Household Science; and for a girl to | 433
take Manual Training was unheard of. Today, boys are busy learning | 447
how to prepare meals, and girls are working lathes and sanding table | 461
tops. My, how times have changed. | 468

| 1 | 2 | 3 | 4 | 5 | 6 | 7 | 8 | 9 | 10 | 11 | 12 | 13 | 14 |

Tracing one's family roots has become a favourite pastime. More	13
and more people are seeing the value of tying their family's past with	27
the present to form a picture for the future. Tracing one's lineage	41
is a lengthy project, but also a highly rewarding one. It promotes a	55
better understanding of oneself. It fosters a sense of pride and	68
belonging. It strengthens family ties.	76

Tracing one's family roots has become a favourite pastime. More and more people are seeing the value of tying their family's past with the present to form a picture for the future. Tracing one's lineage is a lengthy project, but also a highly rewarding one. It promotes a better understanding of oneself. It fosters a sense of pride and belonging. It strengthens family ties.

If you have ever wondered just who you are, from whence you came, and what kind of genes have been at work to help make you what you are, then you have already begun the search for your roots. Perhaps soon you will be ready to take the next step, an active pursuit of your forebears. When you are, the place to start is right in your own home.

First gather information about yourself and your siblings. Then you can work backwards to parents, grandparents, and so on. You will want names, places, dates, and relationships. Search your own memory, family papers, scrapbooks, clippings, letters, the family bible, etc. Even check out the backs of pictures for names and dates. Write down all of the data in a systematic way, such as in chart form.

When your home sources are exhausted, tap into other sources. Phone, write or visit relatives who may have information. Show them what you are doing and offer to share the fruits of your labour with them. Kindle their interest and they will bend over backwards to help. When you are reading or listening, be alert for clues that may not fit into the picture now but may prove to be a missing link later. As well as gleaning the vital details, find out whether someone else has started a family tree; ask about pictures, stories, what people worked at, and traditions of the family. Mark everything down and be sure to record the source of your information in case you should have to retrace your steps.

As a result of some clues, you may find yourself pouring over public records or wandering through graveyards trying to decipher the writing on the stones. Wherever your search leads you, you will find the path interesting and challenging. There is a mystery to solve and you are the detective. Whether your ancestors turn out to be famous or infamous, they are part of your history; and when you are ready to set out on your ancestral journey, they will be waiting to meet you.

| 1 | 2 | 3 | 4 | 5 | 6 | 7 | 8 | 9 | 10 | 11 | 12 | 13 | 14 |

Homemaker

Much has been said which maligns the role of homemaker. No won-der it used to be so hard for me to feel like a person, let alone feel important or interesting or worthy. Then someone suggested that per-haps there was another way of looking at things. A new picture began to emerge of a person who, by choice, is at the centre of things that are important to her, a person who can give love and support and joy to a spouse and child, a person who sees and cherishes the value of peace and quiet contentment and fun, the need to lie in the sun and watch the clouds pass by, the fun of romping in the living room having a pillow fight. Seldom are the virtues of these things extolled, but then their value is beyond reckoning.

The fact is that homemaking poses more challenges than any other lifestyle. Like the job of a senior executive, the role becomes what the person makes of it. There are homemakers who handle a broader spectrum of responsibilities and decisions, and purchase a wider range of goods and services than any other workers, except perhaps the self-employed or the high executive. They may buy everything from skating lessons to a new roof for the house. They may take the car in for repair and supervise tradespeople in the home, in many cases deciding on their own the standards of workmanship which will be acceptable. When guests come for dinner, it is often the homemaker who sets the tone. When the family goes for a weekend outing, the homemaker organ-izes clothing, food, and so on, to make it a success.

What's more, homemakers work on their own – alone and independ-ent. Day after day, they must provide not only the answers, but the questions as well. There is no boss to watch, direct, instruct, or report on their performance. When the homemaker solves a tricky prob-lem, there is no one there to know it. There is no praise from a manager, no pats on the back from colleagues. Homemakers must realize that they deserve these things but must supply the recognition and support from within themselves.

If homemakers should ever disappear from society, and I hope they never will, they will leave behind them a gaping emptiness and an irreplaceable loss.

| 1 | 2 | 3 | 4 | 5 | 6 | 7 | 8 | 9 | 10 | 11 | 12 | 13 | 14 |

13
27
41
55
69
83
97
111
125
139
146
160
174
187
201
215
229
242
256
270
284
298
309
323
337
351
365
378
392
405
411
425
438
442

Down through the ages, the world of fashion has supported a num- | 13
ber of unusual and sometimes amusing styles – at least from our modern | 27
point of view. One of these fashions can be seen in paintings showing | 41
the long fingernails of both men and women of old, upper-class China. | 55
Long nails were a mark of great beauty and a clear sign of status, in- | 69
dicating that the owners did not have to work with their hands. Nails | 83
sometimes grew to over five centimetres long, and special gold or | 96
silver covers were worn to protect them. | 104

Recent generations have not been the only people to put their | 117
money where their mouths are. Instead of using gold, however, the | 130
Mayan Indians filled the cavities in their teeth with pieces of jade. | 144

For a while in Europe, hair was literally the height of ladies' | 158
fashion. With the addition of wigs, coiffures rose to over a metre | 172
high. These were elaborately styled and were decorated with flowers, | 186
ribbons, plumes, and/or veils. Designers got so carried away that | 199
some creations included little figures of people and one was topped | 213
off with a model sailing ship. The hairdos were powdered and coated | 227
with lard to hold them together; however this attracted bugs and mice | 241
so great care had to be taken to avoid these pests. Because the cre- | 255
ations required so much work to construct, they had to last a while | 269
and were often maintained for a few months. The wearers slept on | 282
special pillows and wore huge bonnets to keep their hair in place. | 296

Another curious fashion which women adopted and which got out of | 310
hand was the hooped skirt. As the fad spread, so did the hoops, and | 324
skirts became wider and wider. When a few ladies in their hooped | 337
skirts became wedged together in the entrance to a royal ball and pre- | 351
vented the rest of the guests from getting in, King James I decided | 365
the craze had gone too far. He let it be known that that style of | 378
dress was no longer welcome at court. | 385

At various times throughout history, men have rivalled women in | 399
ornateness of dress. In their zeal, they have donned powdered and | 412
curled wigs and fancy jewellery. They have worn brightly coloured | 425
fabrics, including velvets and brocades with lavish designs. Clothes | 439
have been trimmed with lace, fur, ruffles, and frills, and decorated | 453
with jewels, braid, embroidery, buckles, plumes, buttons, and bows. | 467

| 1 | 2 | 3 | 4 | 5 | 6 | 7 | 8 | 9 | 10 | 11 | 12 | 13 | 14 |

The hog dates back to prehistoric times and is believed to be the | 13
oldest domestic animal still in existence. The hog was introduced to | 27
America by an explorer in the mid-sixteenth century. Indians adopted | 41
the delicious pork meat as part of their diet and raided settlements | 55
to obtain hogs for breeding. Pioneer settlers took hogs with them | 68
when they moved west. They began to develop the pork industry, and | 82
trail drives of as many as three thousand hogs were made to assembly | 96
points. | 97

The hog of today has been bred to provide more meat and less fat | 111
than its ancestors. Ham is the meat from the hind leg of a hog. Most | 125
hams are cured or cured and smoked, and may or may not require further | 139
cooking. If there is no label to say, it is advisable to cook the | 152
ham. Canned ham is always cured and is fully cooked in the process- | 166
ing. Fresh ham is fresh pork; it has not been cured in any way and | 180
should be cooked like any other pork roast. Although it is called ham | 194
because it is from the hind leg, it tastes like pork, not cured ham. | 208

Ham and other pork cuts can be frozen for later use, but should | 222
be used within six months. Because freezing may alter the flavour and | 236
texture of cured meat, it is not usually recommended that cured hams | 250
be frozen. If one does decide to freeze a cured ham, it should not be | 264
kept for more than two months. A whole ham is often cut into several | 278
pieces. The upper half, which is rounder and meatier, is usually | 291
called the butt, but is also known as the rump. The lower half is not | 305
as rounded and is called the shank. Often, centre slices are removed | 319
between the butt and the shank for sale as ham steaks. When meat is | 333
removed in this manner, the remaining cuts are called butt portions or | 347
shank portions. | 350

The danger of contracting trichinosis, a disease caused by eating | 364
meat containing parasitic worms, from eating undercooked pork is well | 378
known. Because of this fear, however, many persons tend to overcook | 392
pork. Recent research has shown that it is not necessary to roast | 405
pork at such high temperatures or for as long as is recommended in | 418
many old cookbooks. For a well-done, tender roast, pork should be | 431
cooked in a moderate oven until the internal temperature reads eighty | 445
degrees Celsius. It is better to rely on an easily-read thermometer | 459
than to determine the cooking time by mass, as roasts of the same | 472
mass vary in length and thickness. | 479

| 1 | 2 | 3 | 4 | 5 | 6 | 7 | 8 | 9 | 10 | 11 | 12 | 13 | 14 |

Fashions Revived

Fashions might be defined as the personal grooming, mode of dress | 13
(or undress), and the ornaments and accessories used to adorn oneself | 28
which are in vogue and enhance one's appearance and status in the eyes | 42
of one's contemporaries. | 47

From early times, men and women have been concerned with fashion. | 61
Body paint; simple garments such as loincloths; strings of shells or | 75
beads around the neck, wrists, and/or ankles; and flowers or feathers | 89
in the hair were common fashions among primitive peoples. As civili- | 103
zation advanced, however, so did fashions. | 111

It is interesting to look back in time and find that many fash- | 125
ions that we consider current or recent are, in fact, revivals of | 138
styles that were popular hundreds of years ago. The bikini, for ex- | 151
ample, was worn by Roman women when they were engaged in exercise or | 165
sports. The wearing of the kilt dates back to ancient Egypt when men | 179
wore skirts that sometimes extended to below their knees. Headbands | 193
were often worn by Egyptian women. Gloves with separate fingers were | 207
worn in the days of the Persian empire, and dress slits were common in | 221
China in days of old. Hair nets, many of which were made with gold | 235
mesh, were the "in" thing nearly a thousand years ago. At that time, | 250
too, linings were attached to gowns and cloaks. Usually in a con- | 263
trasting colour, they added that certain touch of dash. Even leg | 276
warmers were fashionable way back then, although they usually came up | 290
just to the knee and were found on men, rather than on women. | 302

Neither are platform shoes new to this era. Platforms were worn | 316
by the ladies of Venice in the sixteenth century. As the style caught | 330
on, the platforms became higher and higher until they reached an amaz- | 344
ing half a metre. As one can well imagine, walking on these stilts | 358
was rather difficult; however, as a rule, the gentlemen were more than | 372
glad to lend their assistance. | 378

In that same century, men were wearing close-fitting tights that | 392
would have made them feel right at home in today's gymnasiums. It's | 406
hard to say when men began to wear ties that were completely separate | 420
from their shirts, but they must have been the height of fashion in | 434
the early 1800s when, the records tell us, an enterprising fellow | 447
started up a school at which he taught the fine art of knotting ties. | 461

| 1 | 2 | 3 | 4 | 5 | 6 | 7 | 8 | 9 | 10 | 11 | 12 | 13 | 14 |

One of the joys of growing plants indoors is that their beauty | 13
can be enjoyed year-round. It's like having a little bit of summer in | 27
your home all year, even in the middle of winter. | 37

House plants have so many uses – from brightening up a window | 50
sill; to adding a fresh, natural touch to the decor; to making a wel- | 64
come gift for friends and relatives; and even to tempting the taste- | 78
buds. Too, they come in all manner of shapes, sizes, and habits. | 91
They can be small trees, like palms and figs, and require a fair piece | 105
of floor space. They may be medium-sized, like ferns and caladiums, | 119
that rest nicely on a table. Like African violets and geraniums, they | 133
may deliver gorgeous displays of flowers. They may even be vines or | 147
trailers, such as ivy or spider plants, that will cascade over a large | 161
planter or hanging basket, or may be trained on a trellis. Some gar- | 175
deners see indoor gardening in a more culinary light. They grow herbs | 189
and tiny tomatoes which will provide fresh garnishes and seasonings | 203
for their gourmet dishes. | 208

The selection and placement of indoor plants will depend on the | 222
quantity and quality of light that is available. A number of green | 236
plants will prosper in low and medium light; but a far greater number | 250
have high light needs, and most flowering plants require a good share | 264
of sunshine. However, light can be supplemented by artificial lights, | 278
and special grow bulbs are available for that purpose. | 289

Plants also require a moderate temperature and moisture. Just as | 303
people tend to dry up in heated buildings in winter, so do plants. | 316
Most plants love humidity; that is why they perform so well in bath- | 330
rooms and near the kitchen sink. All plants need food and water – how | 344
much depends on the plant. The tendency is to water plants too much, | 358
which keeps the tiny air spaces in the soil filled with water instead | 372
of air, and in time the roots literally drown and rot. | 383

One of the nice things about most plants is that you can propa- | 397
gate them. Depending on the type of plant, this may be done by taking | 411
leaf or stem cuttings and rooting them, or simply by splitting the | 424
plant, roots and all, in two. The new plant can decorate another spot | 438
in the home, replace a plant whose days are numbered, or be given away | 452
as a gift to give pleasure to someone else. | 461

| 1 | 2 | 3 | 4 | 5 | 6 | 7 | 8 | 9 | 10 | 11 | 12 | 13 | 14 |

8 9 0-7730-4319-5 92 91